Second Edition

Case Studies in Health Information Management

Second Edition

Case Studies in Health Information Management

Charlotte McCuen, M.S., RHIA

Nanette B. Sayles, Ed.D., RHIA, CCS, CHPS, CPHIMS, FAHIMA

Patricia Schnering, RHIA, CCS

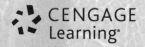

CENGAGE
Learning·

Australia • Brazil • Mexico • Singapore • United Kingdom • United States

Case Studies in Health Information Management, Second Edition

Charlotte McCuen, Nanette B. Sayles, Patricia Schnering

Vice President, Careers and Computing: Dave Garza

Publisher: Stephen Helba

Executive Editor: Rhonda Dearborn

Director, Development-Career and Computing: Marah Bellegarde

Product Development Manager: Juliet Steiner

Product Manager: Lauren Whalen

Editorial Assistant: Courtney Cozzy

Brand Manager: Wendy Mapstone

Market Development Manager: Nancy Bradshaw

Senior Production Director: Wendy Troeger

Production Manager: Andrew Crouth

Content Project Management and Art Direction: PreMediaGlobal

Media Editor: William Overocker

Cover Image: © Shutterstock.com/Pro-Studio

For product information and technology assistance, contact us at **Cengage Learning Customer & Sales Support, 1-800-354-9706**.

For permission to use material from this text or product, submit all requests online at **www.cengage.com/permissions**. Further permissions questions can be e-mailed to **permissionrequest@cengage.com**.

Library of Congress Control Number: 2013934610

ISBN: 978-1-133-60268-2

Cengage Learning
200 First Stamford Place, 4th Floor
Stamford, CT 06902
USA

Cengage Learning is a leading provider of customized learning solutions with office locations around the globe, including Singapore, the United Kingdom, Australia, Mexico, Brazil, and Japan. Locate your local office at **international.cengage.com/region**.

Cengage Learning products are represented in Canada by Nelson Education, Ltd.

To learn more about Cengage Learning, visit **www.cengage.com**. Purchase any of our products at your local college store or at our preferred online store **www.cengagebrain.com**.

Printed in the United States of America
3 4 5 6 7 16 15 14

Contents

Section 2

Clinical Classification Systems and Reimbursement Methods **45**

Section 3   Statistics and Quality Improvement. 161

Section 4   Healthcare Privacy, Confidentiality, Legal, and Ethical Issues 199

Section 5

Information Technology and Systems 257

Section 6   Management and Health Information Services 325

Section 7 — Project and Operations Management 382

Preface

Case Studies in Health Information Management, Second Edition, answers the educational need for a comprehensive case study workbook for Health Information Management (HIM) educators and students. The case format will help the student move from theory to application and analysis. The 240 comprehensive case studies are designed to provide both the AS or BS student with an opportunity to experience a wide range of HIM situations.

Case Study Framework

The cases are based on real-life HIM scenarios and demand thought and action from the HIM student. Critical thinking is a cornerstone of HIM practice. These case studies were designed to assist students at all levels develop and strengthen their critical thinking skills. Each case brings the user into the HIM setting and invites him or her to consider all of the variables that influence the information management situation. The students are then expected to utilize HIM principles in making decisions based on these multiple variables.

Case Studies in Health Information Management, Second Edition, provides instructors with a transitional tool to help guide students in "bridging the gap" between content knowledge and on-the-job performance in actual HIM practice. The cases represent a unique set of variables to offer a breadth of learning experiences and to capture the reality of HIM practice. Therefore, students should not expect to be able to just look up the answers in the textbooks. They will have to draw on everything that they have learned to answer many of the questions in the case studies.

Organization

The cases are grouped into parts based on 7 major HIM topics:

- Health Data Management
- Clinical Classification Systems and Reimbursement Methodology
- Statistics and Quality Improvement
- Healthcare Privacy, Confidentiality, Legal, and Ethical Issues
- Information Technology and Systems
- Management and Health Information Services
- Project and Operations Management

Within each section, we attempted to organize cases by subject area and then from less to more difficult. The classification of the cases is subjective and, as we all know, many of the HIM principles pertain to more than one HIM topic. For example, some cases in different sections may be quite similar but were included in the section for a different focus on the subject (e.g., personal health record [PHR] is addressed in Health Data Management as well as in Information Systems [IS]). Although reimbursement issues and coding go hand in hand, we have not included a variety of coding questions because there are already a myriad of excellent coding texts and workbooks. Our focus is on principles and compliance rather than specific codes.

Features

- *Case study questions* are written in such a way that the answers cannot be looked up in a textbook but instead must be found by drawing on the knowledge acquired during the course of study, promoting critical thinking.

- *True-to-life scenarios* are used throughout, including actual forms, codes, and the like that the HIM professional will utilize on the job.

Instructor Companion Site

All instructor resources can be accessed at http://login.cengage.com with your Cengage instructor account. If you are a first-time user, click New Faculty User and follow the prompts. Online instructor resources at the Instructor Companion site are password protected and include the following:

- The *Online Instructor's Manual* contains answers or suggested answers to every question found in the workbook. The *Online Instructor's Manual* contains Word files that can be easily manipulated by instructors so they can alter the information to meet their individual needs.
- A *Case Study Correlation Grid* illustrates at a glance which case studies contain principles related to the various American Health Information Management Association (AHIMA) Registered Health Information Administrator (RHIA) and Registered Health Information Technician (RHIT) competency statement domains. The cases are aligned with the Commission on Accreditation of Health Informatics and Information Management Education (CAHIIM) standards for accreditation.

Student Companion Site at CengageBrain

Online student resources at the Student Companion site include web links, as referenced in the case studies; spreadsheets to assist in completing individual case studies; and a glossary of key terms.

To access the Student Companion site from CengageBrain, follow these instructions:

- Go to http://www.cengagebrain.com, type author, title, or ISBN in the **Search** window.
- Locate the desired product and click on the title.
- When you arrive at the Product Page, click on the **Free Stuff** tab. Use the **Click Here** link to be brought to the Companion site.
- Click on the Student Resources link on the left navigation pane to access the resources.

Features

- Over 200 case studies mapping to curriculum domains.
- Aligns to Commission on Accreditation of Health Informatics and Information Management Education (CAHIIM) standards for accreditation.
- Promotes application of concepts to real-world problems and situations.
- Realistic presentation and dialogue to prepare students for situations they may encounter on the job.
- Designed to capture student interest with stimulating and fresh graphics.
- Instructor's manual provides complete answer keys.

New to This Edition

Over 30 new case studies have been added to *Case Studies in Health Information Management,* Second Edition, set in a variety of health care environments, including hospitals, ambulatory care centers, nursing facilities, medical centers, long-term care facilities, state departments of health, and physician practices. This variety gives students an idea of the wide range of professional opportunities available to them.

The new and revised case studies are focused on giving students an opportunity to think critically about real-world challenges they may face, with an emphasis on trending health care topics, such as the following:

- Electronic Health Records, Use and Implementation
- Meaningful Use
- Health Information Exchanges
- Personal Health Records
- ICD-10 Implementation
- Compliance

About the Authors

Charlotte McCuen, M.S., RHIA

Charlotte McCuen, M.S., RHIA has 30 years of experience in health information management. She currently is an independent contractor as editor and coauthor of HIM textbooks and Adjunct Faculty in the Health Information Management BS program at University of Cincinnati. She has served as Associate Professor and Clinical Coordinator for 14 years in the Health Information Management Baccalaureate and Associate degree programs at Macon State College in Macon, Georgia. She has also served 15 years as HIM Director of an acute care hospital and a state psychiatric/forensic acute care hospital. She has consulted for long-term care facilities, a behavioral health hospital, physician offices, and renal dialysis centers. She received her Master's Degree from Mercer University in Health Care Policy and Administration and a Baccalaureate Degree from the Medical College of Georgia in Medical Record Administration. Charlotte volunteers professional service to both AHIMA and the Georgia Health Information Management Association (GHIMA), most recently serving on the AHIMA program committee and as president of GHIMA 2011–2012. She was the recipient of the Mentor Award for GHIMA in 2004.

Nanette B. Sayles, Ed.D., RHIA, CCS, CHPS, CPHIMS, FAHIMA

Nanette Sayles is a 1985 graduate of the University of Alabama at Birmingham Medical Record Administration (now Health Information Management) program. She earned her Masters of Science in Health Information Management (1995) and her Masters in Public Administration (1990) from the University of Alabama at Birmingham. She earned her doctorate in Adult Education from the University of Georgia (2003). She is currently Associate Professor in the Health Information Management program at East Central College in Union, Missouri. She has a wide range of health information management experience in hospitals, consulting, system development/implementation, and education. Nanette received the 2005 American Health Information Management Association Triumph Educator Award.

Patricia Schnering, RHIA, CCS

A self-employed entrepreneur, Patricia Schnering, RHIA, CCS, is the founder, owner, author, and publisher for Professional Review Guides, Inc., and PRG Publishing, Inc. In addition to earning a Baccalaureate degree in Business Administration from the University of South Florida, she is a graduate of the Health Information Management program at St. Petersburg College and holds both CCS and RHIA certifications. Prior to entering the Health Information Management field, Patricia worked for 13 years with a national corporation in departmental management. Since 1993, she has worked in health information services supervisory positions as a HIM consultant and as an adjunct HIM instructor at St. Petersburg College. She has served as president of her local professional association (GCHIMA) and a delegate to the state organization (FHIMA), where she has served on the board of directors, been a committee member, and received the FHIMA Literary Award in 2000 and 2006. Currently, Patricia serves as a delegate to the FHIMA and is on the advisory board at St. Petersburg College. She is also a member of AHIMA and the Assembly on Education (AOE).

Acknowledgments

I would like to extend my sincere thanks to my colleagues, Dr. Nanette Sayles and Ms. Patricia Schnering, for their professional experience, dedication, and contribution to the development of this book. Their input of real-world experiences and knowledge of working in the health information field helped in the development of the case studies presented. I thank the peer reviewers for comments and suggestions in development of the book and keeping it applicable to various scenarios. I would like to give thanks to special people in my life. First, I thank my husband and children for their understanding throughout the development of the book. I also extend gratitude to my parents who always encouraged me to strive for my dreams. Their example of work ethic, diligence, and determination has shown me that your goals can be achieved. Without their support, this text would not have been possible.

Charlotte McCuen, M.S., RHIA

This case study book is one that I have wanted to do for a long time. It is a product that I believe will be useful to both health information management educators and students. For this goal to be realized, it took a lot of support from a number of people:

- My husband, Mark, is supportive of the various projects that I am working on, including this project.
- My parents, George and Jeanette Burchfield, who taught me to work hard and the importance of education.
- My coauthors, Pat Schnering and Charlotte McCuen, for their hard work on this book.

Without their hard work, this case study book would not exist. I'm not sure any of us knew what we were getting ourselves into when we decided to commit to this project.

To the students, it is my hope that you find this book a useful part of your preparation to enter the exciting and challenging world of health information management.

To the educators, I hope that you will find this case study book valuable as you develop and continue to refine your courses.

Nanette B. Sayles, Ed.D., RHIA, CCS, CHPS, CPHIMS, FAHIMA

I especially wish to express my gratitude to Nanette Sayles and Charlotte McCuen, who were instrumental in creating this book. Nanette and Charlotte are seasoned professionals and are experienced instructors in HIA and HIT programs. Their level of energy and dedication to the profession is amazing.

I have enjoyed working with the staff at Cengage Learning. They have been quite accommodating and have taught me a lot about the process of publishing. I thank Lauren, Jadin, Rhonda, and all of the other Cengage team members that made this book possible.

There are some very special people in my life who were always there when I needed them. My late husband, Bob, always continued to keep me grounded, as I tended to spin off in space while I worked on the books, and my mother, Emma Miller, was my role model for perseverance leading to success. She embodied grace, courage, strength, and endurance.

My thanks would not be complete without acknowledging all the HIM/HIT professionals, educators, and students who support our efforts by letting us know what would be useful to them and how we can improve the products we produce. Special thanks for the educators who were willing to take personal time to review our product for quality and value. Thank you for the letters and words of encouragement.

My reward is knowing that the materials you use here may assist you in preparing for the challenge of the workplace. I wish you the very best now and throughout your career.

Until we meet...

Patricia Schnering, RHIA, CCS

Reviewers

Melissa H. Edenburn, RHIA, ICD-10 Trainer
Associate Faculty
McLennan Community College
Waco, TX

Marie A. Janes, MEd, RHIA
Associate Lecturer, HIA/CHIA Programs
The University of Toledo
Toledo, OH

Kelli Lewis, RHIA
Clinical Education Coordinator
Polk State College
Lakeland, FL

Rachel Minatee, MBA, RHIA
Professor of Health Information Technology
Rose State College
Midwest City, OK

Alice M. Noblin, PhD, RHIA, CCS
Health Informatics and Information Management Program Director and Instructor
University of Central Florida
Orlando, FL

Everall A. Peele, MPH, LHRM, RHIA, CCS
Privacy Manager–HIM & Training Coordinator
University of Florida
Gainesville, FL

Julia Steff, RHIA, CCS, CCS-P
Assistant Professor/Department Chair of HIM and Medical Information Coder/Biller
Palm Beach State College
Lake Worth, FL

Beverly Walker, RHIA, CCS
Adjunct Faculty
IUPUI School of Informatics, HIA Program
Indianapolis, IN

Linda Whaley, MEd, RHIA, CCS
Director, Health Information Technology Program
Rose State College
Midwest City, OK

SECTION ONE

Health Data
Management

CASE 1-1

Subjective, Objective, Assessment, and Plan (SOAP) Statements and the Problem-Oriented Medical Record (POMR)

Review each of the following unrelated statements abstracted from problem-oriented medical record (POMR) documentation. Determine whether each statement is a subjective (S), objective (O), assessment (A), or plan (P) entry from the patient records.

1. _____ Rule out myocardial infarction.
2. _____ Patient complains of pain in the left ear and upon neck movement.
3. _____ BP 130/80. Pulse 85. Respirations 20. Temperature 98.6. Lungs clear. Heart regular. Abdomen nontender.
4. _____ Compare baseline mammogram 2006 to current mammogram.
5. _____ Uncontrolled hypertension.
6. _____ Chest pain.
7. _____ Pedal edema was 2+.
8. _____ Possible aortic aneurysm.
9. _____ Rule out cancerous tumor following biopsy of thyroid lesion.
10. _____ Patient complained of headache, fatigue, and photosensitivity.
11. _____ Patient states, "I am thirsty all the time."
12. _____ Discharge home with home health nursing and durable medical equipment. Follow-up in 1 week with Dr. Brantley. Home medications of Plavix 75mg, Zetia 10mg, Norvasc 25mg, and Tricor 145mg.
13. _____ BUN 21.0mg/dL, ALB 6.0gm/dL, bilirubin total 6.3mg/dL.
14. _____ Percussion was normal.
15. _____ MRI brain with and without contrast: negative findings.
16. _____ Complaining of pain in the low back.
17. _____ Chest x-ray: negative. EKG: A-fibrillation. Total LDH: 145.
18. _____ Laceration measured 2 cm above right brow.
19. _____ Determine treatment following results of radiology studies.
20. _____ Surgical Pathology Frozen Section: Lung LLL Wedge Biopsy reflects nonsmall cell carcinoma involving pleural nodule.

CASE 1-2

Problem-Oriented Medical Record (POMR) Record Format

Read the patient visit report shown in Figure 1-1 and answer the following questions.

1. What is the patient's chief complaint?

2. What information in the scenario is "subjective"?

3. What information in the scenario is "objective"?

4. Does Dr. Jenkins have a definitive assessment of Ms. Gerry's problem? If so, what is it?

5. What is the plan for this patient?

Patient Visit Report

HISTORY OF PRESENT ILLNESS: Ms. Gerry is an 85-year-old female who fell out of a wheelchair today. She comes in complaining of severe pain in her left hip. X-ray reveals an intertrochanteric fracture of the left hip.

PAST MEDICAL HISTORY: Alzheimer's disease, GERD, COPD, coronary artery disease.

MEDICATIONS: Zantac 75mg in the AM; Synthroid 88 mcg in the AM; Norvasc 2.5mg in the AM; Nebulizer QID; Coumadin 2.5mg Monday, Wednesday, Friday, and Saturday.

PHYSICAL EXAM: Shortening of the left leg; good bilateral pedal pulses.

PLAN: Medical clearance. Vitamin K to decrease protime. Bucks traction. Open reduction and internal fixation of left hip if cleared for surgery.

X-RAY AFTER SURGERY: Diffuse osteopenia present. Patient is post placement of a dynamic hip screw within the proximal left femur. There is near anatomical alignment of the intertrochanteric femoral neck fracture.

Figure 1-1 *Patient Visit Report*

CASE **1-3**

Master Patient Index (MPI) and Duplicate Medical Record Number Assignment

The ad hoc report shown in Table 1-1 (Master Patient Index [MPI] Discrepancy Report) is a reporting function of the MPI system. This system function applies weights for the probability, on a scale from 1 to 15, that the two patient encounters in each case are likely to pertain to the same patient or not. The policy of the hospital is to retain the survivorship record number when correcting duplicate number assignments on the same patient.

Review the ad hoc report provided in Table 1-1 for analysis of duplicate medical record number assignments.

1. For each pair of patients listed, which medical record number should be retained, based on the hospital policy?

2. Which numbers listed do you think require further documentation review to determine if the patients are the same or not?

3. Which record documentation or data elements from the patient record could be used for determining "matches" of the same patient versus different patients?

Table 1-1 *MPI Discrepancy Report*

MPI Discrepancy Report					
Case	Patient Name	MR#	SSN	DOB	Residence	Wt.
1	John Carmichael	016792	256-14-9876	1-5-1982	111 Holly Dr.	14.1
	J. D. Carmichael	019156	256-14-9876	1-5-1982	295 Stream Dr.	
2	Susan A. Pherris	042121	031-55-8642	5-4-2002	Hwy. 24, Box 11	5.0
	Susan Ferris	050377	386-12-7854	5-4-1962	456 First St.	
3	Amanda Johns	114682	487-09-4210	8-2-1984	219 Bates St.	10.4
	Amanda Willis	143022	487-09-4211	8-2-1984	532 Jesse Dr.	
4	Jonathan Allen, III	015467	276-22-9768	1-9-1955	131 Oaks Rd.	2.5
	Jonathan Allen	139878	297-46-2089	9-8-2006	197 Trey Cir.	
5	William Jones	122199	698-28-7667	2-6-2004	100 Windy Rd.	13.0
	Bill Jones	140981	698-28-7661	2-6-2004	100 Windy Rd.	
6	Tracy Lemon	130961	209-88-0120	1-9-2001	28 Hillman Ave.	1.5
	Treina Lemon	098972	462-90-0156	8-5-2006	101 Troy Ct.	

CASE 1-4

Enterprise MPI (E-MPI)

As the assistant health information management (HIM) director of a growing health system network that currently includes 3 hospitals and 16 outpatient clinics, you are a member on the Information Systems Committee. You have been asked to oversee the development of a standardized, system-wide enterprise master patient index (MPI) that will include all patients and their information from all encounters within the system network.

1. *Level 1:* Research the recommended core elements of a single-entity MPI and a multi-facility enterprise MPI through professional journals and list references used (e.g., *Journal of AHIMA*).

2. *Level 2:* Develop a data dictionary, defining each of the data elements needed.

3. *Level 3:* Design a data display screen of a multi-facility enterprise MPI screen.

CASE 1-5

Chart Check-Out Screen Design and Data Quality

You have been recently hired by a vendor who develops chart management software. In your role as the subject matter expert, it is your responsibility to ensure that the system will meet the needs of users in the HIM Department. One of your first duties is to evaluate the screens that have been designed over the past few months when the vendor's company did not have an HIM professional on staff. The first one that you review is the chart check-out screen for the chart locator.

1. Evaluate the screen design in Figure 1-2 to identify ways to improve data quality, including the comprehensiveness and appropriateness of the fields on the screen. Make recommendations for improvement.

To help you in your project, you may reference form design and control in the textbook *Today's Health Information Management: An Integrated Approach, Second Edition* (2013), by Dana McWay.

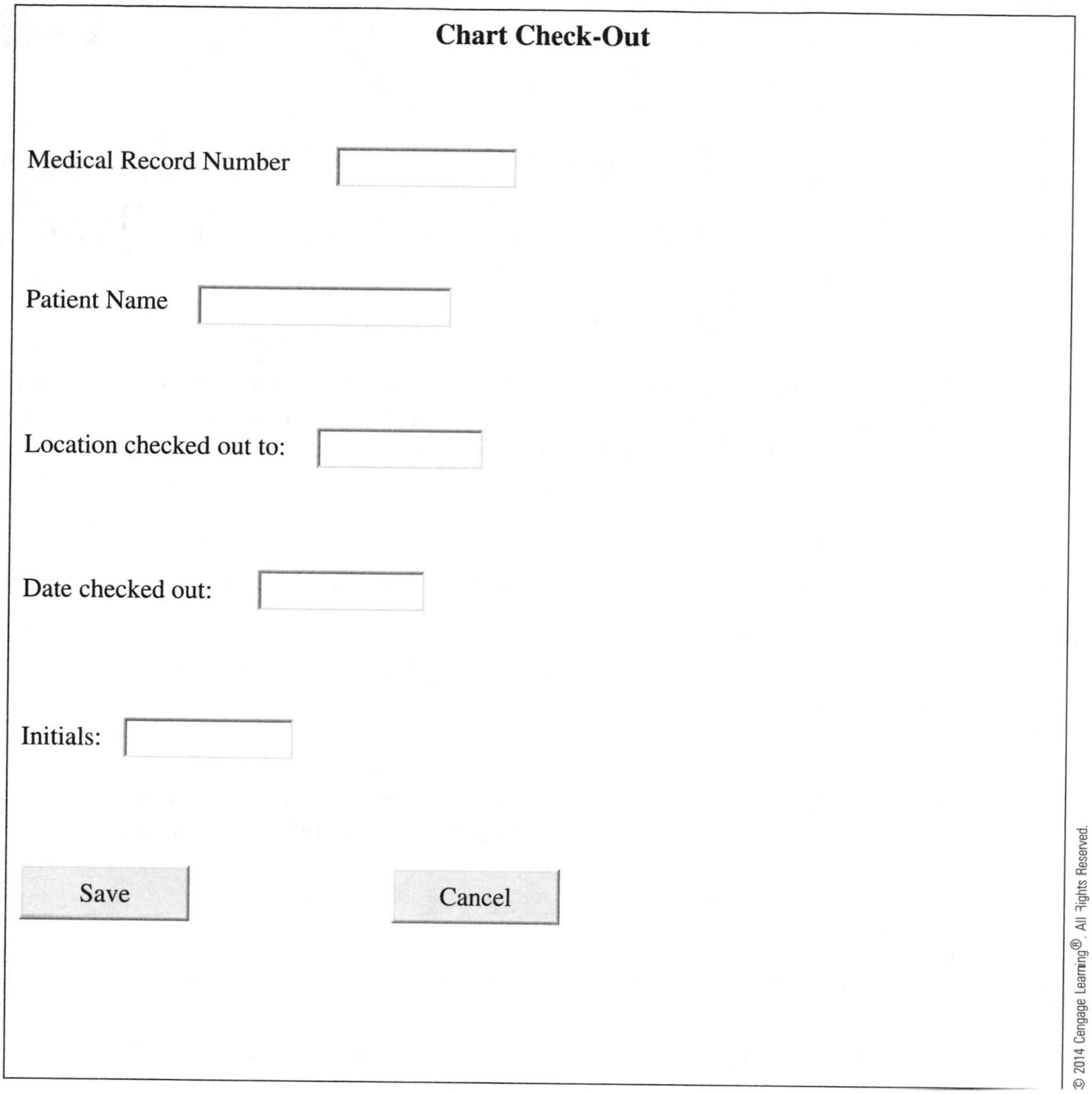

Chart Check-Out

Medical Record Number [ ]

Patient Name [ ]

Location checked out to: [ ]

Date checked out: [ ]

Initials: [ ]

[Save]   [Cancel]

Figure 1-2 *Chart Check-Out Screen*

CASE 1-6

Patient Demographic Data Entry Screen Design and Data Quality

You are the assistant HIM director and you are on the Health Information Systems (HIS) Committee for overseeing screen design for data entry. A screen request for a patient demographic data entry screen has been submitted by the supervisor of the chart locator system.

1. Employ good design principles for data entry and data quality to critique the screen design in Figure 1-3.

2. Evaluate the screen design and content in Figure 1-3 to identify ways to improve data quality, including the comprehensiveness and appropriateness of the data fields as well as field names.

To help you in your project, you may reference form design and control in the textbook *Today's Health Information Management: An Integrated Approach, Second Edition* (2013), by Dana McWay.

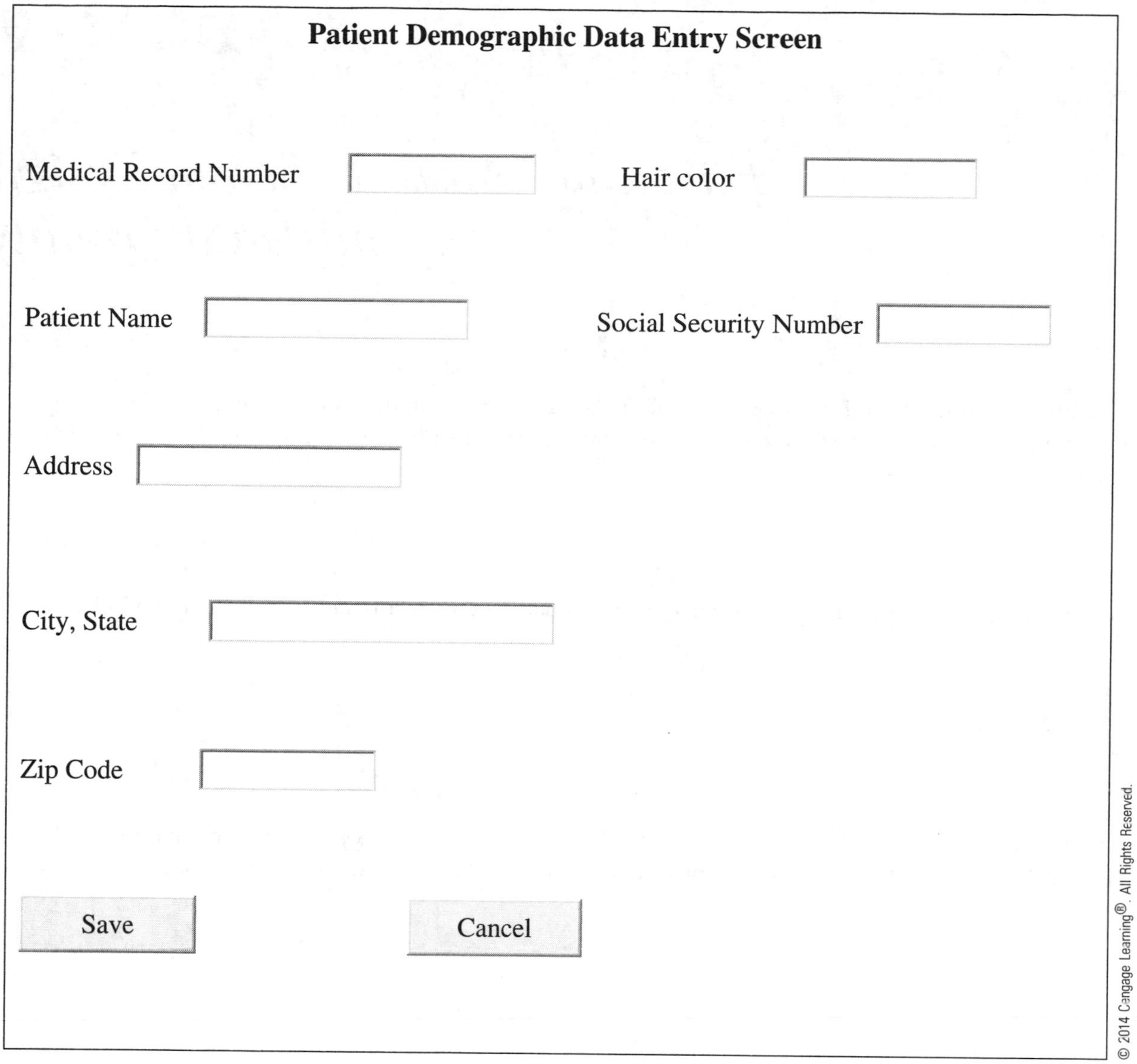

Patient Demographic Data Entry Screen

Medical Record Number [   ]   Hair color [   ]

Patient Name [   ]   Social Security Number [   ]

Address [   ]

City, State [   ]

Zip Code [   ]

[Save]   [Cancel]

Figure 1-3 *Patient Demographic Data Entry Screen*

CASE 1-7

Encounter Abstract Screen Design and Data Quality

You are the assistant HIM director and you are on the HIS Committee for overseeing screen design for data entry. A screen request for an encounter data entry screen has been submitted by the supervisor of the chart locator system.

1. Employ good design principles for data entry and data quality to critique the screen design in Figure 1-4.

2. Evaluate the screen design and content in Figure 1-4 to identify ways to improve data quality, including the comprehensiveness and appropriateness of the data fields as well as field names.

To help you in your project, you may reference form design and control in the textbook *Today's Health Information Management: An Integrated Approach, Second Edition* (2013), by Dana McWay.

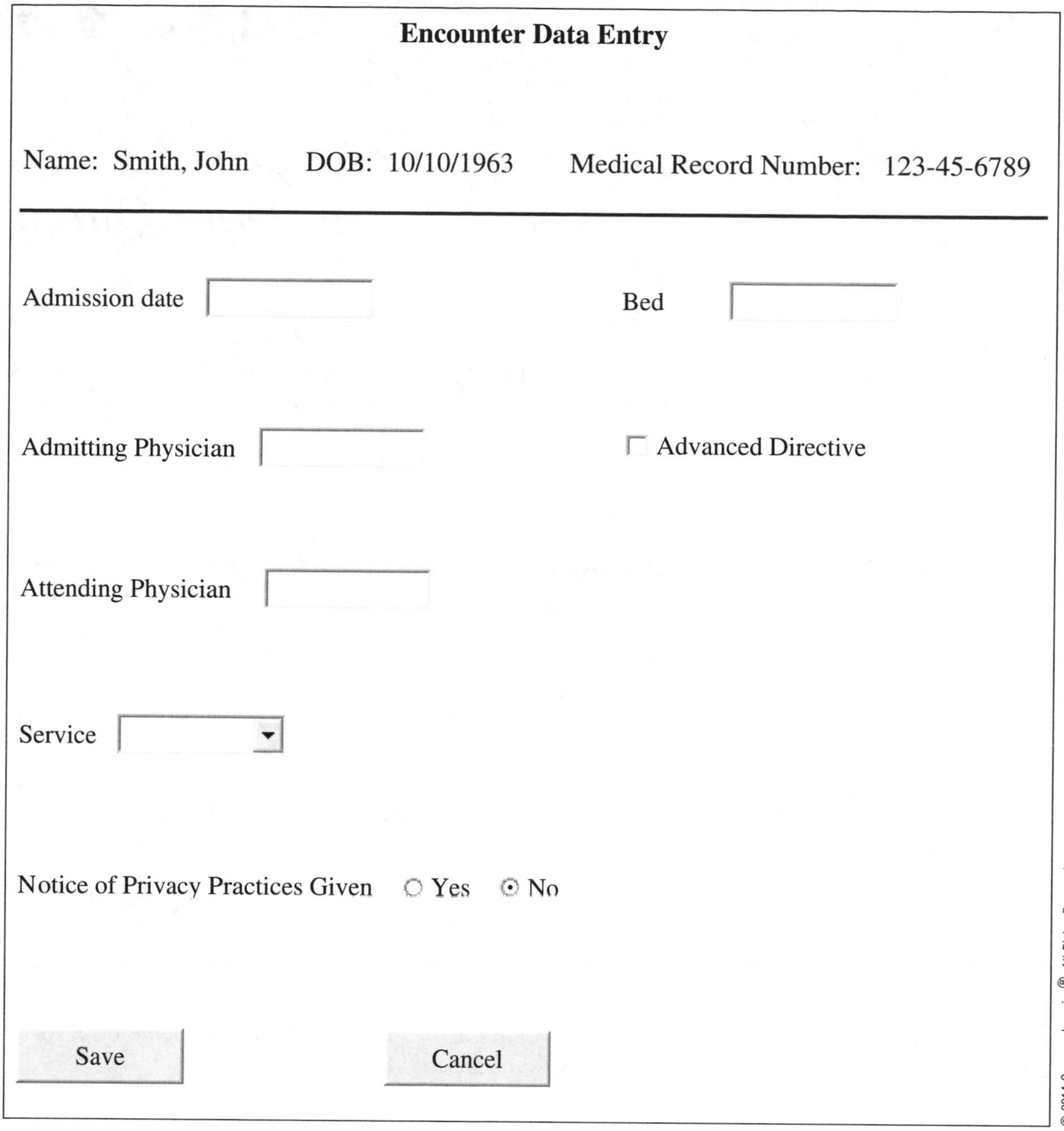

Encounter Data Entry

Name: Smith, John   DOB: 10/10/1963   Medical Record Number: 123-45-6789

Admission date [   ]   Bed [   ]

Admitting Physician [   ]   □ Advanced Directive

Attending Physician [   ]

Service [▼]

Notice of Privacy Practices Given   ○ Yes   ⊙ No

[Save]   [Cancel]

Figure 1-4   *Encounter Abstract Screen*

CASE 1-8

Coding Abstract Data Entry Screen Design and Data Quality

You are the assistant HIM director and you are on the HIS Committee for overseeing screen design for data entry. A screen request for a coding abstract screen has been submitted by the supervisor of the chart locator system.

1. Employ good design principles for data entry and data quality to critique the screen design in Figure 1-5.

2. Evaluate the screen design and content in Figure 1-5 to identify ways to improve data quality, including the comprehensiveness and appropriateness of the data fields as well as field names.

To help you in your project, you may reference form design and control in the textbook *Today's Health Information Management: An Integrated Approach, Second Edition* (2013), by Dana McWay.

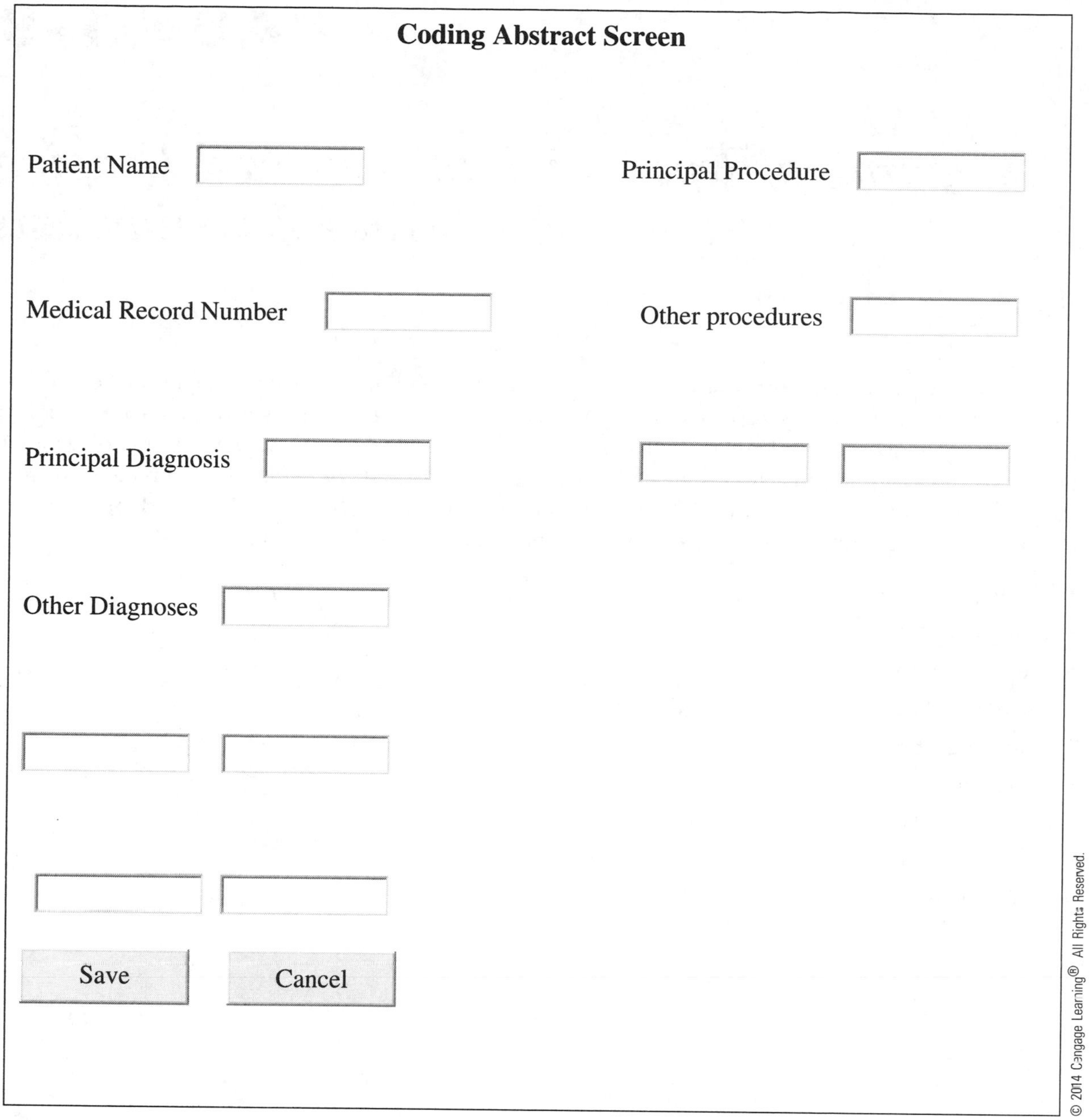

Coding Abstract Screen

Patient Name [   ]   Principal Procedure [   ]

Medical Record Number [   ]   Other procedures [   ]

Principal Diagnosis [   ]   [   ]   [   ]

Other Diagnoses [   ]

[   ]   [   ]

[   ]   [   ]

[Save]   [Cancel]

Figure 1-5   *Coding Abstract Data Entry Screen*

CASE 1-9

Designing a Report for Radiology and Imaging Service Examinations

You are a member of the Forms or Screen Design Committee of an ambulatory diagnostic center. You have been assigned the task of developing a requisition and imaging report to be used for radiology and imaging service exams. The new report needs to combine both the requisition and radiology interpretative report on the same form or electronic health record (EHR) screen. Follow directions of your instructor to design either a form or computer entry screen utilizing Microsoft Access, Microsoft Excel, or Microsoft Word, and include all data elements specified in the following list.

- Patient Name
- Date of Birth
- Medical Record Number
- Encounter Number
- Attending Physician
- Referring Physician
- Encounter Date
- Diagnosis/Condition
- Interpretation

CASE 1-10

Documentation Requirements for the History and Physical Report

As the chart completion supervisor, you are to meet with the HIM director to discuss documentation requirements among various agencies and state laws, such as the timeliness of the History and Physical Report, by which the hospital abides. The purpose of the meeting is to make sure the policy and procedure for analyzing patient record documentation remain current with regulatory agency documentation requirements.

1. Research the history and physical report documentation requirements for the Joint Commission and DNV Healthcare (Det Norske Veritas) accrediting bodies and for your applicable state law.

2. Create a table to report the differences in requirements between the 2 regulatory agencies.

CASE 1-11

Documentation Requirements for the Autopsy Report

You are the chart completion supervisor. You are preparing for a meeting with the HIM director to discuss the documentation requirements for timeliness of the Provisional and Final Autopsy Report. There are various agencies and state laws with requirements that the hospital must meet. The purpose of the meeting is to make sure the policy and procedure for analyzing patient record documentation remains current with regulatory agency documentation requirements.

1. Research the Provisional and Final Autopsy Report documentation requirements for the Joint Commission and DNV Healthcare (Det Norske Veritas) accrediting bodies and for your applicable state law.

2. Create a table to report the differences in requirements between the 2 agencies.

CASE 1-12

Data Collection in Long-Term Care: Minimum Data Set Version 3.0 (MDS 3.0)

The company that you work for owns 25 long-term nursing and rehabilitation centers throughout the state. Your regional director has asked you to develop an audit process for quality review of the Minimum Data Set 3.0 on completion requirements for the (comprehensive) Full Assessment Form. The process will review data collection among the corporation's homes to assess the accuracy and efficiency of reporting MDS data to Center for Medicare and Medicaid Services (CMS) for reimbursement of care.

Please visit the web links section of the student companion website to access the online material referenced in this case study.

1. *Level 1:* For informational purposes, visit the CMS website for "MDS 3.0 training." Review the official MDS and provide the following information:
   a) MDS 3.0 required data sections.
   b) The types of data included under each section.
   c) Where in the medical record you would expect to find the data to complete each section of the MDS.
2. *Level 2:* Listen to the online panel discussion "MDS 3 Interdisciplinary Team" to assist in answering the following questions:
   a) Which MDS 3.0 section requires using the resident's medical record for completion?
   b) What problems are likely to be encountered while completing MDS 3.0?
   c) What suggestions would you make to overcome these problems?
3. *Level 3:* Listen to the CMS presentation "VIVE: Video on Interviewing Vulnerable Elders" to assist in answering the following questions.
   a) What sections of MDS 3.0 must be completed by interview?
   b) What are the advantages of using an interview format for gathering this data?
   c) How long do these interviews typically take, according to the training video?
   d) Describe some of the techniques suggested for the interview process.

CASE 1-13

Data Collection for the Healthcare Effectiveness Data and Information Set (HEDIS) in Managed Care

The managed care delivery system you have been employed with over the past few months is struggling in some areas of patient care and information systems for capturing and reporting patient care. You sit on a committee to develop an organizational quality improvement program for the organization. In preparation for the next administrative staff meeting, you are to report on healthcare effectiveness data and information set (HEDIS) elements reported and benchmarked among managed care providers.

As the HIM manager, you initially plan to visit www.ncqa.org and review professional literature to research HEDIS data element requirements.

1. Develop a list of the care measures tracked among different patient populations. Review National Committee for Quality Assurance (NCQA) report on "The State of Health Care Quality 2011: Continuous Improvement and the Expansion of Quality Measurement."

2. Develop a summary of the patient populations reviewed and report findings relative to different conditions. Briefly summarize the chronic diseases measured, children and adolescent conditions, and older adult conditions from, the 2011 Quality Measurement Report.

CASE 1-14

Birth Certificate Reporting Project

Cabbage County is a rural community in Georgia that still completes and mails birth certificates to the county health department and state vital records office once a week. The hospital had 1 live birth yesterday. You are the birth certificate coordinator at Cabbage Patch Hospital and are responsible for completing birth certificates of newborn babies in the hospital. Pertinent identity information was obtained from an interview with the mother and from her obstetric record.

Valid information from the interview is given in Figure 1-6. The remainder of the prenatal, perinatal, and postnatal information can be found in the mother's medical record (obstetric record) provided in Figure 1-7. Use the information in the interview and abstract information from the obstetric record provided to complete the birth certificate shown in Figure 1-8.

The obstetrician who delivered the baby was James Mercy, MD, license number 52443. His office is at 210 Cabbage Patch Circle, Cleveland, Georgia 31402. The certifier field on the birth certificate will be left blank; notify the doctor to sign before mailing the certificate.

The registrar with the state vital records office will sign the registrar field of the completed birth certificate when it is received, and maintain it on file at the vital records office in Cabbage County, where the baby was born.

Interview with Mother

The mother's name is Diana Lynn Prince, maiden name Quinn, DOB 9-1-1991, Social Security number 251-00-1333. Ms. Prince is a homemaker who was born in Arizona, where she completed her high school education. She later relocated to her new hometown, the city of Cleveland, Georgia. She lives with her husband, Charles Anthony Prince, at 100 Windy Lane, Cleveland, GA 31402. The record indicates Ms. Prince was admitted 1-13-2013 in labor. Charles Anthony Prince was born in Maryland on 10-5-87 and has the Social Security number 231-20-3120. Mr. Prince is a black male of American descent who completed 4 years of college with a bachelor's degree in business. Ms. Prince and her husband chose to name their baby boy Lawrence Anthony Prince. The mother did give consent to release information to the Social Security Administration for issuance of a Social Security number for the baby.

Figure 1-6 *Interview with Mother*

Cabbage Patch Hospital

Admission Information   INPATIENT

Admit Date	Admit Time	Location	Room/Bed	Accom.	Bill. Type	Rel. Info.	Med. Rec. Number	Fin. Cl.
1-13-2013	0530	322	224/03	P	00	Y	09 09 99	8

Patient Name: Diana Lynn Prince   **Nick Name:**   **Maiden Name:**   **Account Number:** 10032145   **Donor:** N

Street Address: 100 Windy Lane   **County:** Cabbage   **City:** Cleveland   **State:** GA   **Zip Code:** 31402   **Facility ID:** 88888

Sex	Race	Marital	Date of Birth	Age	SSN
F	B	M	9-1-1991	22	251-00-1333

Religion: Non   **Place of Worship:**   **City:**   **State:**

Patient Employer: N/A   **Occupation:** homemaker   **Work Phone:**

Address: **City:**   **State:**   **Zip Code:**

Emergency Contact: Charles Anthony Prince   **Relationship:**   **Home Phone:**   **Work Phone:**

Address: 100 Windy Lane,   **County:** Cabbage   **City:** Cleveland   **State:** GA   **Zip Code:** 31402

Insurance Co. 1: Blue Cross/Blue Shield   **Authorization Number:** 012345678 PZ   **Phone:** (912) 999-0000

Insurance Co. 2: N/A   **Authorization Number:**   **Phone:**

Insurance Co. 3:   **Authorization Number:**   **Phone:**

Admission Physician: James Mercy   **Service:** OBS   **Doctor Code:** 018   **Answering Serv. Phone:** 799-8888   **Beeper:** 032   UPIN 52443

Referring Physician: **City:**   **State:**   **Phone Number:**

Admit Diagnosis: OB for delivery at term   **Admit Type:** 1   **Admit Source:** 1   **Accident Date:** N/A   **Accident Time:**

Pre-Admit Clerk: **Admit Clerk:** APT   **Memos:**

Normal Vaginal Delivery, spontaneous
Tubal Ligation

Consulting Physicians:

	Assembly
	Code/Abstract
	Entered
Discharge Date: 1-14-2013 **Discharge Time:** _____ **Days Stay:** _____	Deficiency
Results: ☐ Alive ☐ Post Op Death +48 Hrs. ☐ Death +48 Hrs. ☐ Death with Autopsy	Final Analysis
☐ AMA ☐ Post Op Death −48 Hrs. ☐ Death −48 Hrs.	

Figure 1-7 *Mother's Obstetric Record*

Prince, Diana Lynn
DOB 9/1/1991
MR 09 09 99, 10032145

Cabbage Patch Hospital

Obstetric Admitting Record

ASSESSMENT

Admission Date: 1 / 13 / 2013 Time 0535 Age 22

G	T	P	A	L

EDC 1-16-2013 EGA 39+
LMP 4-18-2012

Perinatal Transfer (From-Place) N/A

Arrival on Unit: ☐ Ambulatory ☐ Wheelchair ☐ Stretcher

Reason for Admission rule out labor

Allergies No known drug allergies

Labor Began: Date 1-13-2013 Time 0500

Membranes on Admission:

☑ Intact ☐ Ruptured: Date _____ Time _____

Fluid: ☐ Clear ☐ Meconium ☐ Foul Smelling

Vaginal Bleeding: ☑ None ☐ Normal Show

☐ Bleeding (Describe): _____

Patient: ☑ Recent URI   ☐ Dentures
         ☐ Been vomiting   ☐ Glasses
         ☐ Exposed to infection ☐ Contact lenses

Prenatal: Care: ☐ No ☑ Yes
Prev. Adm. L&D: ☐ No ☑ Yes   Record: ☐ No ☑ Yes
                             Education: ☑ No ☐ Yes

RISK ASSESSMENT

Risk Factors: ☑ None

Antepartum Tests: ☐ None
Sonogram X 2

Hx Herpes Virus: ☑ No ☐ Yes
  +Culture and/or Herpes Lesion:
    ☐ No ☐ Yes Date _____

Hx Blood Transfusions: ☑ No ☐ Yes

Previous Alcohol and/or Drug Use: ☑ No ☐ Yes

Other _____

Smoker: ☑ No ☐ Yes

Hx Hepatitis: ☑ No ☐ Yes

Blood Type: A+

Last Oral Intake:
  Fluids - Date 1-12-2013 Time 2100
  Solids - Date 1-12-2013 Time 2100

Current Medications: ☐ None

Name/Type of Medication	Last Taken	Brought In

PHYSICAL ASSESSMENT

HT. 5'2"	WT. 149	BP 156/70	FHR 150
T 37	P 115	R 24	

DTR'S + 2?

Mental Status alert + appropriate

Dilation 4 cm.
Effacement 80 %
Station _____
Presentation vertex

Urine dipstick: Protein _____
Glucose _____ Ketone _____
Other: none obtained at admission).

PLAN

Plans for Anesthesia:

Specify Type _____ ☐ None planned

Pt. has: Living Will: ☐ No ☐ Yes   Durable Power of Attorney: ☐ No ☐ Yes
☐ Information regarding Advance Directives given to patient.
☐ Advised of video broadcast
☐ Referred to resource group
☐ Referred to physician

Patient Orientation: ☐ Fetal Monitor
                     ☐ Nurses Call Light
                     ☐ Visiting Policy

Consent Forms: ☐ NA
☐ Preanesthesia Evaluation ☐ Support Person
☐ Metabolic Screening   ☐ Sibling Visitation

Pediatrician Jim Jelanski, MD.
Support Person father of baby
Tubal Ligation: ☐ No ☑ Yes
Desires Circumcision: ☐ No ☑ Yes
Pt. plans: ☐ Private   ☐ Breast feeding
           ☑ Mother/Baby   ☑ Bottle feeding

INTERVENTION
Procedures EFM/VE
Disposition: Admit
Physician's Name James Mercy, M.D.
Notified by _____
Date 1-13-2013 Time 0610

RN SIGNATURE Lucy Aiken, RN

Figure 1-7 *Mother's Obstetric Record (continued)*

Prince, Diana Lynn DOB 9/1/1991 MR 09 09 99, 10032145	Cabbage Patch Hospital Obstetric Admitting Record

ASSESSMENT

Admission Date: _1_ / _10_ / _2013_ Time _0130_ Age _22_

G	T	P	A	L
3	2	0	0	2

EDC _1-16_ EGA _39_
LMP _4-18-2012_

Perinatal Transfer (From-Place) _____

Arrival on Unit: ☐ Ambulatory ☑ Wheelchair ☐ Stretcher

Reason for Admission _rule out labor_

Allergies _no known drug allergies_

Labor Began: Date _1-9-2013_ Time _2300_

Membranes on Admission:
☑ Intact ☐ Ruptured: Date _____ Time _____
Fluid: ☐ Clear ☐ Meconium ☐ Foul Smelling
Vaginal Bleeding: ☑ None ☐ Normal Show
☐ Bleeding (Describe): _____

Patient: ☑ Recent URI ☐ Dentures
☐ Been vomiting ☐ Glasses
☐ Exposed to infection ☐ Contact lenses

Prenatal: Care: ☐ No ☑ Yes
Prev. Adm. L&D: ☑ No ☐ Yes Record: ☐ No ☐ Yes
Education: ☑ No ☐ Yes

RISK ASSESSMENT

Risk Factors: ☑ None
_____
_____
_____

Antepartum Tests: ☐ None
OB sonogram X 2
_____
_____

Hx Herpes Virus: ☑ No ☐ Yes
  +Culture and/or Herpes Lesion:
  ☐ No ☐ Yes Date _____
Hx Blood Transfusions: ☑ No ☐ Yes
Previous Alcohol and/or Drug Use: ☑ No ☐ Yes
Other _____
Smoker: ☑ No ☐ Yes
Hx Hepatitis: ☑ No ☐ Yes _A+_
Blood Type: _____
Last Oral Intake:
  Fluids - Date _1-9-2013_ Time _2200_
  Solids - Date _1-9-2013_ Time _2000_
Current Medications: ☐ None

Name/Type of Medication	Last Taken	Brought In
PNV's + FESO4	_1-9-2013_	

PHYSICAL ASSESSMENT

HT. _5'2"_ WT. _149½_ BP _153/75_
T _37.3 C_ P _82_ R _20_
DTR'S _____
Mental Status _alert + oriented_

FHR _____
Dilation _____
Effacement _____
Station _____
Presentation _____

Urine dipstick: Protein _N_
Glucose _N_ Ketone _N_
Other: _____

PLAN

Plans for Anesthesia:
Specify Type _epidural_ ☐ None planned

Pt. has: Living Will: ☐ No ☐ Yes Durable Power of Attorney: ☑ No ☐ Yes
☐ Information regarding Advance Directives given to patient.
☐ Advised of video broadcast
☐ Referred to resource group
☐ Referred to physician

Patient Orientation: ☑ Fetal Monitor
☑ Nurses Call Light
☑ Visiting Policy

Consent Forms: ☐ NA
☑ Preanesthesia Evaluation ☑ Support Person
☑ Metabolic Screening ☑ Sibling Visitation

Pediatrician _Jim Telanski, M.D._
Support Person _father of baby_
Tubal Ligation: ☐ No ☐ Yes
Desires Circumcision: ☐ No ☐ Yes
Pt. plans: ☐ Private ☐ Breast feeding
☑ Mother/Baby ☑ Bottle feeding

INTERVENTION
Procedures _____
Disposition: _____
Physician's Name _____
Notified by _J. Jones, RN_
Date _1-10-2013_ Time _0200_

RN SIGNATURE _J. Jones, RN_

Figure 1-7 *Mother's Obstetric Record (continued)*

Prince, Diana Lynn
DOB 9/1/1991
MR 09 09 99, 10032145

Cabbage Patch Hospital

OBSTETRIC HISTORY & PHYSICAL

Date _1-13-2013_ Time _0200_ (24 Hr.)

Age _22_ Race _B_ FPAL _2002_
LMP _4-18-12_ EDC _1-16-2013_ EGA _39_
Prev C/S ☐ No ☐ Yes: LTCS ☐ No ☐ Yes ☐ Unknown
Ultrasound ☐ No ☑ Yes
   Date _6-12_ EDC _10-16_ EGA _8.2 mo._
   Date _____ EDC _____ EGA _____
Drug Allergies ☑ No ☐ Yes _____
ACOG Criteria for Elective Delivery Met?
   ☐ Yes ☐ No ☐ N/A _____ Initials

OBSTETRIC LAB PROFILE
ABO _A_ Rh ⊕ MSAFP _____ Cytol _____
Last Hgb/Hct _____ Date _____ Hgb Screen _____
Antibody Screen _____
Rubella _immune_ HBSAg _____
Urine Culture _____
1° Glucose Screen _94_
RPR _WNL_ Date _____ Chlamydia ⊖
Other Lab(s) _____
HIV ⊖

HISTORY

Past Medical History _∅_

Family History _∅_   Social History _⊖ cigarette, ⊖ ETOH, ⊖ drugs_

ROS _∅_

Admission History _22 y/o, P2002, admitted with occasional contractions. Had uneventful antepartum course._

PHYSICAL EXAMINATION

General _WDWN_   Vital Signs T _37.3 c_ P _82_ R _20_ BP _153/75_
Mental Status ☐ Normal ☐ Abnormal _____ Skin _____
HEENT _pupils equal, round, reactive to light_ Neck _____
Heart _regular rate and rhythm_
Lungs _____   Breasts _soft/non-tender_
Abdomen Fundal Ht _____ FHR _130_ EFW _____ Presentation/Lie _vertex_ Other _____
Cervix Dil _3 cm_ Eff _70%_ Stn _-2_ Consist _____ Cx Position _____ Other _____
Pelvic Assessment ☐ Adequate ☐ Borderline ☐ Contracted _____
Membranes ☐ Intact ☐ Ruptured _____ Date _____ Time _____ (24 Hr.)
Rectal _____ Extremities _____ Neuro _____
Other _____

Fetal Monitor Assessment _reactive_

Impressions _39 wks._   Plans _anticipate NSVD_

PHYSICIAN SIGNATURE _James Mercy, M.D._

Figure 1-7 *Mother's Obstetric Record (continued)*

Prince, Diana Lynn DOB 9/1/1991 MR 09 09 99, 10032145	**Cabbage Patch Hospital** **Labor and Delivery Summary**

Labor Summary

G	T	Pt	A	L	Type & Rh
3	2	0	0	2	A+

Maternal transport   ☐ Yes   ☐ No

Presentation   ☐ Position
- ☑ Vertex
- ☐ Face or brow
- ☐ Breech: _____
- ☐ Transverse lie   ☐ Compound
- ☐ Unknown

Complications   ☑ None
- ☐ No prenatal care
- ☐ Preterm labor (<37 weeks)
- ☐ Postterm (>42 weeks)
- ☐ Febrile (> 100.4°) when adm.
- ☐ PROM (> 12 hrs. preadmit)
- ☐ Meconium
- ☐ Foul smelling fluid
- ☐ Hydramnios
- ☐ Abruption
- ☐ Placenta previa
- ☐ Bleeding-site undetermined
- ☐ Toxemia (mild) (severe)
- ☐ Seizure activity
- ☐ Precipitous labor (< 3 hrs.)
- ☐ Prolonged labor (> 20 hrs.)
- ☐ Prolonged latent phase
- ☐ Prolonged active phase
- ☐ Prolonged 2nd stage (> 2.5 hrs.)
- ☐ Secondary arrest of dilation
- ☐ Cephalopelvic disproportion
- ☐ Cord prolapse
- ☐ Decreased FHT variability
- ☐ Extended fetal bradycardia
- ☐ Extended fetal tachycardia
- ☐ Multiple late decelerations
- ☐ Acidosis (pH 7.2)
- ☐ Anesthetic complications
- ☐ Multiple variable decelerations
- ☐ HSV

☐ _____
☐ _____

Scalp pH: ☐ Yes   ☐ No

Induction   ☑ None
- ☐ ARM   ☐ Oxytoc.   ☐ Prostin
- ☐ Serial X: _____ days

Augmentation   ☑ None
- ☐ ARM   ☐ Oxytoc.
☐ _____

Monitor   ☑ LR   ☑ DR   ☐ None
External: ☐ FHT   ☐ UC
Internal: ☐ FHT   ☐ UC

Medications	Total dose
fentanyl	0.1mg

Time of last narcotic: 0615

Delivery Data

Method of Delivery
☐ VBAC
Cephalic
- ☑ Spontaneous
- ☐ Low forceps ⎤
- ☐ Mid forceps ⎦ Type: _____
- ☐ Rotation: _____ to _____
- ☐ Vacuum Extractor

Breech
- ☐ Spontaneous
- ☐ Partial extraction (assisted)
- ☐ Total extraction
- ☐ Forceps to A.C. head

Cesarean (details in operative notes)
- ☐ Primary   ☐ Repeat
- ☐ Low cervical: transverse
- ☐ Low cervical: vertical
- ☐ Classical
- ☐ Cesarean hysterectomy

Placenta	Blood Loss
☑ Spontaneous	☐ < 500 ml.
☐ Expressed	☐ > 500 ml.
☐ Manual	Specify amt.
☐ Adherent	(ml.)
☐ Ut. exploration	Detail in remarks
☐ Configuration	
☐ Normal	
☐ Abn.: _____	

☐ To pathology   ☐ Yes   ☑ No

Cord
- ☐ Nuchal cord X: ___ N/A
- ☐ True knot
- ☑ 2 Umbilical vessels
Cord blood: ☑ Lab   ☐ Not obt.
Cord blood gas: No
pH ___ pCO2 ___ pO2 ___ B.E. ___

Episiotomy   ☑ None
- ☐ Median suture: _____
- ☐ Mediolateral _____
- ☐ Degree: _____

Laceration	☐ None
☑ 1 2 3 4	Degree perineal
☐ Vaginal	
☐ Cervical	
☐ Uterine rupture	
☐ Other: vaginal	

Del. room no.: 03

father of baby
Support person

Maternal BP: _____ P: _____
FHT: _____ Time: _____
James Mercy, MD
Attending physician

_____
Assisting physician

Delivery Data (Cont.)

Surgical Procedures   ☐ None
- ☑ Tubal ligation   ☐ Curettage
- ☐ Specimen to Pathology

Delivery Anesthesia   ☐ None
1=Local   2=Pudendal
3=Paracervical   ④=Epidural
5=Spinal   6=General

Administered by: _____

Delivery Room Meds   ☐ None

Agent/Drug	Dose	Route

Time/Signature

Agent/Drug	Dose	Route

Time/Signature

IV Fluids: _____

Time/Signature _____

Maternal O2:   ☐ Yes   ☐ No
                         ☐ LR   ☐ DR

Chronology

EDC date: 10 / 16 / 2013

Gestation: 39 weeks

	Date	Time
• Admit to hospital	1-13	0535
• Membranes ruptured	1-13	0652
• Onset of labor	1-13	0500
• Complete cervical dil.	1-13	0558
• Delivery of infant	1-13	0659
• Delivery of placenta	1-13	0703

Remarks: _____

RN signature: L. Mimbs, RN.
Physician signature: James Mercy, MD

Infant Data

Assessment

-crying vigorously.
-movement good.

Plan & Intervention
☐ Term   ☐ IMC   ☐ NICU   ☑ MB

Apgar Scores

	Heart rate	Respiration	Muscle tone	Reflex irritation	Skin color	Totals
1 min	2	2	1	1		8
5 min	2	2	2	1		9

Basic Infant Data

Medical rec. no.: _____

ID bracelet no.: 9850

☑ Male   ☐ Female

Birth order: 1 of ① 2 3 4

Weight: 6 lbs 11 ozs.
3050 Grams

Length: 19 1/2 in

☑ Erythromycin oint.

RN: P. Smith, RN.

Deceased N/A
Date: __/__/__ Time: _____
☐ Antepartum   ☐ Intrapartum
☐ Neonatal (in delivery room)

White - Mother's Chart   Yellow - Baby's Chart   Pink - physician

Figure 1-7   *Mother's Obstetric Record (continued)*

Prince, Diana Lynn DOB 9/1/1991 MR 09 09 99, 10032145	Cabbage Patch Hospital
	Labor & Delivery Admission Orders

Admission Date: _1-13-2013_   Time: _0630_

RN Init.	Time	
		Admit to Labor & Delivery
		Allergies: _NKDA_
		Patient may ambulate if desired and labor uncomplicated.
		NPO except for ice chips and medications.
		Measure intake q 8h and output q void.
		Obtain external fetal monitor strip for 30 minutes on admission.
la	0630	Activity: ☑ Bedrest
		☐ Bathroom privileges
		☐ May ambulate ☐ with fetal monitor ☐ without fetal monitor
		Fetal Monitor: ☐ No ☑ External ☐ Internal
la	0634	Labs: ☑ Hemoglobin & Hematocrit: ☐ STAT ☐ Routine
		☑ Urinalysis: ☐ None ☑ Routine ☐ Microscopic ☐ Culture & Sensitivity
		☑ Dipstick urine for protein, glucose, ketone, and nitrite.
		☐ Biochemical Profile I for patient desiring PPS.
		☐ RPR
		☑ Type and Screen
la	0638	☐ Other Labs
		IV Fluids: _D5LR_ @ _125_ cc/hr through 18 gauge intravenous
		catheter. May adjust IV rate as indicated for hydration.
		IV Fluids for epidural bolus: RL only (at least 1500cc intake before epidural placement)
		Maternal and fetal vital signs per intrapartum standard of care.
		Catheterize PRN: if patient bladder distended and patient unable to void.
		Sedation: _Fentanyl 0.1mg IVP q 1-2hr prn pain_

Physician Signature: _James Mercy, MD._

RN Init./Signature: _Lucy Aiken, RN._

Figure 1-7 *Mother's Obstetric Record (continued)*

Prince, Diana Lynn DOB 9/1/1991 MR 09 09 99, 10032145	Cabbage Patch Hospital
Date: mo/day/yr	Health History Summary

Age _22_ Date of birth _9-1-1991_ Race or ethnicity _Black_ Religion _(non)_ Years married _3 yrs_

Social Security Number _251-00-1333_ Work Tel. no. _____ Home Tel. no. _____

Work Tel. no. _____ Home Tel. no. _____

Referring physician _____ Attending physician _James Mercy, MD._ OPTIONAL FOR INSURANCE, ETC.,

Medical History

Check and detail positive findings including date and place of treatment. Precede findings by reference number.

	Patient	Family	
1. Congenital anomalies	☐	☐	
2. Genetic diseases	☐	☐	
3. Multiple births	☑	☐	*Patient is a twin.*
4. Diabetes mellitus	☐	☑	*Mother, Maternal G'mother.*
5. Malignancies	☐	☐	
6. Hypertension	☐	☑	*Maternal G'mother.*
7. Heart disease	☐	☑	*Maternal G'mother.*
8. Rheumatic fever	☐		
9. Pulmonary disease	☐	☑	*Sister.*
10. GL problems	☐		
11. Renal disease	☐	☐	
12. Genitourinary tract problems	☐		
13. Abnormal uterine bleeding	☐		
14. Infertility	☐		
15. Venereal disease	☐	☐	
16. Phlebitis, varicosities	☐		
17. Neurologic disorders	☐	☐	
18. Metabol./endocrine disorders	☐	☐	
19. Anemia/hemoglobinopathy	☐	☐	
20. Blood disorders	☐	☐	
21. Drug abuse	☐		
22. Smoking/alcohol use	☐		
23. Infectious diseases	☐		
24. Operations/accidents	☐		
25. Allergies/meds sensitivity	☐		*NKDA*
26. Blood transfusions	☐		
27. Other hospitalizations	☐		
28. _____	☐	☐	
29. _____	☐	☐	
30. No known disease/problems	☐	☐	

Preexisting Risk Guide

Indicates pregnancy/outcome at risk

- 31. ☐ Age< 15 or > 35
- 32. ☐ < 8th grade education
- 33. ☐ Cardiac disease (class I or II)
- 34. ☐ Tuberculosis, active
- 35. ☐ Chronic pulmonary disease
- 36. ☐ Thrombophlebitis
- 37. ☐ Endocrinopathy
- 38. ☐ Epilepsy (on medication)
- 39. ☐ Infertility (treated)
- 40. ☐ 2 abortions (spontaneous/induced)
- 41. ☐ ≥ 7 deliveries
- 42. ☐ Previous preterm or SGA infants
- 43. ☐ Infants ≥ 4,000 gms
- 44. ☐ Isoimmunization (ABO, etc.)
- 45. ☐ Hemorrhage during previous preg.
- 46. ☐ Previous preeclampsia
- 47. ☐ Surgically scarred uterus
- 48. ☐ Preg. without familial support
- 49. ☐ Second pregnancy in 12 months
- 50. ☐ Smoking (≥ 1 pack per day)
- 51. ☐ _____
- 52. ☐ _____
- 53. ☐ _____

Indicates pregnancy/outcome at high risk

- 54. ☐ Age ≥ 40
- 55. ☐ Diabetes mellitus
- 56. ☐ Hypertension
- 57. ☐ Cardiac disease (class III or IV)
- 58. ☐ Chronic renal disease
- 59. ☐ Congenital/chromosomal anomalies
- 60. ☐ Hemoglobinopathies
- 61. ☐ Isoimmunization (Rh.)
- 62. ☐ Alcohol or drug abuse
- 63. ☐ Habitual abortions
- 64. ☐ Incompetent cervix
- 65. ☐ Prior fetal or neonatal death
- 66. ☐ Prior neurologically damaged infant
- 67. ☐ Significant social problems
- 68. ☐ _____
- 69. ☐ _____
- 70. ☐ _____

Historical Risk Status

- 71. ☑ No risk factors noted
- 72. ☐ At risk
- 73. ☐ At high risk

Signature _Lucy Aiken, RN_

Menstrual History	Onset _13_ age	Cycle q. _28_ days	Length _3_ days	Amount	L M P _4-8-2012_ mo/day/yr quality

Pregnancy History	Grav _3_	Term _2_	Pret _0_	Abort _0_	Live _2_	E D C _1-16-2013_ mo/day/yr

No.	Month/year	Sex	Weight at birth	Wks gest	Hrs. in labor	Type of delivery	Details of delivery: Include anesthesia and maternal or newborn complications. Use Risk Guide numbers where applicable.
1.	9-09	F	5¹⁰6oz	38		NSVD	*without complication*
2.	8-11	M	7¹⁰2oz	39		NSVD	*without complication*
3.							
4.							
5.							
6.							
7.							
8.							

Figure 1-7 *Mother's Obstetric Record (continued)*

| Prince, Diana Lynn
DOB 9/1/1991
MR 09 09 99, 10032145
Date: 6-10-2012 mo/day/yr | Cabbage Patch Hospital

Initial Pregnancy Profile |

History Since LMP (/) Check and detail all positive findings below: Use reference numbers

1. Headaches ☐
2. Nausea/vomiting ☑ *occasional*
3. Abdominal pain ☐
4. Urinary complaints ☐
5. Vaginal discharge ☐
6. Vaginal bleeding ☐
7. Edema (specify area) ☐
8. Febrile episode ☐
9. Rubella exposure ☐
10. Other viral exposure ☐
11. Radiation exposure ☐
12. _____ ☐
13. _____ ☐
14. Contraception prior to conception _____ None ☐

Type *O.Novum 1/35*
Last used _____ mo/day/yr

15. Nutritional Assessment

☑ Adequate   ☐ Inadequate
☐ Nutritional counseling

Remarks: _____
_____
_____

16. Medications Since LMP

☑ None   ☐ Exposure to drugs

Describe: _____
_____
_____
_____
_____

Initial Physical Examination Height `5'2"` Weight `140` Pregravid weight `137` B.P. `120/72` Pulse `82`

OPTIONAL

SYSTEM	Normal	Abn	Check and detail all abnormal findings below: Use reference numbers.
17. Skin	☑	☐	
18. EENT	☑	☐	
19. Mouth	☑	☐	
20. Neck	☑	☐	
21. Chest	☑	☐	
22. Breast	☑	☐	
23. Heart	☑	☐	
24. Lungs	☑	☐	
25. Abdomen	☑	☐	
26. Musculoskeletal	☑	☐	
27. Extremities	☑	☐	
28. Neurologic	☑	☐	

Pelvic Examination

	Normal	Abn
29. Ext. genitalia	☑	☐
30. Vagina	☑	☐
31. Cervix	☑	☐
32. Uterus (describe)	☑	☐
33. Adnexa	☑	☐
34. Rectum	☑	☐
35. Other	☐	☐

Bony Pelvis

36. Diag. conj. _____
37. Shape sacrum _____
38. S.S. notch _____
39. Ischial spines _____
40. Pubic arch _____
41. Trans. outlet _____
42. Post sag.diam. _____
43. Coccyx _____
44. Classification ☐ Gynecoid ☐ Android ☐ Anthropoid ☐ Platypelloid
45. Estimation ☐ Adequate ☐ Borderline ☐ Contracted

Exam done on by: mo/day/yr 6-10-2012 *James Mercy MD*

Figure 1-7 *Mother's Obstetric Record (continued)*

Prince, Diana Lynn
DOB 9/1/1991
MR 09 09 99, 10032145

Cabbage Patch Hospital

Prenatal Flow Record

Historical Risk Factors and Assessment

Chlamydia (+), history

0	Has no known risk
1	Is "at risk"
2	Is at high risk

Continuing Risk Assessment Guide (revise RISK STATUS)

Date	At risk factors	Date	High risk factors
/	Uterine/cervical malformation	/	Diabetes mellitus
/	Suspect pelvis	/	Hypertension
/	Rh negative (nonsensitized)	/	Thrombophlebitis
/	Anemia (Hct <30%: Hgb <10%)	/	Herpes (type 2)
/	Venereal disease	/	Rh sensitization
/	Acute pyelonephritis	/	Uterine bleeding
/	Failure to gain weight	/	Hydramnios
/	Abnormal oresentation	/	Severe preeclampsia
/	Postterm pregnancy	/	Fetal growth retardation
/	Alcohol use	/	Premature rupt. membranes
/		/	Multiple pregnancy (preterm)
/		/	Alcohol and drug abuse
/		/	
/		/	

Initial Prenatal Screen / Additional Lab Findings

Date: mo/day/yr		Test	Date	Result	Date	Result
Hct/Hgb	12/39	Hct/Hgb				
Patient's Blood type and Rh	A+	Blood sugar				
Antibody	NR	Antibody				
Serology	NR					
Rubella titer	Imm					
Urinalysis micro		AFP	WNL			
Pap test		HIV	6/10	neg		
Cervical culture		HEP B	6/10	neg		
		Chlamydia status neg.				

L M P 4-18-2012   Quickening date ____ mo/dy/yr

Medication Sensitivity ☐ None known or. _____

☐ Initial prenatal instructions	**Amniocentesis**
☐ Attends prenatal classes	Explained on ____ mo/day
☐ Do herpes culture	☐ Accepted ☐ Rejected by patient
☐ Do antenatal RhoGam	**VBAC or C-Section**
☐ For sterilization	☐ OR records reviewed
☐ Circumcision	Explained on ____ mo/day
☐ Needs rubella vaccine	☐ Candidate for VBAC
☐ Breast ☐ Bottle feeding	☐ For Cesarean section

G 3	T 2	Pt 0	A 0	L 2

Age ____
Visit date 20 13

Baby's physician _____   Return visit   Sig.

Visit date	Weight this visit	Pre-gravid	Blood pressure	Base line	Urine protein	Urine Sugar	Est. weeks gestation (dates/size)	Fundal height	Fetal heart rate/quadrant	Edema	RISK STATUS (0,1 2)	Notes	Return visit	Sig.
				1							+			
6/10	144	29/72			8/						+	Patient desires prenatal care.		
/		/			/						+	Will obtain prenatal labs,		
/		/			/						+	HIV consent and OB ultrasound		
/		/			/						+	for estimated gestational age.		
/		/			/						+			
/		/			/						+	① Return to lab 4 wks for exam		
/		/			/						+	② PN Vitamins, FESO₄ given		
/		/			/						+	Vitamins D. Berry, RN		
/		/			/						+	* Need urine C+S next visit.		
/		/			/						+	Urine 6-10 ⊕ WBC and		
/		/			/						+	2+ bacteria		
/		/			/						+	Physician's signature James Mercy MD		

Figure 1-7 *Mother's Obstetric Record (continued)*

U.S. STANDARD CERTIFICATE OF LIVE BIRTH

LOCAL FILE NO.   BIRTH NUMBER:

C H I L D	1. CHILD'S NAME (First, Middle, Last, Suffix)	2. TIME OF BIRTH (24 hr) 3. SEX 4. DATE OF BIRTH (Mo/Day/Yr)
	5. FACILITY NAME (If not institution, give street and number)	6. CITY, TOWN, OR LOCATION OF BIRTH 7. COUNTY OF BIRTH
M O T H E R	8a. MOTHER'S CURRENT LEGAL NAME (First, Middle, Last, Suffix)	8b. DATE OF BIRTH (Mo/Day/Yr)
	8c. MOTHER'S NAME PRIOR TO FIRST MARRIAGE (First, Middle, Last, Suffix)	8d. BIRTHPLACE (State, Territory, or Foreign Country)
	9a. RESIDENCE OF MOTHER-STATE 9b. COUNTY	9c. CITY, TOWN, OR LOCATION
	9d. STREET AND NUMBER	9e. APT. NO. 9f. ZIP CODE 9g. INSIDE CITY LIMITS? ☐ Yes ☐ No
F A T H E R	10a. FATHER'S CURRENT LEGAL NAME (First, Middle, Last, Suffix)	10b. DATE OF BIRTH (Mo/Day/Yr) 10c. BIRTHPLACE (State, Territory, or Foreign Country)
CERTIFIER	11. CERTIFIER'S NAME: _____ TITLE: ☐ MD ☐ DO ☐ HOSPITAL ADMIN. ☐ CNM/CM ☐ OTHER MIDWIFE ☐ OTHER (Specify)_____	12. DATE CERTIFIED ____/____/_____ MM DD YYYY 13. DATE FILED BY REGISTRAR ____/____/_____ MM DD YYYY

INFORMATION FOR ADMINISTRATIVE USE

M O T H E R	14. MOTHER'S MAILING ADDRESS: ☐ Same as residence, or: State: City, Town, or Location: Street & Number: Apartment No.: Zip Code:
	15. MOTHER MARRIED? (At birth, conception, or any time between) ☐ Yes ☐ No 16. SOCIAL SECURITY NUMBER REQUESTED 17. FACILITY ID. (NPI) IF NO, HAS PATERNITY ACKNOWLEDGEMENT BEEN SIGNED IN THE HOSPITAL? ☐ Yes ☐ No FOR CHILD? ☐ Yes ☐ No
	18. MOTHER'S SOCIAL SECURITY NUMBER: 19. FATHER'S SOCIAL SECURITY NUMBER:

INFORMATION FOR MEDICAL AND HEALTH PURPOSES ONLY

M O T H E R

20. MOTHER'S EDUCATION (Check the box that best describes the highest degree or level of school completed at the time of delivery)

- ☐ 8th grade or less
- ☐ 9th - 12th grade, no diploma
- ☐ High school graduate or GED completed
- ☐ Some college credit but no degree
- ☐ Associate degree (e.g., AA, AS)
- ☐ Bachelor's degree (e.g., BA, AB, BS)
- ☐ Master's degree (e.g., MA, MS, MEng, MEd, MSW, MBA)
- ☐ Doctorate (e.g., PhD, EdD) or Professional degree (e.g., MD, DDS, DVM, LLB, JD)

21. MOTHER OF HISPANIC ORIGIN? (Check the box that best describes whether the mother is Spanish/Hispanic/Latina. Check the "No" box if mother is not Spanish/Hispanic/Latina)

- ☐ No, not Spanish/Hispanic/Latina
- ☐ Yes, Mexican, Mexican American, Chicana
- ☐ Yes, Puerto Rican
- ☐ Yes, Cuban
- ☐ Yes, other Spanish/Hispanic/Latina

(Specify)_____

22. MOTHER'S RACE (Check one or more races to indicate what the mother considers herself to be)

- ☐ White
- ☐ Black or African American
- ☐ American Indian or Alaska Native (Name of the enrolled or principal tribe)_____
- ☐ Asian Indian
- ☐ Chinese
- ☐ Filipino
- ☐ Japanese
- ☐ Korean
- ☐ Vietnamese
- ☐ Other Asian (Specify)_____
- ☐ Native Hawaiian
- ☐ Guamanian or Chamorro
- ☐ Samoan
- ☐ Other Pacific Islander (Specify)_____
- ☐ Other (Specify)_____

F A T H E R

23. FATHER'S EDUCATION (Check the box that best describes the highest degree or level of school completed at the time of delivery)

- ☐ 8th grade or less
- ☐ 9th - 12th grade, no diploma
- ☐ High school graduate or GED completed
- ☐ Some college credit but no degree
- ☐ Associate degree (e.g., AA, AS)
- ☐ Bachelor's degree (e.g., BA, AB, BS)
- ☐ Master's degree (e.g., MA, MS, MEng, MEd, MSW, MBA)
- ☐ Doctorate (e.g., PhD, EdD) or Professional degree (e.g., MD, DDS, DVM, LLB, JD)

24. FATHER OF HISPANIC ORIGIN? (Check the box that best describes whether the father is Spanish/Hispanic/Latino. Check the "No" box if father is not Spanish/Hispanic/Latino)

- ☐ No, not Spanish/Hispanic/Latino
- ☐ Yes, Mexican, Mexican American, Chicano
- ☐ Yes, Puerto Rican
- ☐ Yes, Cuban
- ☐ Yes, other Spanish/Hispanic/Latino

(Specify)_____

25. FATHER'S RACE (Check one or more races to indicate what the father considers himself to be)

- ☐ White
- ☐ Black or African American
- ☐ American Indian or Alaska Native (Name of the enrolled or principal tribe)_____
- ☐ Asian Indian
- ☐ Chinese
- ☐ Filipino
- ☐ Japanese
- ☐ Korean
- ☐ Vietnamese
- ☐ Other Asian (Specify)_____
- ☐ Native Hawaiian
- ☐ Guamanian or Chamorro
- ☐ Samoan
- ☐ Other Pacific Islander (Specify)_____
- ☐ Other (Specify)_____

Mother's Name | Mother's Medical Record No.

26. PLACE WHERE BIRTH OCCURRED (Check one)
- ☐ Hospital
- ☐ Freestanding birthing center
- ☐ Home Birth: Planned to deliver at home? ☐ Yes ☐ No
- ☐ Clinic/Doctor's office
- ☐ Other (Specify)_____

27. ATTENDANT'S NAME, TITLE, AND NPI
NAME: _____ NPI:_____
TITLE: ☐ MD ☐ DO ☐ CNM/CM ☐ OTHER MIDWIFE ☐ OTHER (Specify)_____

28. MOTHER TRANSFERRED FOR MATERNAL MEDICAL OR FETAL INDICATIONS FOR DELIVERY? ☐ Yes ☐ No
IF YES, ENTER NAME OF FACILITY MOTHER TRANSFERRED FROM:
_____

REV. 11/2003

Figure 1-8 *Manual Birth Certificate*

MOTHER

29a. DATE OF FIRST PRENATAL CARE VISIT	29b. DATE OF LAST PRENATAL CARE VISIT	30. TOTAL NUMBER OF PRENATAL VISITS FOR THIS PREGNANCY
____/____/_____ ☐ No Prenatal Care M M D D YYYY	____/____/_____ M M D D YYYY	_____ (If none, enter ʌ0".)

31. MOTHER'S HEIGHT _____ (feet/inches)	32. MOTHER'S PREPREGNANCY WEIGHT (pounds)	33. MOTHER'S WEIGHT AT DELIVERY (pounds)	34. DID MOTHER GET WIC FOOD FOR HERSELF DURING THIS PREGNANCY? ☐ Yes ☐ No

35. NUMBER OF PREVIOUS LIVE BIRTHS (Do not include this child)	36. NUMBER OF OTHER PREGNANCY OUTCOMES (spontaneous or induced losses or ectopic pregnancies)	37. CIGARETTE SMOKING BEFORE AND DURING PREGNANCY For each time period, enter either the number of cigarettes or the number of packs of cigarettes smoked. IF NONE, ENTER ʌ0".	38. PRINCIPAL SOURCE OF PAYMENT FOR THIS DELIVERY

35a. Now Living	35b. Now Dead	36a. Other Outcomes		38.

Number _____
 	
☐ None
	Number _____
	
	☐ None
		Number _____
		
		☐ None
			Average number of cigarettes or packs of cigarettes smoked per day.
			     # of cigarettes # of packs
			Three Months Before Pregnancy _____ OR _____
			First Three Months of Pregnancy _____ OR _____
			Second Three Months of Pregnancy _____ OR _____
			Third Trimester of Pregnancy _____ OR _____
				☐ Private Insurance
				☐ Medicaid
				☐ Self-pay
				☐ Other
				   (Specify) _____

35c. DATE OF LAST LIVE BIRTH ____/_____ MM YYYY	36b. DATE OF LAST OTHER PREGNANCY OUTCOME ____/_____ MM YYYY	39. DATE LAST NORMAL MENSES BEGAN ____/____/_____ MM DD YYYY	40. MOTHER'S MEDICAL RECORD NUMBER

MEDICAL AND HEALTH INFORMATION

41. RISK FACTORS IN THIS PREGNANCY (Check all that apply)	43. OBSTETRIC PROCEDURES (Check all that apply)	46. METHOD OF DELIVERY

Diabetes
 ☐ Prepregnancy (Diagnosis prior to this pregnancy)
 ☐ Gestational (Diagnosis in this pregnancy)
 	
Hypertension
 ☐ Prepregnancy (Chronic)
 ☐ Gestational (PIH, preeclampsia)
 ☐ Eclampsia
 	
☐ Previous preterm birth
 	
☐ Other previous poor pregnancy outcome (Includes perinatal death, small-for-gestational age/intrauterine growth restricted birth)
 	
☐ Pregnancy resulted from infertility treatment-If yes, check all that apply:
 ☐ Fertility-enhancing drugs, Artificial insemination or Intrauterine insemination
 ☐ Assisted reproductive technology (e.g., in vitro fertilization (IVF), gamete intrafallopian transfer (GIFT))
 	
☐ Mother had a previous cesarean delivery
   If yes, how many _____
 	
☐ None of the above
	☐ Cervical cerclage
	☐ Tocolysis
	
	External cephalic version:
	 ☐ Successful
	 ☐ Failed
	
	☐ None of the above
		A. Was delivery with forceps attempted but unsuccessful?
		    ☐ Yes ☐ No
		
		B. Was delivery with vacuum extraction attempted but unsuccessful?
		    ☐ Yes ☐ No
		
		C. Fetal presentation at birth
		    ☐ Cephalic
		    ☐ Breech
		    ☐ Other
		
		D. Final route and method of delivery (Check one)
		    ☐ Vaginal/Spontaneous
		    ☐ Vaginal/Forceps
		    ☐ Vaginal/Vacuum
		    ☐ Cesarean
		      If cesarean, was a trial of labor attempted?
		       ☐ Yes
		       ☐ No

	44. ONSET OF LABOR (Check all that apply)	
	☐ Premature Rupture of the Membranes (prolonged, ≥12 hrs.) ☐ Precipitous Labor (<3 hrs.) ☐ Prolonged Labor (≥20 hrs.) ☐ None of the above	
	45. CHARACTERISTICS OF LABOR AND DELIVERY (Check all that apply)	47. MATERNAL MORBIDITY (Check all that apply) (Complications associated with labor and delivery)
42. INFECTIONS PRESENT AND/OR TREATED DURING THIS PREGNANCY (Check all that apply) ☐ Gonorrhea ☐ Syphilis ☐ Chlamydia ☐ Hepatitis B ☐ Hepatitis C ☐ None of the above	☐ Induction of labor ☐ Augmentation of labor ☐ Non-vertex presentation ☐ Steroids (glucocorticoids) for fetal lung maturation received by the mother prior to delivery ☐ Antibiotics received by the mother during labor ☐ Clinical chorioamnionitis diagnosed during labor or maternal temperature ≥38°C (100.4°F) ☐ Moderate/heavy meconium staining of the amniotic fluid ☐ Fetal intolerance of labor such that one or more of the following actions was taken: in-utero resuscitative measures, further fetal assessment, or operative delivery ☐ Epidural or spinal anesthesia during labor ☐ None of the above	☐ Maternal transfusion ☐ Third or fourth degree perineal laceration ☐ Ruptured uterus ☐ Unplanned hysterectomy ☐ Admission to intensive care unit ☐ Unplanned operating room procedure following delivery ☐ None of the above

NEWBORN INFORMATION

NEWBORN

48. NEWBORN MEDICAL RECORD NUMBER	54. ABNORMAL CONDITIONS OF THE NEWBORN (Check all that apply)	55. CONGENITAL ANOMALIES OF THE NEWBORN (Check all that apply)
49. BIRTHWEIGHT (grams preferred, specify unit) _____ 9 grams 9 lb/oz	☐ Assisted ventilation required immediately following delivery ☐ Assisted ventilation required for more than six hours ☐ NICU admission ☐ Newborn given surfactant replacement therapy ☐ Antibiotics received by the newborn for suspected neonatal sepsis ☐ Seizure or serious neurologic dysfunction ☐ Significant birth injury (skeletal fracture(s), peripheral nerve injury, and/or soft tissue/solid organ hemorrhage which requires intervention) 9 None of the above	☐ Anencephaly ☐ Meningomyelocele/Spina bifida ☐ Cyanotic congenital heart disease ☐ Congenital diaphragmatic hernia ☐ Omphalocele ☐ Gastroschisis ☐ Limb reduction defect (excluding congenital amputation and dwarfing syndromes) ☐ Cleft Lip with or without Cleft Palate ☐ Cleft Palate alone ☐ Down Syndrome ☐ Karyotype confirmed ☐ Karyotype pending ☐ Suspected chromosomal disorder ☐ Karyotype confirmed ☐ Karyotype pending ☐ Hypospadias ☐ None of the anomalies listed above
50. OBSTETRIC ESTIMATE OF GESTATION: _____ (completed weeks)		
51. APGAR SCORE: Score at 5 minutes: _____ **If 5 minute score is less than 6,** Score at 10 minutes: _____		
52. PLURALITY - Single, Twin, Triplet, etc. (Specify) _____		
53. IF NOT SINGLE BIRTH - Born First, Second, Third, etc. (Specify) _____		

Mother's Name

Mother's Medical Record No. _____

56. WAS INFANT TRANSFERRED WITHIN 24 HOURS OF DELIVERY? 9 Yes 9 No IF YES, NAME OF FACILITY INFANT TRANSFERRED TO: _____	57. IS INFANT LIVING AT TIME OF REPORT? ☐ Yes ☐ No ☐ Infant transferred, status unknown	58. IS THE INFANT BEING BREASTFED AT DISCHARGE? ☐ Yes ☐ No

Centers for Disease Control and Prevention (http://www.cdc.gov/nchs/vital_certs_rev.htm)

Figure 1-8 *Manual Birth Certificate (continued)*

CASE 1-15

Clinical Coding Systems and Technology

Research literature to collect information to distinguish similarities and differences among various technologies used for coding diagnoses and procedures by coders. Technologies used include an encoder system of a logic-based automated codebook, the automated code assignment technology in natural language processing (NLP), and computer assisted coding (CAC).

Reference resources would likely include the American Health Information Management Association (AHIMA) website (www.ahima.org), *The Journal of AHIMA*, or AHIMA Body of Knowledge.

1. Compare and contrast how each might be used differently.

2. Summarize your analysis to state which technology you feel is most advantageous and why. Include the reference sources you utilized in your analysis.

CASE 1-16

External Core Measure Reporting Requirements: ORYX Performance Measures for the Joint Commission and CMS

You will be having a meeting with the community's medical society to present information on external core measure requirements of hospitals and core measure reporting for the Joint Commission and CMS.

You may reference the Joint Commission website at http://www.jointcommission.org and the CMS website at http://cms.gov.

1. What have been the ORYX performance measure requirements in the past for hospitals?

2. Explain how ORYX and performance measure data are used in the accreditation process.

CASE 1-17

Joint Commission Mock Survey

You are on a Mock Joint Commission Survey team for the hospital. The hospital will conduct an unannounced mock survey sometime during the next 3 months. The team leader has asked you to bring suggestions of activities to include in the upcoming internal (mock) survey to share at the next meeting. You want to include activities that simulate a real Joint Commission on-site survey. You have several ideas from networking with your peers on the regional, state, and national levels of your professional association and by participating in AHIMA's Communities of Practice (CoP) for Joint Commission Accreditation. Your next step is to visit the Joint Commission website at http://www.jointcommission. org and review the current survey process to gain a better understanding of what is being done during the on-site survey.

What suggestions would you include for the next mock survey conducted?

CASE 1-18

Authentication Compliance

Huffman Medical Center is accredited by the Joint Commission and is licensed by the state to accept Medicare and Medicaid reimbursement. The hospital's Quality Improvement (QI) Director chairs the committee and has sent you an agenda draft for next month's committee meeting, where you are to report on the topic of medical staff authentication of the medical record. He calls you in advance to inquire if Huffman Medical Center is in compliance on medical record documentation requirements. He is concerned that the hospital is not meeting authentication requirements of medical reports such as verbal orders, histories and physicals, consultations, and discharge summaries. The current practice by the medical staff is that only signatures are required of all reports, except for verbal orders that require the physician to date his or her authentication. The committee chair specifically inquires whether all medical reports must reflect date and time of signatures and/or authentications.

You have been charged with researching the Joint Commission standard and Federal Register for authentication requirements and preparing a brief report on the subject matter to distribute at the next Accreditation Committee meeting to educate members and alleviate concerns.

You may reference the Joint Commission website at http://www.jointcommission.org and the CMS website at http://cms.gov.

CASE 1-19

Primary Ambulatory Care Center EHR and Meaningful Use

You are the HIM director of a multi-physician-owned primary ambulatory care practice, and the board of directors has agreed to implement an EHR system. The board has met with you to receive your input and has delegated responsibility to you of proposing a system to purchase and implement. The only specifications given by the board are to ensure that the system has components necessary to meet the meaningful use requirements of the American Recovery and Reinvestment Act (ARRA) in order to participate in stage I of the HITECH/ARRA incentive program, and to streamline the registration, billing, and patient record documentation processes.

This group practice has expanded over the past 20 years. There are now 4 different offices around the suburban area with a total of 16 primary care physicians in practice.

To assist you with your project, you may visit the following web sites.

For information on the Office of National Coordinator (ONC) certification, you may visit: http://healthit.hhs.gov/certification

For information about the Medicare and Medicaid incentive programs, you may visit: http://www.cms.gov/EHRincentiveprograms

What major elements do you need to consider in the project to propose a selected EHR system and become a meaningful user?

CASE 1-20

Case Finding for Tumor Registry

You are the Tumor Registrar of the county hospital and work under the HIM Department. Although it is a small hospital of only 150 beds, it offers general medical and surgical inpatient care, a radiation treatment center, emergency care, and a surgical center for outpatient procedures. Services include medicine, surgery, gynecology, orthopedics, neurology, urology, and oncology, with ancillary service departments supporting diagnostic clinical care and treatment to patients. The HIM Department is responsible for usual services to ensure that complete, timely, and accurate records are maintained, as well as for oversight of the hospital Cancer Registry Program. The Chief Operations Officer has asked you to compile a demographic origin list of every identifiable reportable bladder and colon cancer case from the past 6 months, for strategic planning of hospital services.

What are your sources for obtaining the information to compile a list?

CASE 1-21

Face Validity of QI Study on Births

The Obstetric (OB) Service of the hospital is conducting a QI study on the July OB admissions. As HIM Director, you have requested that your assistant write the following report that identifies reproductive histories from the antepartum records of the July OB admissions. It is important to realize that gravida in the reproductive history represents number of pregnancies, inclusive of the current pregnancy. The subsequent data (i.e., TPAL) in the reproductive history represent birth data from prior pregnancies. You have asked her to send the report to you so that you can review it for validity before submitting to the OB Service director. Respond to the following questions for face validity.

- Gravida (G) – number of pregnancies
- Term (T) – number of full-term infants born (born at 37 weeks or after)
- Para (P) – number of preterm infants born (born before 37 weeks)
- Abortion (A) – number of spontaneous or induced abortions (pregnancy terminated before the age of viability). Age of viability is 24 weeks.
- Living children (L) – number of living children.

Utilizing the report provided in Table 1-2, answer the questions presented:

1. How many patients are primigravida?

2. How many total pregnancies have these 17 patients had?

3. How many full-term births are reported?

4. How many premature births are reported?

5. How many aborted pregnancies are reported?

6. How many living children are reported?

Table 1-2 *July Obstetric Report*

	July Obstetric Report	
Unit MR #	Admission Date	Reproductive History G-T-P-A-L
042194	07/03/XX	2-1-0-0-1
037901	07/03/XX	1-0-0-0-0
048458	07/07/XX	4-2-1-1-2
051092	07/08/XX	3-0-0-0-2
046098	07/10/XX	5-3-1-1-3
048820	07/11/XX	3-1-0-1-1
050987	07/14XX	1-0-0-0-0
051488	07/14/XX	2-0-1-0-1
038965	07/16/XX	3-2-0-0-2
054082	07/19/XX	1-0-0-0-0
050390	07/19/XX	2-1-0-0-1
042884	07/19/XX	2-1-0-0-1
047910	07/22/XX	3-2-0-0-2
047738	07/25/XX	4-2-1-0-2
057534	07/26/XX	3-2-0-0-2
050185	07/29/XX	2-1-0-1-0
049127	07/31/XX	1-0-0-0-0

CASE 1-22

Reproductive History Interpretation

Utilizing the report from Table 1-2 in Case 1-21, identify the following OB patients and explain each of their reproductive histories at the time of their July admission.

1. MR #050309

2. MR #047738

3. MR #050185

CASE 1-23

Abstract of Pertinent Inpatient Medical Documentation

You are an HIM manager at a Critical Access Hospital (CAH). Find below a list of health data items frequently accessed for reporting purposes in hospitals. Review the list of data requested and indicate from which medical report or electronic health record (EHR) screen you would most likely find the inpatient record data.

1. Patient demographic data
2. Evidence that the patient was informed of benefits, risks, and alternatives prior to a particular surgery
3. Reason for admission and review of body systems
4. An evaluation of patient prior to induction of anesthesia
5. Chest radiology interpretation
6. Name of surgeon and assistant surgeon, and estimated blood loss
7. Family and social history
8. CBC and urinalysis test results
9. Course of events throughout hospital stay
10. Vital signs; fluid input and urine output
11. Chronological entries made about patient's condition by nurses
12. Chronological entries made about patient's condition by physician
13. Patient's blood type and Rh factor
14. Discharge diagnosis and discharge instructions with follow-up care
15. Date, time, name of drug; drug dose and route of administration
16. Name of person designated by patient to make healthcare decisions should patient become incapacitated

CASE 1-24

Choosing a Personal Health Record (PHR)

You have had a variety of illnesses, hospitalizations, and surgeries. Physicians who treat you include a primary care physician; an ear, nose, and throat specialist (ENT); a cardiologist; a nephrologist; a retinal specialist; a glaucoma specialist; a psychiatrist; and a urologist. It seems that you are visiting the health information department frequently for copies of your health record for one physician or another. An HIM professional said that you could benefit from having a personal health record (PHR). You have decided that you want to learn more about it.

Review 3 of the web-based PHRs found at http://www.myphr.org.

Use the following categories to conduct your investigation of the web-based PHRs:

* Back-up
* Robustness of content that can be entered
* Uptime
* Ease of use
* Expense
* Storage size
* Privacy and security

1. What benefits would you expect to encounter when you implement your PHR?

2. What other information might the patient want to know?

CASE 1-25

Personal Health Record (PHR) Education

As the patient advocate at your facility and a member of an EHR task force, you have been asked to write a patient information sheet for the PHR your facility is rolling out. This is to be a 1-page information sheet that defines the PHR, explains the benefits of the PHR, and tells about the PHR that your facility is offering. With the PHR, patients will have access to test results, key clinical findings, and secure e-mail to communicate with their doctors.

Create this PHR information sheet. Keep in mind that it is being written for the patient to use.

Clinical Classification Systems and Reimbursement Methods

CASE 2-1

Official Coding Resource

You are training a new coder, Elizabeth. She is a new graduate and just passed her registered health information technician (RHIT) exam last month. Elizabeth is a delight to work with and is anxious to learn everything she can. One of the things you have noticed in working with her is that she is having trouble using the coding references. Specifically, she does not understand how to use *Coding Clinic, CPT Assistant,* and the official coding guidelines. The encoder has these resources built into the system, so it is not a problem with knowing where to find them. She does know how to access and use the encoder, but just does not understand how *Coding Clinic, CPT Assistant,* and other resources tie into the coding software. Help her identify which official coding reference can help her assign the proper codes to the diagnoses and procedures listed in Table 2-1.

What other training issues should you address with Elizabeth?

Table 2-1 *Coding Resources for Diagnosis and/or Procedure*

Coding Resources for Diagnosis and/or Procedure	
Diagnosis and/or Procedure	Proper Code According to Official Coding Resources
Uvulopalatoplasty—laser assisted	
Tangent bone grafts	
Needle aspiration of the intervertebral disk using CT guidance	
Vertebral stapling	

CASE 2-2

Coding Quality in ICD-9-CM

You have been the coding supervisor for about 6 months at General Hospital. You are settling in and getting a strong grasp of what has been happening in the areas of quality, quantity, work ethic, policies, etc.

You have been at the hospital long enough to know that there is a problem with the quality of coding performed. You know that you need to strengthen the quality audits being conducted in order to gain a better understanding of the coding quality problems. There is a lot of work ahead to improve the coding function to achieve a 98% accuracy rate. The last audit showed only an 87% accuracy rate.

You decide to begin by conducting a face validity audit of the codes. You print a report of the most recent discharge diagnosis codes to see if you can identify any glaring problems.

Perform a face validity review of the first nine discharges shown in Table 2-2 to ensure compliance to official coding guidelines. Report any coding quality issues you identify from your review.

Table 2-2 *Worksheet for Identifying Coding Quality Problems*

Worksheet for Identifying Coding Quality Problems
Case 1   Principal Diagnosis: 041.4 E. Coli infection Secondary Diagnosis: 599.0 Urinary tract infection (UTI)
Problem(s) Identified:
Case 2   Principal Diagnosis: 038.10 Staphylococcal septicemia Secondary Diagnosis: 041.10 Staphylococcal infection
Problem(s) Identified:
Case 3   Principal Diagnosis: 414.01 Coronary artery disease (CAD) Principal Procedure: 36.12 Coronary artery bypass graft (CABG) 2 vessel
Problem(s) Identified:
Case 4   Principal Diagnosis: 550.92 Bilateral inguinal hernia Principal Procedure: 53.14 Repair, bilateral inguinal hernia
Problem(s) Identified:
Case 5   Principal Diagnosis: 402.90 Hypertensive heart disease Secondary Diagnosis: 401.9 Hypertension
Problem(s) Identified:
Case 6   Principal Diagnosis: 780.01 Coma Secondary Diagnosis: 191.9 Adenocarcinoma brain Secondary Diagnosis: M8104/3
Problem(s) Identified:
Case 7   Principal Diagnosis: 850.0 Concussion Secondary Diagnosis: 784.0 Headache
Problem(s) Identified:
Case 8   Principal Diagnosis: *V58.ll* Admission for chemotherapy Secondary Diagnosis: 174.9 Adenocarcinoma breast Secondary Diagnosis: M8140/3 Adenocarcinoma Principal Procedure: 99.25 Chemotherapy
Problem(s) Identified:
Case 9   Principal Diagnosis: 426.0 Atrioventricular block, complete Principal Procedure: 37.81 Initial insertion of single chamber device, not specified as rate responsive (no physiologic stimuli)
Problem(s) Identified:

CASE 2-3

Documentation Support for Principal Diagnosis

You are the coding supervisor at Vale Community General Hospital. An HIM student, Javier, is working with you today. He is looking at some charts and has asked you how you determine if the documentation supports the codes. You decide to walk through the charts with him and explain each one. The principal diagnoses are shown in Table 2-3.

What would you tell Javier about each?

Table 2-3 *Principal Diagnosis and Explanation*

Principal Diagnosis and Explanation	
Principal Diagnosis: Explanation:	Pneumonia
Principal Diagnosis: Explanation:	Septicemia
Principal Diagnosis: Explanation:	Respiratory failure
Principal Diagnosis: Explanation:	Congestive heart failure
Principal Diagnosis: Explanation:	Cholecystectomy with cholelithiasis
Principal Diagnosis: Explanation:	Preeclampsia
Principal Diagnosis: Explanation:	Thrombophlebitis
Principal Diagnosis: Explanation:	Cerebrovascular accident (CVA)

CASE 2-4

Improving Coding Quality

Coding quality is your responsibility as coding supervisor. Lately you have been doing a lot of coding audits and have recognized some patterns in the coding errors that you have identified. You have found 3 problem areas where coders are consistently miscoding: skin coronary artery bypass grafts (CABGs), respiratory failure, and heart catheterizations.

1. What can you do to improve coding quality?

2. What role can the encoder play in coding quality?

CASE 2-5

Chargemaster Audit

You are part of the chargemaster maintenance team, but the day-to-day operations tend to fall to you. As the chargemaster coordinator, you spend a lot of your time each day auditing the chargemaster. You have printed out a portion of the chargemaster to review. These entries from the Chargemaster Report shown in Table 2-4 are to be audited; the audit will look for comprehensiveness of information and data quality.

What problem(s) can you identify?

Table 2-4 *Chargemaster Report to Audit*

	Chargemaster Report to Audit		
CM#	Description	(CPT) Code	Charge
12355	EKG—12 lead	93000	$78.00
12356	Echocardiography—transesophageal (TEE)	93318	$379.00
12357	R heart catheterization	93501	$1,234.00
12358	L heart catheterization retrograde-percutaneous	93546	$1,234.00
12359	Bundle of HIS	93600	$257.00

Current Procedural Terminology © 2012 American Medical Association. All Rights Reserved.

Chargemaster Maintenance

You are the assistant director of the HIM department. You have just been given the responsibility of maintaining the chargemaster. The person who was maintaining the chargemaster just quit, and to save money, administration has decided to add this to your current duties instead of filling the position. You only spent a day with the person who resigned to learn about what you need to do. This is what you learned:

- The chargemaster coordinator did 100% of the maintenance on the chargemaster.
- If she had a question, she would call and ask the appropriate department.
- She was about 3 months behind in her maintenance.
- When departments started new services, she usually learned about them a week after they started, when billing problems arose.
- The reason that she quit was because she was so frustrated with her job.

You are concerned about what you have gotten yourself into. You know that you cannot do this alone, especially on top of your other duties, which were not decreased when this responsibility was added. You drag out your old textbooks, surf the Internet, and order a new book on chargemaster maintenance. After studying up on the subject, you decide to draft a proposal on a better way to manage the chargemaster. You want to do a good job because the director has agreed to send the final report to administration.

What plan would you come up with?

CASE 2-7

Selecting Coding Classification Systems

You are the director of HIM. The administrator, Stan, comes to you to discuss a change that he wants to make. Stan wants you either to stop using ICD-9-CM (or ICD-10-CM and PCS) and CPT codes and start coding all of your records in Systematized Nomenclature of Medicine (SNOMED), or to add SNOMED to your coding responsibilities—without additional staff of course. He has heard that SNOMED is much more detailed. He wants to use it so that he can have as much information as possible to make decisions affecting the hospital.

How would you respond? Apply either the ICD-9 or ICD-10 classification system, as assigned by your instructor.

CASE 2-8

Presentation on ICD-10-CM and ICD-10-PCS

You have been assigned the responsibility of giving a presentation on ICD-10-CM and ICD-10-PCS to people within your hospital who are involved with reimbursement. This includes the business office staff, coders, chargemaster committee, and others. The goal of the presentation is not to teach them how to code but to get them to understand the importance of ICD-10-CM and ICD-10-PCS, the information provided by the code, and the impact that changing to ICD-10 will have on your organization.

Develop PowerPoint slides to be used for your lecture.

CASE 2-9

Encoder Functional Requirements

You are part of a team charged with the selection of the new encoder. You are in the process of developing the request for proposal—specifically, the functional requirements. Last week you sent out a questionnaire asking coders and coding managers about their needs in an encoder. The questionnaires have been returned and combined, and the responses to which functional requirements the coders and coding managers want in an encoder are shown in Table 2-5.

Your job is to identify which of these functions are mandatory and which are optional requirements for the system that you choose. Justify your classification for each functional requirement.

Table 2-5 *Encoder Functional Requirements*

Response to Questionnaire on *Encoder Functional Requirements*
• Ability to connect to MPI for demographic information download
• Ability to update codes each year when new codes come out
• Coding resources available online
• Ability to show estimated reimbursement for our facility
• Provides a list of charts not coded
• Ability to enter code(s) directly
• Ability to write notes
• Ability to transfer codes and other information back into hospital financial system
• Ability to sort codes
• Ability to create and print out physician queries
• Ability to save codes when you are unable to complete the coding
• Includes multiple groupers

CASE 2-10

Encoder Selection

Administration wanted a choice for encoders made quickly, so the decision was to have the process be as informal as possible. There are 2 encoder systems to choose from: PerfectCode and JustCoding.

PerfectCode is an automated codebook with numerous reference materials, and it has an interface with the hospital information system and the ability to enter facility policies.

JustCoding is a logic-based system and also has reference materials, an interface with the hospital information system, and the ability to enter hospital policies into the system.

It was decided that the coders would vote for the system they preferred, and that you, as the coding supervisor, would cast the deciding vote in the event of a tie. Half of your coders want PerfectCode and half want JustCoding, and the coders are adamant about their choices.

1. How would you handle this situation?

2. What questions would you ask as part of the investigation?

3. If price, quality of system, references, and other evaluations are relatively equal, which system would you choose and why? (Be sure to include management, computer, and reimbursement issues.)

CASE 2-11

Request for Information (RFI) for Encoder Systems

As part of the encoder selection team, you have been asked to identify 4 encoders on the market that your facility can investigate further. A request for information (RFI) will be sent to these vendors. You have been asked to gather some basic information on the vendors and their products. The specific information to be collected for each encoder is listed in Table 2-6.

Table 2-6 *Information for Request for Information (RFI) on Encoders*

Information for RFI on Encoders				
Information	Vendor 1	Vendor 2	Vendor 3	Vendor 4
Name of company				
Name of product				
Logic or automated				
Phone number of vendor				
Address				
Summary of additional coding/compliance resources beyond encoder				
Number of years on market				

CASE 2-12

Physician Query Policy

You have suspected there are problems in the physician query process for a while now, and you have planned to review the policy and query form to look for any compliance issues. You would rather find the problems yourself before the Office of the Inspector General (OIG) finds them. Your task today is to evaluate the physician query process at your facility.

1. Review Figures 2-1 and 2-2 for appropriateness.

2. Evaluate the policy and procedure on all aspects, including:
   - Standards for completion of a proper physician query
   - Appropriate format of the policy
   - Grammar
   - Form design
   - Process described
   - Need to meet discharged not final billed (DNFB) standards

Honolulu General Hospital

Policy Title: Physician Queries

Policy: Physician Queries are used as the sole method of communication between coders and physicians. It should be used when there are problems with incomplete documentation, conflicting diagnoses, recommendations for improvement in medical practices, incomplete histories and physicals, incomplete discharge summaries, and other documentation issues.

Procedure:

Task	Person Responsible
1. Review medical record to determine principal diagnoses, secondary diagnoses, principal procedure, and other procedures	Coder
2. Complete physician query form (see attached)	Coder
3. Complete envelope with physician's mailing address	Coder
4. Mail physician query with a self-addressed, stamped envelope enclosed	Coder
5. When query is returned, review physician documentation and make the necessary adjustments to the code assignment	Coder
6. File the physician query in the medical record	Coder
7. Give copy of the completed query to the coding supervisor	Coder

Effective date: May 1, 2012

Figure 2-1 *Policy and Procedure for Physician Queries*

Honolulu General Hospital

Physician Query Form

Patient Name: _____

Dr. _____

Upon review of the above-mentioned chart for the purpose of coding, the following issue(s) were identified:

Please answer the above question(s) and return to Macon General Hospital in the enclosed stamped, self-addressed envelope. If you have any questions, please contact:

Coder: _____ Phone: (___)___-___ Date:___/___/_____

Response:

Physician Signature: _____ Date:___/___/_____

Figure 2-2 *Physician Query Form*

CASE 2-13

Physician Query Evaluation

As coding supervisor, you are responsible for monitoring the queries generated by the coders. You want to make sure that the queries are written appropriately with regard to content, appropriately worded questions, and documentation.

Review the sample queries in Figures 2-3 through 2-10 and critique the content of each of these queries.

1. Is the query well written?

2. What recommendations do you have for improvement?

3. Do you see any trends?

4. Which coders are better at writing physician queries?

Physician Query

Patient name:	Timothy Brown
MRN:	1125851
Dates of service:	8/12–8/14/12
Attending physician:	Johnson
Query:	Please add Pneumonia, as it is indicated by the CXR.
Financial impact:	$357.25
Coder:	Sabrina

Figure 2-3 *Physician Query 1*

Physician Query

Patient name:	Tyler Smith
MRN:	1257863
Dates of service:	8/14–8/17/12
Attending physician:	Grant, James, MD

Query:

Dr. Grant, the progress note dated 8/15 states that the patient has new onset of asthma. The progress note on 8/16 states that the patient has chronic asthma with status asthmaticus. Please advise me on the proper diagnosis.

Financial impact:	$542.24
Coder:	Toni

Figure 2-4 *Physician Query 2*

Physician Query

Patient name:	Tiffany Bradford
MRN:	0985688
Dates of service:	8/23–8/26/12
Attending physician:	Rogers, Anthony, MD

Query:

Dr. Rogers, the pathology report states that the patient had cervical dysplasia. Dr. Brown wrote that the patient had carcinoma in situ. Please advise regarding the proper diagnosis.

Financial impact:	$1.256.10
Coder:	Clarice

Figure 2-5   *Physician Query 3*

Physician Query

Patient name:	Grover Lake
MRN:	1015483
Dates of service:	8/01–8/03/12
Attending physician:	Finebaum, Frederick, MD

Query:

Does the electrolyte imbalance indicate dehydration? Please circle: Yes or No.

Financial impact:	$854.22
Coder:	Lonna

Figure 2-6   *Physician Query 4*

Physician Query

Patient name:	Simone Hardcastle
MRN:	1122557
Dates of service:	08/10–8/21/12
Attending physician:	Colgate, James, MD

Query:

Dr. Colgate, if you will document the BBB in the progress notes, we can increase reimbursement.

Financial impact:	$2,345.98
Coder:	Claire

Figure 2-7 *Physician Query 5*

Physician Query

Patient name:	Harold Sykes
MRN:	0865521
Dates of service:	8/1–8/5/12
Attending physician:	Dodd, Geraldine, MD

Query:

The low potassium is significant, isn't it?

Financial impact:	$567.98
Coder:	Glenda

Figure 2-8 *Physician Query 6*

Physician Query

Patient name:	Susan Stokes
MRN:	1054437
Dates of service:	08/27–08/30/12
Attending physician:	Lawrence, Lynne, MD
Query:	Should hematuria be coded?
Financial impact:	$1,123.87
Coder:	Bob

Figure 2-9 *Physician Query 7*

Physician Query

Patient name:	Frank Byron
MRN:	1597799
Dates of service:	8/13–8/16/12
Attending physician:	Zeigler, Clark, MD

Query:

The operative report indicates that 1130 cc of blood was lost. A CBC on the first POD shows a low RBC. Does this indicate a postoperative complication?

Financial impact:	$2,321.65
Coder:	Jennie

Figure 2-10 *Physician Query 8*

CASE 2-14

Physician Education

Two of your physicians are constantly writing "urosepsis" as the principal diagnosis. You send a physician query every time, but they still keep doing it. Both you and the 2 physicians have become very frustrated. Obviously, the informal education through the physician query process is not working, so you need to try another approach.

1. What would you recommend?

2. Why did you choose this method?

CASE 2-15

Using Workflow Technology in Physician Query Management

Janice, the coding supervisor, is excited about the implementation of the new EHR. Currently, to get responses to their queries, the coders have to wait for physicians to come in and complete their charts. This can sometimes take several weeks. With administration asking why the DNFB is not lower, Janice plans to use workflow technology to assist in the query process.

How can this help?

CASE 2-16

Physician Orders for Outpatient Testing

You are an admissions clerk in an acute care hospital. A patient comes to your facility and says that Dr. Jackson has sent him over to have a chest x-ray. You ask the patient for the order for the test, and the patient tells you that Dr. Jackson did not give him a written order for the test.

1. How should the admissions clerk handle this situation?

2. Why is having the order so important?

CASE 2-17

Report Generation

Dr. Smith came to the HIM department research coordinator and asked for a list of all of his patients with a diagnosis code of 486 (ICD-9-CM) or J18.9 (ICD-10-CM). The coordinator promptly printed out a list and presented it to him. Dr. Smith exploded, "I have lots more pneumonia patients than this!"

1. How should the research coordinator respond?

2. What could the research coordinator have done to get Dr. Smith the information that he wanted without upsetting the physician?

CASE 2-18

Monitoring Compliance Activities

You are the chief compliance officer for Tybee Healthcare. You have only been in this position for 6 months. One of the things that you have learned is that there is no system in place to monitor the compliance efforts. You have decided to identify 10 indicators that you will monitor on a routine basis.

1. What are the 10 indicators that you recommend?

2. What threshold do you recommend that the organization should strive to meet?

3. Justify your recommendations.

CASE 2-19

Potential Compliance Issue

As compliance coordinator, you spend a lot of time looking for compliance issues that need correcting. Today, you are looking at various reports and charts. You cannot tell from the information provided to you if there is a compliance problem, but you can identify areas that need further investigation.

Review the information in Table 2-7 for potential compliance issues.

1. Write a Y if the situation indicates a potential compliance problem; write an N if the situation describes a simple error or insignificant finding.

2. Justify your responses.

Table 2-7 *Potential Compliance Problems*

Potential Compliance Problems	
Situation	Yes/No? Why?
Principal Diagnosis (Dx): fractured humerus Secondary Dx: crushed larynx Procedure: repair larynx and temporary tracheostomy	
Principal Dx: septicemia Secondary Dx: urinary tract infection Procedure: none	
National percent of simple pneumonia: 76% (Your hospital's is 77%)	
Your case mix index (CMI) is 1.5678 The average CMI for a comparable facility is 1.2094.	
98% of physician queries ask questions that would increase reimbursement.	
The number of advance beneficiary notices (ABNs) for the past year: 1	
Medicare reviewed 100 heart cath charts. The MS-DRG was changed on two of the cases.	
A review of the remittance advice shows 50 denials over the past month, with 42 of these denials for medical necessity.	
An audit was performed on rebills: 62% were for higher-weighted MS-DRGS; 38% were for lower.	
The annual report of compliance activities shows the following: • number of discharges: 22,000 • 50% of the medical services were audited • only inpatient services were audited • 50 charts were audited	
A new compliance software package was installed in January. In March, HR evaluated salary ranges for all of the jobs in the hospital. The admissions coordinator position's salary was decreased by 25%. The new hires have a high school education and strong typing skills.	
The coding supervisor reviews a random sample of inpatient, outpatient, and ER records for correct coding.	
The sample is taken from all services, all physicians, and all coders.	

CASE 2-20

Discharge Planning

The case manager has been following a patient who has been in your facility for about a month now. The patient was critical at one time, but has now progressed to a point where the hospital can do little more to help the patient. The patient is going to need 24-hour nursing care, but not at a level that requires acute care hospitalization. Since the patient does not meet criteria required to remain in the facility, the UR coordinator refers the patient to the physician advisor for review. The physician advisor agrees that the patient does not need acute care hospitalization.

1. What do you recommend?

2. What actions do you hope have been taking place over the past month in preparation for the patient's expected discharge?

CASE 2-21

Documentation Improvement

Laura just finished a documentation audit. She was not surprised to learn that there were significant documentation problems. The top 3 problems identified were the following:

- History and physicals (H&Ps) do not meet Joint Commission and medical staff regulations for time of completion and content.
- Discharge summaries do not meet Joint Commission and medical staff regulations for completion and content.
- Progress notes are very brief and do not adequately describe the patient's improvement or lack thereof.

1. What should Laura recommend to the HIM director to improve documentation?

2. Who should be involved in this documentation improvement program?

3. What else would you want to know?

4. What type of follow-up should be performed? When?

CASE 2-22

Strategic Management of ICD-10 Implementation

As the HIM Director, you sit on the ICD-10 Management Committee. The goals of this committee are to assess and plan for ICD-10 implementation, analyze the financial impact that ICD-10 will have on the hospital, and make a recommendation to the Chief Operating Officer (COO) for successful transition to the new classification system.

What recommendation and input would you give to the committee for a systematic method to forecast the financial implications ICD-10 will have for your hospital?

CASE 2-23

Developing a Coding Quality Plan

You have just been promoted to coding supervisor at a 300-physician clinic. The previous supervisor was terminated for incompetence. The coding section is a disaster. There is no coding quality program in place. There are no coding standards for either quality or productivity. There is a high denial rate due to the coding problems. Your job is to resolve the coding section deficiencies. Since you have been promoted from within the facility, you are already aware of many of the problems. Your facility is in serious trouble with the Quality Improvement Organization (QIO), and you fear that the OIG will show up on your doorstep soon. Although not all of the financial difficulties the physician practice is having can be related to coding, many can, as the facility is not receiving proper reimbursement.

1. What should you do to resolve the problems with quality of coding?

2. What should you do to reduce the denial rate?

3. What standard for quality of coding will you recommend?

4. What standard(s) for productivity will you recommend?

CASE 2-24

High-Risk Medicare-Severity Diagnosis-Related Groups (MS-DRGs)

You are the coding supervisor at a 250-bed acute care hospital. The facility averages about 1,050 discharges per month. About 41% of the discharges are Medicare. You have been given the responsibility of ensuring that there are no problems with the OIG's MS-DRG target areas.

1. On the www.pepperresources.com website, identify the current target area MS-DRGs for improper reimbursement.

2. Create a plan for monitoring these MS-DRGs. In this plan include at least:
   - The types of monitoring to be performed
   - Sample size to monitor
   - Frequency of the monitoring
   - Case selection criteria
   - Documentation of monitoring activities
   - A format for reporting the monitoring results
   - A corrective action plan

CASE 2-25

Medicare-Severity Diagnosis-Related Group (MS-DRG) Comparisons

Your chief financial officer (CFO) has asked you to gather some information for him. He wants to compare the average length of stay (ALOS), average charges, and average reimbursement for specific MS-DRGs at your facility to the geometric mean length of stay and determine if there are any statistically significant differences at the 0.5 level.

1. Identify the MS-DRG geometric mean length of stay for the MS-DRGs in Table 2-8 from Table 2-11. Compare the national geometric mean length of stay to your average length of stay. Determine if the difference between them is statistically significant.

2. Determine the national average charges information for the MS-DRGs in Table 2-9 by using Table 2-11. Compare the 2 figures. Determine if the difference between them is statistically significant.

3. Determine the average reimbursement data for the MS-DRGS in Table 2-10. The national data can be found in Table 2-11. Compare the 2 figures. Determine if the difference between them is statistically significant

4. Complete Tables 2-8 through 2-10 and write a memo to the CFO describing your findings.

Table 2-8 *Geometric Mean Length of Stay (GMLOS)*

Average LOS			
Medicare-Severity Diagnosis Related Group	Hospital ALOS	Geometric Mean LOS	Statistically Significant
061	3.6		
062	5.6		
063	3.1		
088	4.6		
089	3.1		
090	2.3		
190	4.4		
191	3.8		
192	3.9		
215	7.1		

Table 2-9 *Average Charges*

Average Charges			
MS-Diagnosis-Related Group	Hospital	National	Statistically Significant
061	$74,842		
062	$51,235		
063	$46,789		
088	$45,952		
089	$6,205		
090	$24,452		
190	$28,568		
191	$22,301		
192	$17,633		
215	$342,000		

Table 2-10 *Average Reimbursements*

Average Reimbursements			
MS-Diagnosis-Related Group	Hospital	National	Statistically Significant
061	$3,960		
062	$9,900		
063	$8,425		
088	$6,521		
089	$4,753		
090	$3,573		
190	$5,821		
191	$4,503		
192	$3,523		
215	$53,245		

Table 2-11 *Medicare Provider Analysis and Review (MEDPAR) 2010 Diagnosis-Related Groups*

Centers for Medicare and Medicaid Services 100% MEDPAR Inpatient Hospital
National Data for Fiscal Year 2010 Short Stay Inpatient Diagnosis-Related Groups

MS-DRG	Total Charges	Covered Charges	Medicare Reimbursement	Total Days	Number of Discharges	Average Total Day
088	$52,123,005	$51,653,662	$10,009,231	6,832	1,307	5.2
089	$92,022,041	$90,873,741	$15,145,663	12,051	3,487	3.5
215	$61,906,042	$61,904,603	$16,289,873	2,283	174	13.1
281	$1,367,838,891	$1,358,407,898	$1,358,407,898	192,510	49,942	3.9
302	$293,691,918	$387,738,340	$63,449,856	48,075	12,188	3.9
344	$104,227,028	$1,020,803,70	$2,370,2255	14,413	1,308	11.0

Extracted from http://www.cms.gov/Research-Statistics-Data-and-Systems/Statistics-Trends-and-Reports/MedicareFeeforSvcPartsAB/Downloads/DRG10.pdf

CASE 2-26

Medicare-Severity Diagnosis-Related Group (MS-DRG) Changes

You just received a MS-DRG change letter from the QIO. The medical record shows that the patient was admitted to the hospital with a high fever and difficulty breathing. A chest x-ray was taken and showed no signs of pneumonia. White blood cell count (WBC) was 17.4; blood cultures grew pseudomonas; arterial blood gases (ABGs) CO_2 rate was 49.6; and the O_2 rate was 53.2. The patient was diagnosed with septicemia and new-onset asthma. The patient was treated with intravenous (IV) antibiotics, respiratory therapy, and bronchodilators. Since both of the diagnoses met the definition of principal diagnosis, the coder chose septicemia as the principal diagnosis since it paid more money. The MS-DRG change notice said that the principal diagnosis should have been asthma.

Write a letter to support your choice of principal diagnosis.

CASE 2-27

Complication/Comorbidity (CC) Medicare-Severity Diagnosis-Related Group (MS-DRG) Analysis

As compliance coordinator, it is important that you compare your facility to other facilities and the national figures. One of your analyses is to compare the major complication/comorbidity (mcc) rate of MS-DRGs for your facility to the national average.

Use the information in Table 2-12 to calculate a MCC percentage for your facility and then determine if there is a statistically significant difference between the 2 figures at the 0.05 level.

Table 2-12 *Major Complication/'Comorbidity Medicare-Severity Diagnosis-Related Group (MS-DRG) Analysis*

Complication/Comorbidity MS-DRG Analysis				
MS-DRG	Number of Cases	National % with cc/mcc	Hospital % with cc	Statistically Significant?
MS-DRG 001	157	87.0%		
MS-DRG 002	24			
MS-DRG 56	123	78.4%		
MS- DRG 57	155			
MS-DRG	21	69.3%		
MS-DRG 73	18			
MS-DRG 74	2	71.5%		
MS-DRG 75	5			
MS-DRG 76	55	65.4%		
MS-DRG 80	43			
MS-DRG 81	123	84.1%		
MS-DRG 100	175			
MS-DRG 101	54	71.2%		
MS-DRG 183	78			
MS-DRG 121	175	37.2%		
MS-DRG 122	154			
MS-DRG 304	63	83.5%		
MS-DRG 305	54			
MS-DRG 493	32	62.4%		
MS-DRG 494	45			

CASE 2-28

Estimated Medicare-Severity Diagnosis-Related Group (MS-DRG) Payments

Administration wants to know the estimated MS-DRG payment for several MS-DRGs. The grouper on your system has crashed. Administration needs this information immediately, so you need to calculate the MS-DRG payments manually. The add-on percentage for your facility is 1.03%. The hospital's base rate is $6,321.67. The MS-DRGs that administration is concerned about are shown in Table 2-13.

Use Table 2-13 to enter the relative weight from Table 2-14 and calculate the estimated payment.

Table 2-13 *Medicare-Severity Diagnosis-Related Groups (MS-DRGs) with Relative Weight and Estimated Payment*

MS-DRGs with Relative Weight and Estimated Payment			
MS-DRG	MS-DRG Title	Relative Weight	Estimated Payment
190	Chronic Obstructive Pulmonary Disease without MCC		
193	Simple Pneumonia & Pleurisy with MCC		
231	Coronary Bypass with PTCA with MCC		
281	Acute Myocardial Infarction Discharged Alive with CC		
304	Hypertension with MCC		
334	Rectal Resection without MCC/CC		
374	Digestive Malignancy with MCC		
389	GI Obstruction with CC		
472	Cervical Spinal Fusion with CC		
509	Arthroscopy		

Table 2-14 *MS-DRG Titles of MS-DRGs Used in Tables 2-12 and 2-13*

MS-DRG	MS-DRG Title	Relative Weight
190	Chronic Obstructive Pulmonary Disease without MCC	1.1924
193	Simple Pneumonia & Pleurisy with MCC	1.4796
231	Coronary Bypass with PTCA with MCC	7.8582
281	Acute Myocardial Infarction Discharged Alive with CC	1.1912
304	Hypertension with MCC	1.0263
334	Rectal Resection without MCC/CC	1.6267
374	Digestive Malignancy with MCC	2.0674
389	GI Obstruction with CC	0.9344
472	Cervical Spinal Fusion with CC	2.7722
509	Arthroscopy	2.7722

CASE 2-29

Case Mix Index (CMI) Trends

You have a committee meeting tomorrow where you have to report on any patterns that are appearing in the case mix index (CMI) for your facility. You have been asked to compare your CMI to the national CMI graphically. The national CMI for 2011 was 1.3638, and for 2012 it was 1.4279. Use the data in Table 2-15 to review the CMI for 2011 and 2012.

1. Create an appropriate graph for this information.

2. What trend(s) do you see from the comparison?

3. What information would you want to know if you were analyzing the reasons behind the trends?

4. Give 3 possible reasons that would explain any trend(s).

Table 2-15 *Quarterly Case Mix Index (CMI)*

Quarterly CMI	
Quarter	CMI
First quarter 2011	1.2354
Second quarter 2011	1.2456
Third quarter 2011	1.2156
Fourth quarter 2011	1.4354
First quarter 2012	1.3541
Second quarter 2012	1.3251
Third quarter 2012	1.3296
Fourth quarter 2012	1.3357

CASE 2-30

Case Mix Index (CMI) Investigation

The CFO just called. He was supposed to have asked you to get him the CMI for 2010, 2011, and 2012 a month ago. He has just realized that he never asked you for the data. He must have it for the board of directors meeting that takes place in 3 hours, but he actually needs the information in an hour so that it can be copied and placed in the packet for the board members. He needs you to create a bar graph to show the trending. He also needs you to provide an analysis of the trends so that he can report it to the board.

1. Use the information in Table 2-16 to make a line graph of the CMI for calendar years 2010, 2011, and 2012.

2. What trends can you identify?

3. Can you identify any cause for concern?

4. What investigation would you want to conduct?

Table 2-16 *Case Mix Index (CMI) for Years 2010, 2011, and 2012 by Month*

Month	Year		
	2010	2011	2012
January	1.4321	1.3276	1.3756
February	1.3215	1.2535	1.4544
March	1.2487	1.2478	1.2489
April	1.5789	2.2435	1.2570
May	1.5789	1.5248	1.5278
June	1.5321	1.4245	1.5741
July	1.2635	1.2857	1.2576
August	1.5227	1.4456	1.5700
September	1.4568	1.2357	1.2768
October	1.2748	1.2575	1.2578
November	1.3578	1.3574	1.4456
December	1.2357	1.6574	1.5788
Annual			

CMI by Month
Years 2010, 2011, and 2012

CASE 2-31

Top 10 Medicare-Severity Diagnosis-Related Groups (MS-DRGs)

Your facility has been investigating your patient population's age, insurance type, and other demographic characteristics to identify who your patients are. Now that you know your patients, the focus is turning to services that you provide. The first round of reports identifies the top 10 MS-DRGs based on the number of discharges and the revenue brought in. You have been asked to report on this at the department director's meeting next week. You have run a report that shows the relative weight for each MS-DRG and the number of discharges for each MS-DRG. Even though you are using the Medicare grouper and MS-DRGs for the report, all patients are included—not just Medicare patients.

Use Table 2-17 to identify the top 10 MS-DRG for your facility based on:
1. Number of discharges
2. Revenue brought in

Table 2-17 *Diagnosis-Related Group (DRG) Relative Weights*

MS-DRG	FY 2011 Final Rule Post-Acute DRG	FY 2011 Final Rule Special Pay DRG	MDC	TYPE	MS-DRG Title	Weights	Discharges
001	No	No	PRE	SURG	HEART TRANSPLANT OR IMPLANT OF HEART ASSIST SYSTEM W MCC	26.3441	0
002	No	No	PRE	SURG	HEART TRANSPLANT OR IMPLANT OF HEART ASSIST SYSTEM W/O MCC	13.6127	0
003	Yes	No	PRE	SURG	ECMO OR TRACH W MV 96+ HRS OR PDX EXC FACE, MOUTH & NECK W MAJ O.R.	18.1239	2
004	Yes	No	PRE	SURG	TRACH W MV 96+ HRS OR PDX EXC FACE, MOUTH & NECK W/O MAJ O.R.	11.2403	2
005	No	No	PRE	SURG	LIVER TRANSPLANT W MCC OR INTESTINAL TRANSPLANT	10.1771	2
006	No	No	PRE	SURG	LIVER TRANSPLANT W/O MCC	4.8353	0
007	No	No	PRE	SURG	LUNG TRANSPLANT	9.3350	0
008	No	No	PRE	SURG	SIMULTANEOUS PANCREAS/KIDNEY TRANSPLANT	4.9632	17
010	No	No	PRE	SURG	PANCREAS TRANSPLANT	3.7831	23
011	No	No	PRE	SURG	TRACHEOSTOMY FOR FACE,MOUTH & NECK DIAGNOSES W MCC	4.7666	1
012	No	No	PRE	SURG	TRACHEOSTOMY FOR FACE,MOUTH & NECK DIAGNOSES W CC	3.1311	1
013	No	No	PRE	SURG	TRACHEOSTOMY FOR FACE,MOUTH & NECK DIAGNOSES W/O CC/MCC	1.9505	1
014	No	No	PRE	SURG	ALLOGENEIC BONE MARROW TRANSPLANT	11.5947	51
015	No	No	PRE	SURG	AUTOLOGOUS BONE MARROW TRANSPLANT	5.9504	30
020	No	No	01	SURG	INTRACRANIAL VASCULAR PROCEDURES W PDX HEMORRHAGE W MCC	8.2479	79
021	No	No	01	SURG	INTRACRANIAL VASCULAR PROCEDURES W PDX HEMORRHAGE W CC	6.2886	100
022	No	No	01	SURG	INTRACRANIAL VASCULAR PROCEDURES W PDX HEMORRHAGE W/O CC/MCC	4.1581	128
023	No	No	01	SURG	CRANIO W MAJOR DEV IMPL/ACUTE COMPLEX CNS PDX W MCC OR CHEMO IMPLANT	5.0883	53
024	No	No	01	SURG	CRANIO W MAJOR DEV IMPL/ACUTE COMPLEX CNS PDX W/O MCC	3.4952	86
025	Yes	No	01	SURG	CRANIOTOMY & ENDOVASCULAR INTRACRANIAL PROCEDURES W MCC	4.7575	21
026	Yes	No	01	SURG	CRANIOTOMY & ENDOVASCULAR INTRACRANIAL PROCEDURES W CC	2.9825	7
027	Yes	No	01	SURG	CRANIOTOMY & ENDOVASCULAR INTRACRANIAL PROCEDURES W/O CC/MCC	2.1307	2
028	Yes	Yes	01	SURG	SPINAL PROCEDURES W MCC	5.3549	0
029	Yes	Yes	01	SURG	SPINAL PROCEDURES W CC OR SPINAL NEUROSTIMULATORS	2.8741	0
030	Yes	Yes	01	SURG	SPINAL PROCEDURES W/O CC/MCC	1.6433	7

					Description	Weight	Count
031	SURG	01	Yes	No	VENTRICULAR SHUNT PROCEDURES W MCC	4.1261	17
032	SURG	01	Yes	No	VENTRICULAR SHUNT PROCEDURES W CC	1.9220	1
033	SURG	01	Yes	No	VENTRICULAR SHUNT PROCEDURES W/O CC/MCC	1.3626	23
034	SURG	01	No	No	CAROTID ARTERY STENT PROCEDURE W MCC	3.5242	54
035	SURG	01	No	No	CAROTID ARTERY STENT PROCEDURE W CC	2.1437	123
036	SURG	01	No	No	CAROTID ARTERY STENT PROCEDURE W/O CC/MCC	1.6390	12
037	SURG	01	No	No	EXTRACRANIAL PROCEDURES W MCC	3.1543	175
038	SURG	01	No	No	EXTRACRANIAL PROCEDURES W CC	1.5462	123
039	SURG	01	No	No	EXTRACRANIAL PROCEDURES W/O CC/MCC	1.0185	23
040	SURG	01	Yes	Yes	PERIPH/CRANIAL NERVE & OTHER NERV SYST PROC W MCC	3.9353	7
041	SURG	01	Yes	Yes	PERIPH/CRANIAL NERVE & OTHER NERV SYST PROC W CC OR PERIPH NEUROSTIM	2.1430	87
042	SURG	01	Yes	Yes	PERIPH/CRANIAL NERVE & OTHER NERV SYST PROC W/O CC/MCC	1.6905	0
052	MED	01	No	No	SPINAL DISORDERS & INJURIES W CC/MCC	1.6109	0
053	MED	01	No	No	SPINAL DISORDERS & INJURIES W/O CC/MCC	0.8441	0
054	MED	01	Yes	No	NERVOUS SYSTEM NEOPLASMS W MCC	1.4863	0
055	MED	01	Yes	No	NERVOUS SYSTEM NEOPLASMS W/O MCC	1.0649	0
056	MED	01	Yes	No	DEGENERATIVE NERVOUS SYSTEM DISORDERS W MCC	1.6748	0
057	MED	01	Yes	No	DEGENERATIVE NERVOUS SYSTEM DISORDERS W/O MCC	0.9350	0
058	MED	01	No	No	MULTIPLE SCLEROSIS & CEREBELLAR ATAXIA W MCC	1.5856	0
059	MED	01	No	No	MULTIPLE SCLEROSIS & CEREBELLAR ATAXIA W CC	0.9811	0
060	MED	01	No	No	MULTIPLE SCLEROSIS & CEREBELLAR ATAXIA W/O CC/MCC	0.7578	0
061	MED	01	No	No	ACUTE ISCHEMIC STROKE W USE OF THROMBOLYTIC AGENT W MCC	2.9568	0
062	MED	01	No	No	ACUTE ISCHEMIC STROKE W USE OF THROMBOLYTIC AGENT W CC	1.9479	0
063	MED	01	No	No	ACUTE ISCHEMIC STROKE W USE OF THROMBOLYTIC AGENT W/O CC/MCC	1.5251	0
064	MED	01	Yes	No	INTRACRANIAL HEMORRHAGE OR CEREBRAL INFARCTION W MCC	1.8674	75
065	MED	01	Yes	No	INTRACRANIAL HEMORRHAGE OR CEREBRAL INFARCTION W CC	1.1667	1
066	MED	01	Yes	No	INTRACRANIAL HEMORRHAGE OR CEREBRAL INFARCTION W/O CC/MCC	0.8198	1

(Continued)

Table 2-17   *(Continued)*

MS-DRG	FY 2011 Final Rule Post-Acute DRG	FY 2011 Final Rule Special Pay DRG	MDC	TYPE	MS-DRG Title	Weights	Discharges
067	No	No	01	MED	NONSPECIFIC CVA & PRECEREBRAL OCCLUSION W/O INFARCT W MCC	1.4231	6
068	No	No	01	MED	NONSPECIFIC CVA & PRECEREBRAL OCCLUSION W/O INFARCT W/O MCC	0.8751	2
069	No	No	01	MED	TRANSIENT ISCHEMIA	0.7311	2
070	Yes	No	01	MED	NONSPECIFIC CEREBROVASCULAR DISORDERS W MCC	1.8417	5
071	Yes	No	01	MED	NONSPECIFIC CEREBROVASCULAR DISORDERS W CC	1.1054	76
072	Yes	No	01	MED	NONSPECIFIC CEREBROVASCULAR DISORDERS W/O CC/MCC	0.7499	12
073	No	No	01	MED	CRANIAL & PERIPHERAL NERVE DISORDERS W MCC	1.2907	45
074	No	No	01	MED	CRANIAL & PERIPHERAL NERVE DISORDERS W/O MCC	0.8606	2
075	No	No	01	MED	VIRAL MENINGITIS W CC/MCC	1.6567	12
076	No	No	01	MED	VIRAL MENINGITIS W/O CC/MCC	0.9050	0
077	No	No	01	MED	HYPERTENSIVE ENCEPHALOPATHY W MCC	1.7376	1
078	No	No	01	MED	HYPERTENSIVE ENCEPHALOPATHY W CC	1.0154	17
079	No	No	01	MED	HYPERTENSIVE ENCEPHALOPATHY W/O CC/MCC	0.7533	3
080	No	No	01	MED	NONTRAUMATIC STUPOR & COMA W MCC	1.1909	7
081	No	No	01	MED	NONTRAUMATIC STUPOR & COMA W/O MCC	0.7392	0
082	No	No	01	MED	TRAUMATIC STUPOR & COMA, COMA >1 HR W MCC	2.0130	1
083	No	No	01	MED	TRAUMATIC STUPOR & COMA, COMA >1 HR W CC	1.3264	0
084	No	No	01	MED	TRAUMATIC STUPOR & COMA, COMA >1 HR W/O CC/MCC	0.8959	0
085	Yes	No	01	MED	TRAUMATIC STUPOR & COMA, COMA <1 HR W MCC	2.1423	0
086	Yes	No	01	MED	TRAUMATIC STUPOR & COMA, COMA <1 HR W CC	1.2051	0
087	Yes	No	01	MED	TRAUMATIC STUPOR & COMA, COMA <1 HR W/O CC/MCC	0.7929	14
088	No	No	01	MED	CONCUSSION W MCC	1.4872	13
089	No	No	01	MED	CONCUSSION W CC	0.9667	15
090	No	No	01	MED	CONCUSSION W/O CC/MCC	0.6927	117
091	Yes	No	01	MED	OTHER DISORDERS OF NERVOUS SYSTEM W MCC	1.6318	89
092	Yes	No	01	MED	OTHER DISORDERS OF NERVOUS SYSTEM W CC	0.9404	57
093	Yes	No	01	MED	OTHER DISORDERS OF NERVOUS SYSTEM W/O CC/MCC	0.6827	14
094	No	No	01	MED	BACTERIAL & TUBERCULOUS INFECTIONS OF NERVOUS SYSTEM W MCC	3.6769	115
095	No	No	01	MED	BACTERIAL & TUBERCULOUS INFECTIONS OF NERVOUS SYSTEM W CC	2.3977	157

096	MED	01	No	No	BACTERIAL & TUBERCULOUS INFECTIONS OF NERVOUS SYSTEM W/O CC/MCC	1.9247	17
097	MED	01	No	No	NON-BACTERIAL INFECT OF NERVOUS SYS EXC VIRAL MENINGITIS W MCC	3.2191	134
098	MED	01	No	No	NON-BACTERIAL INFECT OF NERVOUS SYS EXC VIRAL MENINGITIS W CC	1.9106	54
099	MED	01	No	No	NON-BACTERIAL INFECT OF NERVOUS SYS EXC VIRAL MENINGITIS W/O CC/MCC	1.2084	45
100	MED	01	No	Yes	SEIZURES W MCC	1.5107	100
101	MED	01	No	Yes	SEIZURES W/O MCC	0.7619	78
102	MED	01	No	No	HEADACHES W MCC	1.0288	47
103	MED	01	No	No	HEADACHES W/O MCC	0.6701	275
113	SURG	02	No	No	ORBITAL PROCEDURES W CC/MCC	1.8311	154
114	SURG	02	No	No	ORBITAL PROCEDURES W/O CC/MCC	0.8989	112
115	SURG	02	No	No	EXTRAOCULAR PROCEDURES EXCEPT ORBIT	1.2084	15
116	SURG	02	No	No	INTRAOCULAR PROCEDURES W CC/MCC	1.2675	1
117	SURG	02	No	No	INTRAOCULAR PROCEDURES W/O CC/MCC	0.7305	2
121	MED	02	No	No	ACUTE MAJOR EYE INFECTIONS W CC/MCC	0.9104	6
122	MED	02	No	No	ACUTE MAJOR EYE INFECTIONS W/O CC/MCC	0.6522	1
123	MED	02	No	No	NEUROLOGICAL EYE DISORDERS	0.7144	214
124	MED	02	No	No	OTHER DISORDERS OF THE EYE W MCC	1.1903	187
125	MED	02	No	No	OTHER DISORDERS OF THE EYE W/O MCC	0.6859	21
129	SURG	03	No	No	MAJOR HEAD & NECK PROCEDURES W CC/MCC OR MAJOR DEVICE	2.2349	44
130	SURG	03	No	No	MAJOR HEAD & NECK PROCEDURES W/O CC/MCC	1.2299	52
131	SURG	03	No	No	CRANIAL/FACIAL PROCEDURES W CC/MCC	2.0915	4
132	SURG	03	No	No	CRANIAL/FACIAL PROCEDURES W/O CC/MCC	1.2447	7
133	SURG	03	No	No	OTHER EAR, NOSE, MOUTH & THROAT O.R. PROCEDURES W CC/MCC	1.7000	0
134	SURG	03	No	No	OTHER EAR, NOSE, MOUTH & THROAT O.R. PROCEDURES W/O CC/MCC	0.8514	0
135	SURG	03	No	No	SINUS & MASTOID PROCEDURES W CC/MCC	1.9082	0

(Continued)

Table 2-17 *(Continued)*

MS-DRG	FY 2011 Final Rule Post-Acute DRG	FY 2011 Final Rule Special Pay DRG	MDC	TYPE	MS-DRG Title	Weights	Discharges
136	No	No	03	SURG	SINUS & MASTOID PROCEDURES W/O CC/MCC	0.9751	0
137	No	No	03	SURG	MOUTH PROCEDURES W CC/MCC	1.3007	0
138	No	No	03	SURG	MOUTH PROCEDURES W/O CC/MCC	0.7841	0
139	No	No	03	SURG	SALIVARY GLAND PROCEDURES	0.8756	0
146	No	No	03	MED	EAR, NOSE, MOUTH & THROAT MALIGNANCY W MCC	2.1886	14
147	No	No	03	MED	EAR, NOSE, MOUTH & THROAT MALIGNANCY W CC	1.2413	24
148	No	No	03	MED	EAR, NOSE, MOUTH & THROAT MALIGNANCY W/O CC/MCC	0.8066	101
149	No	No	03	MED	DYSEQUILIBRIUM	0.6389	156
150	No	No	03	MED	EPISTAXIS W MCC	1.2808	1
151	No	No	03	MED	EPISTAXIS W/O MCC	0.6393	65
152	No	No	03	MED	OTITIS MEDIA & URI W MCC	0.9584	115
153	No	No	03	MED	OTITIS MEDIA & URI W/O MCC	0.6290	156
154	No	No	03	MED	OTHER EAR, NOSE, MOUTH & THROAT DIAGNOSES W MCC	1.3965	54
155	No	No	03	MED	OTHER EAR, NOSE, MOUTH & THROAT DIAGNOSES W CC	0.9017	87
156	No	No	03	MED	OTHER EAR, NOSE, MOUTH & THROAT DIAGNOSES W/O CC/MCC	0.6226	44
157	No	No	03	MED	DENTAL & ORAL DISEASES W MCC	1.5794	2
158	No	No	03	MED	DENTAL & ORAL DISEASES W CC	0.9027	276
159	No	No	03	MED	DENTAL & ORAL DISEASES W/O CC/MCC	0.5897	22
163	Yes	No	04	SURG	MAJOR CHEST PROCEDURES W MCC	5.0828	0
164	Yes	No	04	SURG	MAJOR CHEST PROCEDURES W CC	2.6236	33
165	Yes	No	04	SURG	MAJOR CHEST PROCEDURES W/O CC/MCC	1.7758	21
166	Yes	No	04	SURG	OTHER RESP SYSTEM O.R. PROCEDURES W MCC	3.7383	12
167	Yes	No	04	SURG	OTHER RESP SYSTEM O.R. PROCEDURES W CC	2.0567	21
168	Yes	No	04	SURG	OTHER RESP SYSTEM O.R. PROCEDURES W/O CC/MCC	1.3008	114
175	Yes	No	04	MED	PULMONARY EMBOLISM W MCC	1.6096	12
176	Yes	No	04	MED	PULMONARY EMBOLISM W/O MCC	1.0706	21
177	Yes	No	04	MED	RESPIRATORY INFECTIONS & INFLAMMATIONS W MCC	2.0667	99
178	Yes	No	04	MED	RESPIRATORY INFECTIONS & INFLAMMATIONS W CC	1.4887	224
179	Yes	No	04	MED	RESPIRATORY INFECTIONS & INFLAMMATIONS W/O CC/MCC	0.9861	155
180	No	No	04	MED	RESPIRATORY NEOPLASMS W MCC	1.7361	65

181	04	MED	RESPIRATORY NEOPLASMS W CC	No	No	1.2182	54
182	04	MED	RESPIRATORY NEOPLASMS W/O CC/MCC	No	No	0.8096	67
183	04	MED	MAJOR CHEST TRAUMA W MCC	No	No	1.4942	185
184	04	MED	MAJOR CHEST TRAUMA W CC	No	No	0.9755	119
185	04	MED	MAJOR CHEST TRAUMA W/O CC/MCC	No	No	0.6803	106
186	04	MED	PLEURAL EFFUSION W MCC	No	Yes	1.5637	2
187	04	MED	PLEURAL EFFUSION W CC	No	Yes	1.1027	5
188	04	MED	PLEURAL EFFUSION W/O CC/MCC	No	Yes	0.7678	118
189	04	MED	PULMONARY EDEMA & RESPIRATORY FAILURE	No	No	1.2809	226
190	04	MED	CHRONIC OBSTRUCTIVE PULMONARY DISEASE W MCC	No	Yes	1.1924	5
191	04	MED	CHRONIC OBSTRUCTIVE PULMONARY DISEASE W CC	No	Yes	0.9735	4
192	04	MED	CHRONIC OBSTRUCTIVE PULMONARY DISEASE W/O CC/MCC	No	Yes	0.7220	194
193	04	MED	SIMPLE PNEUMONIA & PLEURISY W MCC	No	Yes	1.4796	186
194	04	MED	SIMPLE PNEUMONIA & PLEURISY W CC	No	Yes	1.0152	103
195	04	MED	SIMPLE PNEUMONIA & PLEURISY W/O CC/MCC	No	Yes	0.7096	87
196	04	MED	INTERSTITIAL LUNG DISEASE W MCC	No	Yes	1.6062	1
197	04	MED	INTERSTITIAL LUNG DISEASE W CC	No	Yes	1.1176	17
198	04	MED	INTERSTITIAL LUNG DISEASE W/O CC/MCC	No	Yes	0.8203	2
199	04	MED	PNEUMOTHORAX W MCC	No	No	1.7895	2
200	04	MED	PNEUMOTHORAX W CC	No	No	1.0252	7
201	04	MED	PNEUMOTHORAX W/O CC/MCC	No	No	0.7210	12
202	04	MED	BRONCHITIS & ASTHMA W CC/MCC	No	No	0.8424	18
203	04	MED	BRONCHITIS & ASTHMA W/O CC/MCC	No	No	0.6081	1
204	04	MED	RESPIRATORY SIGNS & SYMPTOMS	No	No	0.6714	204
205	04	MED	OTHER RESPIRATORY SYSTEM DIAGNOSES W MCC	No	Yes	1.2972	191
206	04	MED	OTHER RESPIRATORY SYSTEM DIAGNOSES W/O MCC	No	Yes	0.7575	44
207	04	MED	RESPIRATORY SYSTEM DIAGNOSIS W VENTILATOR SUPPORT 96+ HOURS	No	Yes	5.2068	12
208	04	MED	RESPIRATORY SYSTEM DIAGNOSIS W VENTILATOR SUPPORT <96 HOURS	No	No	2.2630	2
215	05	SURG	OTHER HEART ASSIST SYSTEM IMPLANT	No	No	12.6086	5

(Continued)

Table 2-17 (Continued)

MS-DRG	FY 2011 Final Rule Post-Acute DRG	FY 2011 Final Rule Special Pay DRG	MDC	TYPE	MS-DRG Title	Weights	Discharges
216	Yes	No	05	SURG	CARDIAC VALVE & OTH MAJ CARDIOTHORACIC PROC W CARD CATH W MCC	10.0238	4
217	Yes	No	05	SURG	CARDIAC VALVE & OTH MAJ CARDIOTHORACIC PROC W CARD CATH W CC	6.8038	51
218	Yes	No	05	SURG	CARDIAC VALVE & OTH MAJ CARDIOTHORACIC PROC W CARD CATH W/O CC/MCC	5.3293	75
219	Yes	Yes	05	SURG	CARDIAC VALVE & OTH MAJ CARDIOTHORACIC PROC W/O CARD CATH W MCC	8.0831	53
220	Yes	Yes	05	SURG	CARDIAC VALVE & OTH MAJ CARDIOTHORACIC PROC W/O CARD CATH W CC	5.3787	142
221	Yes	Yes	05	SURG	CARDIAC VALVE & OTH MAJ CARDIOTHORACIC PROC W/O CARD CATH W/O CC/MCC	4.4801	44
222	No	No	05	SURG	CARDIAC DEFIB IMPLANT W CARDIAC CATH W AMI/HF/SHOCK W MCC	8.5230	24
223	No	No	05	SURG	CARDIAC DEFIB IMPLANT W CARDIAC CATH W AMI/HF/SHOCK W/O MCC	6.4250	12
224	No	No	05	SURG	CARDIAC DEFIB IMPLANT W CARDIAC CATH W/O AMI/HF/SHOCK W MCC	7.5819	42
225	No	No	05	SURG	CARDIAC DEFIB IMPLANT W CARDIAC CATH W/O AMI/HF/SHOCK W/O MCC	6.0202	17
226	No	No	05	SURG	CARDIAC DEFIBRILLATOR IMPLANT W/O CARDIAC CATH W MCC	6.4510	62
227	No	No	05	SURG	CARDIAC DEFIBRILLATOR IMPLANT W/O CARDIAC CATH W/O MCC	5.1936	56
228	Yes	No	05	SURG	OTHER CARDIOTHORACIC PROCEDURES W MCC	7.5881	177
229	Yes	No	05	SURG	OTHER CARDIOTHORACIC PROCEDURES W CC	4.7745	150
230	Yes	No	05	SURG	OTHER CARDIOTHORACIC PROCEDURES W/O CC/MCC	3.5451	1
231	No	No	05	SURG	CORONARY BYPASS W PTCA W MCC	7.8582	0
232	No	No	05	SURG	CORONARY BYPASS W PTCA W/O MCC	5.8183	0
233	Yes	No	05	SURG	CORONARY BYPASS W CARDIAC CATH W MCC	7.2081	0
234	Yes	No	05	SURG	CORONARY BYPASS W CARDIAC CATH W/O MCC	4.8281	12
235	Yes	No	05	SURG	CORONARY BYPASS W/O CARDIAC CATH W MCC	5.8530	2
236	Yes	No	05	SURG	CORONARY BYPASS W/O CARDIAC CATH W/O MCC	3.7707	1
237	No	No	05	SURG	MAJOR CARDIOVASC PROCEDURES W MCC OR THORACIC AORTIC ANEURYSM REPAIR	5.1903	1

DRG	MDC	Type			Description	Weight	Count
238	05	SURG	No	No	MAJOR CARDIOVASC PROCEDURES W/O MCC	3.0830	1
239	05	SURG	No	Yes	AMPUTATION FOR CIRC SYS DISORDERS EXC UPPER LIMB & TOE W MCC	4.5544	5
240	05	SURG	No	Yes	AMPUTATION FOR CIRC SYS DISORDERS EXC UPPER LIMB & TOE W CC	2.6589	6
241	05	SURG	No	Yes	AMPUTATION FOR CIRC SYS DISORDERS EXC UPPER LIMB & TOE W/O CC/MCC	1.4631	74
242	05	SURG	No	Yes	PERMANENT CARDIAC PACEMAKER IMPLANT W MCC	3.7277	23
243	05	SURG	No	Yes	PERMANENT CARDIAC PACEMAKER IMPLANT W CC	2.6508	1
244	05	SURG	No	Yes	PERMANENT CARDIAC PACEMAKER IMPLANT W/O CC/MCC	2.0398	2
245	05	SURG	No	No	AICD GENERATOR PROCEDURES	4.2486	4
246	05	SURG	No	No	PERC CARDIOVASC PROC W DRUG-ELUTING STENT W MCC OR 4+ VESSELS/STENTS	3.1802	35
247	05	SURG	No	No	PERC CARDIOVASC PROC W DRUG-ELUTING STENT W/O MCC	1.9691	1
248	05	SURG	No	No	PERC CARDIOVASC PROC W NON-DRUG-ELUTING STENT W MCC OR 4+ VES/STENTS	2.9248	2
249	05	SURG	No	No	PERC CARDIOVASC PROC W NON-DRUG-ELUTING STENT W/O MCC	1.7732	4
250	05	SURG	No	No	PERC CARDIOVASC PROC W/O CORONARY ARTERY STENT W MCC	2.8836	1
251	05	SURG	No	No	PERC CARDIOVASC PROC W/O CORONARY ARTERY STENT W/O MCC	1.7992	26
252	05	SURG	No	No	OTHER VASCULAR PROCEDURES W MCC	2.9754	21
253	05	SURG	No	No	OTHER VASCULAR PROCEDURES W CC	2.4014	12
254	05	SURG	No	No	OTHER VASCULAR PROCEDURES W/O CC/MCC	1.6152	1
255	05	SURG	No	Yes	UPPER LIMB & TOE AMPUTATION FOR CIRC SYSTEM DISORDERS W MCC	2.5043	165
256	05	SURG	No	Yes	UPPER LIMB & TOE AMPUTATION FOR CIRC SYSTEM DISORDERS W CC	1.5969	123
257	05	SURG	No	Yes	UPPER LIMB & TOE AMPUTATION FOR CIRC SYSTEM DISORDERS W/O CC/MCC	0.9750	0
258	05	SURG	No	No	CARDIAC PACEMAKER DEVICE REPLACEMENT W MCC	2.8880	0
259	05	SURG	No	No	CARDIAC PACEMAKER DEVICE REPLACEMENT W/O MCC	1.8334	3
260	05	SURG	No	No	CARDIAC PACEMAKER REVISION EXCEPT DEVICE REPLACEMENT W MCC	3.5500	7
261	05	SURG	No	No	CARDIAC PACEMAKER REVISION EXCEPT DEVICE REPLACEMENT W CC	1.6469	2

(Continued)

Table 2-17 (*Continued*)

MS-DRG	FY 2011 Final Rule Post-Acute DRG	FY 2011 Final Rule Special Pay DRG	MDC	TYPE	MS-DRG Title	Weights	Discharges
262	No	No	05	SURG	CARDIAC PACEMAKER REVISION EXCEPT DEVICE REPLACEMENT W/O CC/MCC	1.1246	4
263	No	No	05	SURG	VEIN LIGATION & STRIPPING	1.7565	3
264	Yes	No	05	SURG	OTHER CIRCULATORY SYSTEM O.R. PROCEDURES	2.5305	18
265	No	No	05	SURG	AICD LEAD PROCEDURES	2.3157	15
280	Yes	No	05	MED	ACUTE MYOCARDIAL INFARCTION, DISCHARGED ALIVE W MCC	1.8503	1
281	Yes	No	05	MED	ACUTE MYOCARDIAL INFARCTION, DISCHARGED ALIVE W CC	1.1912	7
282	Yes	No	05	MED	ACUTE MYOCARDIAL INFARCTION, DISCHARGED ALIVE W/O CC/MCC	0.8064	12
283	No	No	05	MED	ACUTE MYOCARDIAL INFARCTION, EXPIRED W MCC	1.7151	1
284	No	No	05	MED	ACUTE MYOCARDIAL INFARCTION, EXPIRED W CC	0.8888	2
285	No	No	05	MED	ACUTE MYOCARDIAL INFARCTION, EXPIRED W/O CC/MCC	0.5712	54
286	No	No	05	MED	CIRCULATORY DISORDERS EXCEPT AMI, W CARD CATH W MCC	2.0014	1
287	No	No	05	MED	CIRCULATORY DISORDERS EXCEPT AMI, W CARD CATH W/O MCC	1.0879	34
288	Yes	No	05	MED	ACUTE & SUBACUTE ENDOCARDITIS W MCC	2.9397	45
289	Yes	No	05	MED	ACUTE & SUBACUTE ENDOCARDITIS W CC	1.8492	74
290	Yes	No	05	MED	ACUTE & SUBACUTE ENDOCARDITIS W/O CC/MCC	1.2959	54
291	Yes	No	05	MED	HEART FAILURE & SHOCK W MCC	1.4943	6
292	Yes	No	05	MED	HEART FAILURE & SHOCK W CC	1.0302	1
293	Yes	No	05	MED	HEART FAILURE & SHOCK W/O CC/MCC	0.6853	15
294	No	No	05	MED	DEEP VEIN THROMBOPHLEBITIS W CC/MCC	1.0373	2
295	No	No	05	MED	DEEP VEIN THROMBOPHLEBITIS W/O CC/MCC	0.6403	2
296	No	No	05	MED	CARDIAC ARREST, UNEXPLAINED W MCC	1.1692	0
297	No	No	05	MED	CARDIAC ARREST, UNEXPLAINED W CC	0.6792	98
298	No	No	05	MED	CARDIAC ARREST, UNEXPLAINED W/O CC/MCC	0.4497	5
299	Yes	No	05	MED	PERIPHERAL VASCULAR DISORDERS W MCC	1.4072	4
300	Yes	No	05	MED	PERIPHERAL VASCULAR DISORDERS W CC	0.9776	1
301	Yes	No	05	MED	PERIPHERAL VASCULAR DISORDERS W/O CC/MCC	0.6615	4
302	No	No	05	MED	ATHEROSCLEROSIS W MCC	0.9755	3
303	No	No	05	MED	ATHEROSCLEROSIS W/O MCC	0.5830	1
304	No	No	05	MED	HYPERTENSION W MCC	1.0263	0

#						Description	Weight	Count
305	MED	05	No	No	No	HYPERTENSION W/O MCC	0.6138	0
306	MED	05	No	No	No	CARDIAC CONGENITAL & VALVULAR DISORDERS W MCC	1.4667	0
307	MED	05	No	No	No	CARDIAC CONGENITAL & VALVULAR DISORDERS W/O MCC	0.7974	0
308	MED	05	No	No	No	CARDIAC ARRHYTHMIA & CONDUCTION DISORDERS W MCC	1.2339	0
309	MED	05	No	No	No	CARDIAC ARRHYTHMIA & CONDUCTION DISORDERS W CC	0.8387	0
310	MED	05	No	No	No	CARDIAC ARRHYTHMIA & CONDUCTION DISORDERS W/O CC/MCC	0.5709	18
311	MED	05	No	No	No	ANGINA PECTORIS	0.5070	156
312	MED	05	No	No	No	SYNCOPE & COLLAPSE	0.7172	143
313	MED	05	No	No	No	CHEST PAIN	0.5499	87
314	MED	05	No	Yes	No	OTHER CIRCULATORY SYSTEM DIAGNOSES W MCC	1.8145	46
315	MED	05	No	Yes	No	OTHER CIRCULATORY SYSTEM DIAGNOSES W CC	0.9681	23
316	MED	05	No	Yes	No	OTHER CIRCULATORY SYSTEM DIAGNOSES W/O CC/MCC	0.6147	12
326	SURG	06	No	Yes	No	STOMACH, ESOPHAGEAL & DUODENAL PROC W MCC	5.8142	42
327	SURG	06	No	Yes	No	STOMACH, ESOPHAGEAL & DUODENAL PROC W CC	2.7231	14
328	SURG	06	No	Yes	No	STOMACH, ESOPHAGEAL & DUODENAL PROC W/O CC/MCC	1.4298	25
329	SURG	06	No	Yes	No	MAJOR SMALL & LARGE BOWEL PROCEDURES W MCC	5.2807	47
330	SURG	06	No	Yes	No	MAJOR SMALL & LARGE BOWEL PROCEDURES W CC	2.5830	0
331	SURG	06	No	Yes	No	MAJOR SMALL & LARGE BOWEL PROCEDURES W/O CC/MCC	1.6267	14
332	SURG	06	No	Yes	No	RECTAL RESECTION W MCC	4.8635	25
333	SURG	06	No	Yes	No	RECTAL RESECTION W CC	2.4960	45
334	SURG	06	No	Yes	No	RECTAL RESECTION W/O CC/MCC	1.5979	24
335	SURG	06	No	Yes	No	PERITONEAL ADHESIOLYSIS W MCC	4.2777	2
336	SURG	06	No	Yes	No	PERITONEAL ADHESIOLYSIS W CC	2.3456	2
337	SURG	06	No	Yes	No	PERITONEAL ADHESIOLYSIS W/O CC/MCC	1.4789	74
338	SURG	06	No	No	No	APPENDECTOMY W COMPLICATED PRINCIPAL DIAG W MCC	3.2115	54
339	SURG	06	No	No	No	APPENDECTOMY W COMPLICATED PRINCIPAL DIAG W CC	1.8659	12
340	SURG	06	No	No	No	APPENDECTOMY W COMPLICATED PRINCIPAL DIAG W/O CC/MCC	1.2393	32
341	SURG	06	No	No	No	APPENDECTOMY W/O COMPLICATED PRINCIPAL DIAG W MCC	2.2643	54
342	SURG	06	No	No	No	APPENDECTOMY W/O COMPLICATED PRINCIPAL DIAG W CC	1.3246	1
343	SURG	06	No	No	No	APPENDECTOMY W/O COMPLICATED PRINCIPAL DIAG W/O CC/MCC	0.9568	0

(Continued)

Table 2-17 *(Continued)*

MS-DRG	FY 2011 Final Rule Post-Acute DRG	FY 2011 Final Rule Special Pay DRG	MDC	TYPE	MS-DRG Title	Weights	Discharges
344	No	No	06	SURG	MINOR SMALL & LARGE BOWEL PROCEDURES W MCC	3.1586	0
345	No	No	06	SURG	MINOR SMALL & LARGE BOWEL PROCEDURES W CC	1.7035	0
346	No	No	06	SURG	MINOR SMALL & LARGE BOWEL PROCEDURES W/O CC/MCC	1.1883	0
347	No	No	06	SURG	ANAL & STOMAL PROCEDURES W MCC	2.4183	0
348	No	No	06	SURG	ANAL & STOMAL PROCEDURES W CC	1.3705	41
349	No	No	06	SURG	ANAL & STOMAL PROCEDURES W/O CC/MCC	0.7981	0
350	No	No	06	SURG	INGUINAL & FEMORAL HERNIA PROCEDURES W MCC	2.4877	25
351	No	No	06	SURG	INGUINAL & FEMORAL HERNIA PROCEDURES W CC	1.3539	62
352	No	No	06	SURG	INGUINAL & FEMORAL HERNIA PROCEDURES W/O CC/MCC	0.8628	1
353	No	No	06	SURG	HERNIA PROCEDURES EXCEPT INGUINAL & FEMORAL W MCC	2.7510	27
354	No	No	06	SURG	HERNIA PROCEDURES EXCEPT INGUINAL & FEMORAL W CC	1.5523	0
355	No	No	06	SURG	HERNIA PROCEDURES EXCEPT INGUINAL & FEMORAL W/O CC/MCC	1.0329	5
356	Yes	No	06	SURG	OTHER DIGESTIVE SYSTEM O.R. PROCEDURES W MCC	4.0293	4
357	Yes	No	06	SURG	OTHER DIGESTIVE SYSTEM O.R. PROCEDURES W CC	2.1466	178
358	Yes	No	06	SURG	OTHER DIGESTIVE SYSTEM O.R. PROCEDURES W/O CC/MCC	1.3010	46
368	No	No	06	MED	MAJOR ESOPHAGEAL DISORDERS W MCC	1.7578	74
369	No	No	06	MED	MAJOR ESOPHAGEAL DISORDERS W CC	1.0772	56
370	No	No	06	MED	MAJOR ESOPHAGEAL DISORDERS W/O CC/MCC	0.7546	1
371	Yes	No	06	MED	MAJOR GASTROINTESTINAL DISORDERS & PERITONEAL INFECTIONS W MCC	2.0986	0
372	Yes	No	06	MED	MAJOR GASTROINTESTINAL DISORDERS & PERITONEAL INFECTIONS W CC	1.2935	3
373	Yes	No	06	MED	MAJOR GASTROINTESTINAL DISORDERS & PERITONEAL INFECTIONS W/O CC/MCC	0.8599	5
374	Yes	No	06	MED	DIGESTIVE MALIGNANCY W MCC	2.0674	0
375	Yes	No	06	MED	DIGESTIVE MALIGNANCY W CC	1.2801	57
376	Yes	No	06	MED	DIGESTIVE MALIGNANCY W/O CC/MCC	0.8478	45
377	Yes	No	06	MED	G.I. HEMORRHAGE W MCC	1.7541	54
378	Yes	No	06	MED	G.I. HEMORRHAGE W CC	1.0274	78
379	Yes	No	06	MED	G.I. HEMORRHAGE W/O CC/MCC	0.7146	52

380	MED	06	No	Yes	COMPLICATED PEPTIC ULCER W MCC	1.9656	42
381	MED	06	No	Yes	COMPLICATED PEPTIC ULCER W CC	1.1207	12
382	MED	06	No	Yes	COMPLICATED PEPTIC ULCER W/O CC/MCC	0.8130	106
383	MED	06	No	No	UNCOMPLICATED PEPTIC ULCER W MCC	1.1982	123
384	MED	06	No	No	UNCOMPLICATED PEPTIC ULCER W/O MCC	0.8326	21
385	MED	06	No	No	INFLAMMATORY BOWEL DISEASE W MCC	1.9102	1
386	MED	06	No	No	INFLAMMATORY BOWEL DISEASE W CC	1.0435	0
387	MED	06	No	No	INFLAMMATORY BOWEL DISEASE W/O CC/MCC	0.7813	1
388	MED	06	No	Yes	G.I. OBSTRUCTION W MCC	1.6457	98
389	MED	06	No	Yes	G.I. OBSTRUCTION W CC	0.9344	3
390	MED	06	No	Yes	G.I. OBSTRUCTION W/O CC/MCC	0.6369	54
391	MED	06	No	No	ESOPHAGITIS, GASTROENT & MISC DIGEST DISORDERS W MCC	1.1550	24
392	MED	06	No	No	ESOPHAGITIS, GASTROENT & MISC DIGEST DISORDERS W/O MCC	0.7173	117
393	MED	06	No	No	OTHER DIGESTIVE SYSTEM DIAGNOSES W MCC	1.6593	189
394	MED	06	No	No	OTHER DIGESTIVE SYSTEM DIAGNOSES W CC	0.9939	4
395	MED	06	No	No	OTHER DIGESTIVE SYSTEM DIAGNOSES W/O CC/MCC	0.6749	75
405	SURG	07	No	Yes	PANCREAS, LIVER & SHUNT PROCEDURES W MCC	5.5743	24
406	SURG	07	No	Yes	PANCREAS, LIVER & SHUNT PROCEDURES W CC	2.7791	2
407	SURG	07	No	Yes	PANCREAS, LIVER & SHUNT PROCEDURES W/O CC/MCC	1.8665	4
408	SURG	07	No	No	BILIARY TRACT PROC EXCEPT ONLY CHOLECYST W OR W/O C.D.E. W MCC	3.9368	5
409	SURG	07	No	No	BILIARY TRACT PROC EXCEPT ONLY CHOLECYST W OR W/O C.D.E. W CC	2.4875	4
410	SURG	07	No	No	BILIARY TRACT PROC EXCEPT ONLY CHOLECYST W OR W/O C.D.E. W/O CC/MCC	1.6114	6
411	SURG	07	No	No	CHOLECYSTECTOMY W C.D.E. W MCC	3.6818	4
412	SURG	07	No	No	CHOLECYSTECTOMY W C.D.E. W CC	2.4912	4
413	SURG	07	No	No	CHOLECYSTECTOMY W C.D.E. W/O CC/MCC	1.7180	45
414	SURG	07	No	Yes	CHOLECYSTECTOMY EXCEPT BY LAPAROSCOPE W/O C.D.E. W MCC	3.6675	3
415	SURG	07	No	Yes	CHOLECYSTECTOMY EXCEPT BY LAPAROSCOPE W/O C.D.E. W CC	2.0897	18

(Continued)

Table 2-17 *(Continued)*

MS-DRG	FY 2011 Final Rule Post-Acute DRG	FY 2011 Final Rule Special Pay DRG	MDC	TYPE	MS-DRG Title	Weights	Discharges
416	Yes	No	07	SURG	CHOLECYSTECTOMY EXCEPT BY LAPAROSCOPE W/O C.D.E. W/O CC/MCC	1.3080	12
417	No	No	07	SURG	LAPAROSCOPIC CHOLECYSTECTOMY W/O C.D.E. W MCC	2.5029	68
418	No	No	07	SURG	LAPAROSCOPIC CHOLECYSTECTOMY W/O C.D.E. W CC	1.6996	98
419	No	No	07	SURG	LAPAROSCOPIC CHOLECYSTECTOMY W/O C.D.E. W/O CC/MCC	1.1698	14
420	No	No	07	SURG	HEPATOBILIARY DIAGNOSTIC PROCEDURES W MCC	3.6443	22
421	No	No	07	SURG	HEPATOBILIARY DIAGNOSTIC PROCEDURES W CC	1.8910	4
422	No	No	07	SURG	HEPATOBILIARY DIAGNOSTIC PROCEDURES W/O CC/MCC	1.2742	7
423	No	No	07	SURG	OTHER HEPATOBILIARY OR PANCREAS O.R. PROCEDURES W MCC	4.4577	0
424	No	No	07	SURG	OTHER HEPATOBILIARY OR PANCREAS O.R. PROCEDURES W CC	2.4335	0
425	No	No	07	SURG	OTHER HEPATOBILIARY OR PANCREAS O.R. PROCEDURES W/O CC/MCC	1.6273	6
432	No	No	07	MED	CIRRHOSIS & ALCOHOLIC HEPATITIS W MCC	1.7001	4
433	No	No	07	MED	CIRRHOSIS & ALCOHOLIC HEPATITIS W CC	0.9548	12
434	No	No	07	MED	CIRRHOSIS & ALCOHOLIC HEPATITIS W/O CC/MCC	0.6152	5
435	No	No	07	MED	MALIGNANCY OF HEPATOBILIARY SYSTEM OR PANCREAS W MCC	1.8018	66
436	No	No	07	MED	MALIGNANCY OF HEPATOBILIARY SYSTEM OR PANCREAS W CC	1.2215	54
437	No	No	07	MED	MALIGNANCY OF HEPATOBILIARY SYSTEM OR PANCREAS W/O CC/MCC	0.9004	4
438	No	No	07	MED	DISORDERS OF PANCREAS EXCEPT MALIGNANCY W MCC	1.8342	4
439	No	No	07	MED	DISORDERS OF PANCREAS EXCEPT MALIGNANCY W CC	1.0089	1
440	No	No	07	MED	DISORDERS OF PANCREAS EXCEPT MALIGNANCY W/O CC/MCC	0.6890	19
441	Yes	No	07	MED	DISORDERS OF LIVER EXCEPT MALIG,CIRR,ALC HEPA W MCC	1.8242	5
442	Yes	No	07	MED	DISORDERS OF LIVER EXCEPT MALIG,CIRR,ALC HEPA W CC	0.9857	15
443	Yes	No	07	MED	DISORDERS OF LIVER EXCEPT MALIG,CIRR,ALC HEPA W/O CC/MCC	0.6615	21
444	No	No	07	MED	DISORDERS OF THE BILIARY TRACT W MCC	1.5586	1
445	No	No	07	MED	DISORDERS OF THE BILIARY TRACT W CC	1.0688	42
446	No	No	07	MED	DISORDERS OF THE BILIARY TRACT W/O CC/MCC	0.7411	21
453	No	No	08	SURG	COMBINED ANTERIOR/POSTERIOR SPINAL FUSION W MCC	10.2653	5
454	No	No	08	SURG	COMBINED ANTERIOR/POSTERIOR SPINAL FUSION W CC	7.2559	5
455	No	No	08	SURG	COMBINED ANTERIOR/POSTERIOR SPINAL FUSION W/O CC/MCC	5.4308	6

MS-DRG			MDC	Type	MS-DRG Title	Weight	Count
456	No	No	08	SURG	SPINAL FUS EXC CERV W SPINAL CURV/MALIG/INFEC OR 9+ FUS W MCC	9.2885	4
457	No	No	08	SURG	SPINAL FUS EXC CERV W SPINAL CURV/MALIG/INFEC OR 9+ FUS W CC	6.2024	3
458	No	No	08	SURG	SPINAL FUS EXC CERV W SPINAL CURV/MALIG/INFEC OR 9+ FUS W/O CC/MCC	4.9379	1
459	Yes	No	08	SURG	SPINAL FUSION EXCEPT CERVICAL W MCC	6.5065	12
460	Yes	No	08	SURG	SPINAL FUSION EXCEPT CERVICAL W/O MCC	3.8713	12
461	No	No	08	SURG	BILATERAL OR MULTIPLE MAJOR JOINT PROCS OF LOWER EXTREMITY W MCC	4.9385	6
462	No	No	08	SURG	BILATERAL OR MULTIPLE MAJOR JOINT PROCS OF LOWER EXTREMITY W/O MCC	3.3425	42
463	Yes	No	08	SURG	WND DEBRID & SKN GRFT EXC HAND, FOR MUSCULO-CONN TISS DIS W MCC	4.9983	72
464	Yes	No	08	SURG	WND DEBRID & SKN GRFT EXC HAND, FOR MUSCULO-CONN TISS DIS W CC	2.8528	456
465	Yes	No	08	SURG	WND DEBRID & SKN GRFT EXC HAND, FOR MUSCULO-CONN TISS DIS W/O CC/MGC	1.7905	854
466	Yes	No	08	SURG	REVISION OF HIP OR KNEE REPLACEMENT W MCC	4.9144	1065
467	Yes	No	08	SURG	REVISION OF HIP OR KNEE REPLACEMENT W CC	3.2321	165
468	Yes	No	08	SURG	REVISION OF HIP OR KNEE REPLACEMENT W/O CC/MCC	2.5728	6
469	Yes	No	08	SURG	MAJOR JOINT REPLACEMENT OR REATTACHMENT OF LOWER EXTREMITY W MCC	3.4724	12
470	Yes	No	08	SURG	MAJOR JOINT REPLACEMENT OR REATTACHMENT OF LOWER EXTREMITY W/O MCC	2.1039	21
471	No	No	08	SURG	CERVICAL SPINAL FUSION W MCC	4.7301	42
472	No	No	08	SURG	CERVICAL SPINAL FUSION W CC	2.7722	62
473	No	No	08	SURG	CERVICAL SPINAL FUSION W/O CC/MCC	2.0768	1
474	Yes	No	08	SURG	AMPUTATION FOR MUSCULOSKELETAL SYS & CONN TISSUE DIS W MCC	3.4905	6
475	Yes	No	08	SURG	AMPUTAITON FOR MUSCULOSKELETAL SYS & CONN TISSUE DIS W CC	1.9594	45

(Continued)

Table 2-17 *(Continued)*

MS-DRG	FY 2011 Final Rule Post-Acute DRG	FY 2011 Final Rule Special Pay DRG	MDC	TYPE	MS-DRG Title	Weights	Discharges
476	Yes	No	08	SURG	AMPUTATION FOR MUSCULOSKELETAL SYS & CONN TISSUE DIS W/O CC/MCC	0.9920	85
477	Yes	Yes	08	SURG	BIOPSIES OF MUSCULOSKELETAL SYSTEM & CONNECTIVE TISSUE W MCC	3.3286	92
478	Yes	Yes	08	SURG	BIOPSIES OF MUSCULOSKELETAL SYSTEM & CONNECTIVE TISSUE W CC	2.2546	362
479	Yes	Yes	08	SURG	BIOPSIES OF MUSCULOSKELETAL SYSTEM & CONNECTIVE TISSUE W/O CC/MCC	1.6367	89
480	Yes	Yes	08	SURG	HIP & FEMUR PROCEDURES EXCEPT MAJOR JOINT W MCC	3.0939	24
481	Yes	Yes	08	SURG	HIP & FEMUR PROCEDURES EXCEPT MAJOR JOINT W CC	1.8886	55
482	Yes	Yes	08	SURG	HIP & FEMUR PROCEDURES EXCEPT MAJOR JOINT W/O CC/MCC	1.5372	41
483	Yes	No	08	SURG	MAJOR JOINT & LIMB REATTACHMENT PROC OF UPPER EXTREMITY W CC/MCC	2.4019	2
484	Yes	No	08	SURG	MAJOR JOINT & LIMB REATTACHMENT PROC OF UPPER EXTREMITY W/O CC/MCC	1.9554	2101
485	No	No	08	SURG	KNEE PROCEDURES W PDX OF INFECTION W MCC	3.2131	25
486	No	No	08	SURG	KNEE PROCEDURES W PDX OF INFECTION W CC	2.0339	3
487	No	No	08	SURG	KNEE PROCEDURES W PDX OF INFECTION W/O CC/MCC	1.4724	1
488	Yes	No	08	SURG	KNEE PROCEDURES W/O PDX OF INFECTION W CC/MCC	1.7217	24
489	Yes	No	08	SURG	KNEE PROCEDURES W/O PDX OF INFECTION W/O CC/MCC	1.2141	1
490	No	No	08	SURG	BACK & NECK PROC EXC SPINAL FUSION W CC/MCC OR DISC DEVICE/NEUROSTIM	1.7916	3
491	No	No	08	SURG	BACK & NECK PROC EXC SPINAL FUSION W/O CC/MCC	0.9914	0
492	Yes	Yes	08	SURG	LOWER EXTREM & HUMER PROC EXCEPT HIP,FOOT,FEMUR W MCC	3.0670	0
493	Yes	Yes	08	SURG	LOWER EXTREM & HUMER PROC EXCEPT HIP,FOOT,FEMUR W CC	1.8519	1
494	Yes	Yes	08	SURG	LOWER EXTREM & HUMER PROC EXCEPT HIP,FOOT,FEMUR W/O CC/MCC	1.3140	56
495	Yes	Yes	08	SURG	LOCAL EXCISION & REMOVAL INT FIX DEVICES EXC HIP & FEMUR W MCC	2.8683	45
496	Yes	Yes	08	SURG	LOCAL EXCISION & REMOVAL INT FIX DEVICES EXC HIP & FEMUR W CC	1.6207	5
497	Yes	Yes	08	SURG	LOCAL EXCISION & REMOVAL INT FIX DEVICES EXC HIP & FEMUR W/O CC/MCC	1.0770	12

Code				Type	Description		Count
498	No	No	08	SURG	LOCAL EXCISION & REMOVAL INT FIX DEVICES OF HIP & FEMUR W CC/MCC	1.9912	5
499	No	No	08	SURG	LOCAL EXCISION & REMOVAL INT FIX DEVICES OF HIP & FEMUR W/O CC/MCC	0.9917	6
500	Yes	Yes	08	SURG	SOFT TISSUE PROCEDURES W MCC	3.0288	4
501	Yes	Yes	08	SURG	SOFT TISSUE PROCEDURES W CC	1.5846	275
502	Yes	Yes	08	SURG	SOFT TISSUE PROCEDURES W/O CC/MCC	1.0305	675
503	No	No	08	SURG	FOOT PROCEDURES W MCC	2.2809	0
504	No	No	08	SURG	FOOT PROCEDURES W CC	1.5685	14
505	No	No	08	SURG	FOOT PROCEDURES W/O CC/MCC	1.0770	2
506	No	No	08	SURG	MAJOR THUMB OR JOINT PROCEDURES	1.1815	4
507	No	No	08	SURG	MAJOR SHOULDER OR ELBOW JOINT PROCEDURES W CC/MCC	1.8711	0
508	No	No	08	SURG	MAJOR SHOULDER OR ELBOW JOINT PROCEDURES W/O CC/MCC	1.3956	117
509	No	No	08	SURG	ARTHROSCOPY	1.3148	41
510	Yes	Yes	08	SURG	SHOULDER,ELBOW OR FOREARM PROC,EXC MAJOR JOINT PROC W MCC	2.1704	7
511	Yes	No	08	SURG	SHOULDER,ELBOW OR FOREARM PROC,EXC MAJOR JOINT PROC W CC	1.4690	6
512	Yes	No	08	SURG	SHOULDER,ELBOW OR FOREARM PROC,EXC MAJOR JOINT PROC W/O CC/MCC	1.0461	21
513	No	No	08	SURG	HAND OR WRIST PROC, EXCEPT MAJOR THUMB OR JOINT PROC W CC/MCC	1.3007	2
514	No	No	08	SURG	HAND OR WRIST PROC, EXCEPT MAJOR THUMB OR JOINT PROC W/O CC/MCC	0.8209	1
515	Yes	Yes	08	SURG	OTHER MUSCULOSKELET SYS & CONN TISS O.R. PROC W MCC	3.1894	0
516	Yes	Yes	08	SURG	OTHER MUSCULOSKELET SYS & CONN TISS O.R. PROC W CC	1.9244	0
517	Yes	Yes	08	SURG	OTHER MUSCULOSKELET SYS & CONN TISS O.R. PROC W/O CC/MCC	1.4797	0
533	Yes	No	08	MED	FRACTURES OF FEMUR W MCC	1.5657	0
534	Yes	No	08	MED	FRACTURES OF FEMUR W/O MCC	0.7601	0
535	Yes	No	08	MED	FRACTURES OF HIP & PELVIS W MCC	1.3527	0
536	Yes	No	08	MED	FRACTURES OF HIP & PELVIS W/O MCC	0.7191	0

(Continued)

Table 2-17 (Continued)

MS-DRG	FY 2011 Final Rule Post-Acute DRG	FY 2011 Final Rule Special Pay DRG	MDC	TYPE	MS-DRG Title	Weights	Discharges
537	No	No	08	MED	SPRAINS, STRAINS, & DISLOCATIONS OF HIP, PELVIS & THIGH W CC/MCC	0.8275	0
538	No	No	08	MED	SPRAINS, STRAINS, & DISLOCATIONS OF HIP, PELVIS & THIGH W/O CC/MCC	0.6108	0
539	Yes	No	08	MED	OSTEOMYELITIS W MCC	2.0467	0
540	Yes	No	08	MED	OSTEOMYELITIS W CC	1.3126	0
541	Yes	No	08	MED	OSTEOMYELITIS W/O CC/MCC	0.8713	65
542	Yes	No	08	MED	PATHOLOGICAL FRACTURES & MUSCULOSKELET & CONN TISS MALIG W MCC	1.9521	14
543	Yes	No	08	MED	PATHOLOGICAL FRACTURES & MUSCULOSKELET & CONN TISS MALIG W CC	1.1597	25
544	Yes	No	08	MED	PATHOLOGICAL FRACTURES & MUSCULOSKELET & CONN TISS MALIG W/O CC/MCC	0.7775	56
545	Yes	No	08	MED	CONNECTIVE TISSUE DISORDERS W MCC	2.5467	10
546	Yes	No	08	MED	CONNECTIVE TISSUE DISORDERS W CC	1.1712	21
547	Yes	No	08	MED	CONNECTIVE TISSUE DISORDERS W/O CC/MCC	0.7348	32
548	No	No	08	MED	SEPTIC ARTHRITIS W MCC	1.9648	4
549	No	No	08	MED	SEPTIC ARTHRITIS W CC	1.2035	6
550	No	No	08	MED	SEPTIC ARTHRITIS W/O CC/MCC	0.8276	1
551	Yes	No	08	MED	MEDICAL BACK PROBLEMS W MCC	1.6398	1
552	Yes	No	08	MED	MEDICAL BACK PROBLEMS W/O MCC	0.8204	5
553	No	No	08	MED	BONE DISEASES & ARTHROPATHIES W MCC	1.1355	3
554	No	No	08	MED	BONE DISEASES & ARTHROPATHIES W/O MCC	0.6812	6
555	No	No	08	MED	SIGNS & SYMPTOMS OF MUSCULOSKELETAL SYSTEM & CONN TISSUE W MCC	1.0954	4
556	No	No	08	MED	SIGNS & SYMPTOMS OF MUSCULOSKELETAL SYSTEM & CONN TISSUE W/O MCC	0.6568	1
557	Yes	No	08	MED	TENDONITIS, MYOSITIS & BURSITIS W MCC	1.6021	2
558	Yes	No	08	MED	TENDONITIS, MYOSITIS & BURSITIS W/O MCC	0.8823	0
559	Yes	No	08	MED	AFTERCARE, MUSCULOSKELETAL SYSTEM & CONNECTIVE TISSUE W MCC	1.7717	0

560	MED	08	No	Yes	AFTERCARE, MUSCULOSKELETAL SYSTEM & CONNECTIVE TISSUE W CC	1.0022	6
561	MED	08	No	Yes	AFTERCARE, MUSCULOSKELETAL SYSTEM & CONNECTIVE TISSUE W/O CC/MCC	0.6211	24
562	MED	08	No	Yes	FX, SPRN, STRN & DISL EXCEPT FEMUR, HIP, PELVIS & THIGH W MCC	1.3944	0
563	MED	08	No	Yes	FX, SPRN, STRN & DISL EXCEPT FEMUR, HIP, PELVIS & THIGH W/O MCC	0.7153	0
564	MED	08	No	No	OTHER MUSCULOSKELETAL SYS & CONNECTIVE TISSUE DIAGNOSES W MCC	1.4702	0
565	MED	08	No	No	OTHER MUSCULOSKELETAL SYS & CONNECTIVE TISSUE DIAGNOSES W CC	0.9095	85
566	MED	08	No	No	OTHER MUSCULOSKELETAL SYS & CONNECTIVE TISSUE DIAGNOSES W/O CC/MCC	0.6625	0
573	SURG	09	No	Yes	SKIN GRAFT &/OR DEBRID FOR SKN ULCER OR CELLULITIS W MCC	3.2461	0
574	SURG	09	No	Yes	SKIN GRAFT &/OR DEBRID FOR SKN ULCER OR CELLULITIS W CC	1.8675	0
575	SURG	09	No	Yes	SKIN GRAFT &/OR DEBRID FOR SKN ULCER OR CELLULITIS W/O CC/MCC	1.0899	6
576	SURG	09	No	No	SKIN GRAFT &/OR DEBRID EXC FOR SKIN ULCER OR CELLULITIS W MCC	3.9248	152
577	SURG	09	No	No	SKIN GRAFT &/OR DEBRID EXC FOR SKIN ULCER OR CELLULITIS W CC	1.7035	6
578	SURG	09	No	No	SKIN GRAFT &/OR DEBRID EXC FOR SKIN ULCER OR CELLULITIS W/O CC/MCC	1.0416	78
579	SURG	09	No	Yes	OTHER SKIN, SUBCUT TISS & BREAST PROC W MCC	2.9576	36
580	SURG	09	No	Yes	OTHER SKIN, SUBCUT TISS & BREAST PROC W CC	1.4959	0
581	SURG	09	No	Yes	OTHER SKIN, SUBCUT TISS & BREAST PROC W/O CC/MCC	0.9223	0
582	SURG	09	No	No	MASTECTOMY FOR MALIGNANCY W CC/MCC	1.0567	6
583	SURG	09	No	No	MASTECTOMY FOR MALIGNANCY W/O CC/MCC	0.8454	4
584	SURG	09	No	No	BREAST BIOPSY, LOCAL EXCISION & OTHER BREAST PROCEDURES W CC/MCC	1.5153	0
585	SURG	09	No	No	BREAST BIOPSY, LOCAL EXCISION & OTHER BREAST PROCEDURES W/O CC/MCC	1.0411	45

(Continued)

Table 2-17 *(Continued)*

MS-DRG	FY 2011 Final Rule Post-Acute DRG	FY 2011 Final Rule Special Pay DRG	MDC	TYPE	MS-DRG Title	Weights	Discharges
592	Yes	No	09	MED	SKIN ULCERS W MCC	1.7669	54
593	Yes	No	09	MED	SKIN ULCERS W CC	1.0709	6
594	Yes	No	09	MED	SKIN ULCERS W/O CC/MCC	0.7591	2
595	No	No	09	MED	MAJOR SKIN DISORDERS W MCC	1.8690	4
596	No	No	09	MED	MAJOR SKIN DISORDERS W/O MCC	0.8779	0
597	No	No	09	MED	MALIGNANT BREAST DISORDERS W MCC	1.5596	14
598	No	No	09	MED	MALIGNANT BREAST DISORDERS W CC	1.0611	32
599	No	No	09	MED	MALIGNANT BREAST DISORDERS W/O CC/MCC	0.6265	21
600	No	No	09	MED	NON-MALIGNANT BREAST DISORDERS W CC/MCC	0.9602	0
601	No	No	09	MED	NON-MALIGNANT BREAST DISORDERS W/O CC/MCC	0.6728	12
602	Yes	No	09	MED	CELLULITIS W MCC	1.4748	32
603	Yes	No	09	MED	CELLULITIS W/O MCC	0.8377	62
604	No	No	09	MED	TRAUMA TO THE SKIN, SUBCUT TISS & BREAST W MCC	1.2361	189
605	No	No	09	MED	TRAUMA TO THE SKIN, SUBCUT TISS & BREAST W/O MCC	0.7182	204
606	No	No	09	MED	MINOR SKIN DISORDERS W MCC	1.3082	2
607	No	No	09	MED	MINOR SKIN DISORDERS W/O MCC	0.6857	3
614	No	No	10	SURG	ADRENAL & PITUITARY PROCEDURES W CC/MCC	2.4554	6
615	No	No	10	SURG	ADRENAL & PITUITARY PROCEDURES W/O CC/MCC	1.3970	0
616	Yes	No	10	SURG	AMPUTAT OF LOWER LIMB FOR ENDOCRINE,NUTRIT,& METABOL DIS W MCC	4.4934	0
617	Yes	No	10	SURG	AMPUTAT OF LOWER LIMB FOR ENDOCRINE,NUTRIT,& METABOL DIS W CC	2.0006	0
618	Yes	No	10	SURG	AMPUTAT OF LOWER LIMB FOR ENDOCRINE,NUTRIT,& METABOL DIS W/O CC/MCC	1.2006	0
619	No	No	10	SURG	O.R. PROCEDURES FOR OBESITY W MCC	3.5214	0
620	No	No	10	SURG	O.R. PROCEDURES FOR OBESITY W CC	1.8627	0
621	No	No	10	SURG	O.R. PROCEDURES FOR OBESITY W/O CC/MCC	1.4747	0
622	Yes	No	10	SURG	SKIN GRAFTS & WOUND DEBRID FOR ENDOC, NUTRIT & METAB DIS W MCC	3.4166	0
623	Yes	No	10	SURG	SKIN GRAFTS & WOUND DEBRID FOR ENDOC, NUTRIT & METAB DIS W CC	1.8558	0

624	Yes	No	10	SURG	SKIN GRAFTS & WOUND DEBRID FOR ENDOC, NUTRIT & METAB DIS W/O CC/MCC	1.0122	0
625	No	No	10	SURG	THYROID, PARATHYROID & THYROGLOSSAL PROCEDURES W MCC	2.2423	14
626	No	No	10	SURG	THYROID, PARATHYROID & THYROGLOSSAL PROCEDURES W CC	1.1701	23
627	No	No	10	SURG	THYROID, PARATHYROID & THYROGLOSSAL PROCEDURES W/O CC/MCC	0.7821	54
628	Yes	No	10	SURG	OTHER ENDOCRINE, NUTRIT & METAB O.R. PROC W MCC	3.3819	54
629	Yes	No	10	SURG	OTHER ENDOCRINE, NUTRIT & METAB O.R. PROC W CC	2.2650	0
630	Yes	No	10	SURG	OTHER ENDOCRINE, NUTRIT & METAB O.R. PROC W/O CC/MCC	1.4164	0
637	Yes	No	10	MED	DIABETES W MCC	1.4462	0
638	Yes	No	10	MED	DIABETES W CC	0.8306	75
639	Yes	No	10	MED	DIABETES W/O CC/MCC	0.5544	25
640	Yes	No	10	MED	NUTRITIONAL & MISC METABOLIC DISORDERS W MCC	1.1400	41
641	Yes	No	10	MED	NUTRITIONAL & MISC METABOLIC DISORDERS W/O MCC	0.6916	3
642	No	No	10	MED	INBORN ERRCRS OF METABOLISM	1.0290	4
643	Yes	No	10	MED	ENDOCRINE DISORDERS W MCC	1.8159	51
644	Yes	No	10	MED	ENDOCRINE DISORDERS W CC	1.0655	12
645	Yes	No	10	MED	ENDOCRINE DISORDERS W/O CC/MCC	0.7198	5
652	No	No	11	SURG	KIDNEY TRANSPLANT	3.0442	4
653	Yes	No	11	SURG	MAJOR BLADDER PROCEDURES W MCC	6.0929	32
654	Yes	No	11	SURG	MAJOR BLADDER PROCEDURES W CC	3.0054	62
655	Yes	No	11	SURG	MAJOR BLADDER PROCEDURES W/O CC/MCC	1.9567	42
656	No	No	11	SURG	KIDNEY & URETER PROCEDURES FOR NEOPLASM W MCC	3.5713	52
657	No	No	11	SURG	KIDNEY & URETER PROCEDURES FOR NEOPLASM W CC	2.0004	12
658	No	No	11	SURG	KIDNEY & URETER PROCEDURES FOR NEOPLASM W/O CC/MCC	1.4224	54
659	Yes	No	11	SURG	KIDNEY & URETER PROCEDURES FOR NON-NEOPLASM W MCC	3.4988	24
660	Yes	No	11	SURG	KIDNEY & URETER PROCEDURES FOR NON-NEOPLASM W CC	1.9030	7
661	Yes	No	11	SURG	KIDNEY & URETER PROCEDURES FOR NON-NEOPLASM W/O CC/MCC	1.2641	1
662	No	No	11	SURG	MINOR BLADDER PROCEDURES W MCC	3.0158	12
663	No	No	11	SURG	MINOR BLADDER PROCEDURES W CC	1.4718	17

(Continued)

Table 2-17 *(Continued)*

MS-DRG	FY 2011 Final Rule Post-Acute DRG	FY 2011 Final Rule Special Pay DRG	MDC	TYPE	MS-DRG Title	Weights	Discharges
664	No	No	11	SURG	MINOR BLADDER PROCEDURES W/O CC/MCC	1.1074	21
665	No	No	11	SURG	PROSTATECTOMY W MCC	2.8653	0
666	No	No	11	SURG	PROSTATECTOMY W CC	1.6440	0
667	No	No	11	SURG	PROSTATECTOMY W/O CC/MCC	0.7919	0
668	No	No	11	SURG	TRANSURETHRAL PROCEDURES W MCC	2.5175	0
669	No	No	11	SURG	TRANSURETHRAL PROCEDURES W CC	1.2597	65
670	No	No	11	SURG	TRANSURETHRAL PROCEDURES W/O CC/MCC	0.7770	41
671	No	No	11	SURG	URETHRAL PROCEDURES W CC/MCC	1.4400	55
672	No	No	11	SURG	URETHRAL PROCEDURES W/O CC/MCC	0.7885	63
673	No	No	11	SURG	OTHER KIDNEY & URINARY TRACT PROCEDURES W MCC	2.9260	6
674	No	No	11	SURG	OTHER KIDNEY & URINARY TRACT PROCEDURES W CC	2.0934	12
675	No	No	11	SURG	OTHER KIDNEY & URINARY TRACT PROCEDURES W/O CC/MCC	1.3379	56
682	Yes	No	11	MED	RENAL FAILURE W MCC	1.6407	54
683	Yes	No	11	MED	RENAL FAILURE W CC	1.0243	12
684	Yes	No	11	MED	RENAL FAILURE W/O CC/MCC	0.6587	77
685	No	No	11	MED	ADMIT FOR RENAL DIALYSIS	0.8944	85
686	No	No	11	MED	KIDNEY & URINARY TRACT NEOPLASMS W MCC	1.8238	35
687	No	No	11	MED	KIDNEY & URINARY TRACT NEOPLASMS W CC	1.0838	12
688	No	No	11	MED	KIDNEY & URINARY TRACT NEOPLASMS W/O CC/MCC	0.6479	11
689	Yes	No	11	MED	KIDNEY & URINARY TRACT INFECTIONS W MCC	1.2185	5
690	Yes	No	11	MED	KIDNEY & URINARY TRACT INFECTIONS W/O MCC	0.7864	3
691	No	No	11	MED	URINARY STONES W ESW LITHOTRIPSY W CC/MCC	1.6156	0
692	No	No	11	MED	URINARY STONES W ESW LITHOTRIPSY W/O CC/MCC	1.1186	0
693	No	No	11	MED	URINARY STONES W/O ESW LITHOTRIPSY W MCC	1.3505	0
694	No	No	11	MED	URINARY STONES W/O ESW LITHOTRIPSY W/O MCC	0.7096	0
695	No	No	11	MED	KIDNEY & URINARY TRACT SIGNS & SYMPTOMS W MCC	1.2082	88
696	No	No	11	MED	KIDNEY & URINARY TRACT SIGNS & SYMPTOMS W/O MCC	0.6590	56
697	No	No	11	MED	URETHRAL STRICTURE	0.7771	41
698	Yes	No	11	MED	OTHER KIDNEY & URINARY TRACT DIAGNOSES W MCC	1.6098	5
699	Yes	No	11	MED	OTHER KIDNEY & URINARY TRACT DIAGNOSES W CC	0.9999	4

700	Yes	No	11	MED	OTHER KIDNEY & URINARY TRACT DIAGNOSES W/O CC/MCC	0.6757	3
707	No	No	12	SURG	MAJOR MALE PELVIC PROCEDURES W CC/MCC	1.7747	3
708	No	No	12	SURG	MAJOR MALE PELVIC PROCEDURES W/O CC/MCC	1.2581	2
709	No	No	12	SURG	PENIS PROCEDURES W CC/MCC	1.8630	3
710	No	No	12	SURG	PENIS PROCEDURES W/O CC/MCC	1.2712	1
711	No	No	12	SURG	TESTES PROCEDURES W CC/MCC	1.7639	5
712	No	No	12	SURG	TESTES PROCEDURES W/O CC/MCC	0.8084	2
713	No	No	12	SURG	TRANSURETHRAL PROSTATECTOMY W CC/MCC	1.1802	3
714	No	No	12	SURG	TRANSURETHRAL PROSTATECTOMY W/O CC/MCC	0.6544	2
715	No	No	12	SURG	OTHER MALE REPRODUCTIVE SYSTEM O.R. PROC FOR MALIGNANCY W CC/MCC	1.7433	4
716	No	No	12	SURG	OTHER MALE REPRODUCTIVE SYSTEM O.R. PROC FOR MALIGNANCY W/O CC/MCC	0.9974	1
717	No	No	12	SURG	OTHER MALE REPRODUCTIVE SYSTEM O.R. PROC EXC MALIGNANCY W CC/MCC	1.6138	5
718	No	No	12	SURG	OTHER MALE REPRODUCTIVE SYSTEM O.R. PROC EXC MALIGNANCY W/O CC/MCC	0.8044	114
722	No	No	12	MED	MALIGNANCY, MALE REPRODUCTIVE SYSTEM W MCC	1.6891	54
723	No	No	12	MED	MALIGNANCY, MALE REPRODUCTIVE SYSTEM W CC	1.0190	68
724	No	No	12	MED	MALIGNANCY, MALE REPRODUCTIVE SYSTEM W/O CC/MCC	0.6211	95
725	No	No	12	MED	BENIGN PROSTATIC HYPERTROPHY W MCC	1.2742	95
726	No	No	12	MED	BENIGN PROSTATIC HYPERTROPHY W/O MCC	0.7013	54
727	No	No	12	MED	INFLAMMATION OF THE MALE REPRODUCTIVE SYSTEM W MCC	1.3657	5
728	No	No	12	MED	INFLAMMATION OF THE MALE REPRODUCTIVE SYSTEM W/O MCC	0.7612	3
729	No	No	12	MED	OTHER MALE REPRODUCTIVE SYSTEM DIAGNOSES W CC/MCC	0.9892	4
730	No	No	12	MED	OTHER MALE REPRODUCTIVE SYSTEM DIAGNOSES W/O CC/MCC	0.6414	2
734	No	No	13	SURG	PELVIC EVISCERATION, RAD HYSTERECTOMY & RAD VULVECTOMY W CC/MCC	2.4364	5
735	No	No	13	SURG	PELVIC EVISCERATION, RAD HYSTERECTOMY & RAD VULVECTOMY W/O CC/MCC	1.1684	2

(Continued)

Table 2-17 *(Continued)*

MS-DRG	FY 2011 Final Rule Post-Acute DRG	FY 2011 Final Rule Special Pay DRG	MDC	TYPE	MS-DRG Title	Weights	Discharges
736	No	No	13	SURG	UTERINE & ADNEXA PROC FOR OVARIAN OR ADNEXAL MALIGNANCY W MCC	4.3943	12
737	No	No	13	SURG	UTERINE & ADNEXA PROC FOR OVARIAN OR ADNEXAL MALIGNANCY W CC	2.0375	25
738	No	No	13	SURG	UTERINE & ADNEXA PROC FOR OVARIAN OR ADNEXAL MALIGNANCY W/O CC/MCC	1.2324	63
739	No	No	13	SURG	UTERINE,ADNEXA PROC FOR NON-OVARIAN/ADNEXAL MALIG W MCC	3.4300	45
740	No	No	13	SURG	UTERINE,ADNEXA PROC FOR NON-OVARIAN/ADNEXAL MALIG W CC	1.5280	12
741	No	No	13	SURG	UTERINE,ADNEXA PROC FOR NON-OVARIAN/ADNEXAL MALIG W/O CC/MCC	1.0979	56
742	No	No	13	SURG	UTERINE & ADNEXA PROC FOR NON-MALIGNANCY W CC/MCC	1.3883	51
743	No	No	13	SURG	UTERINE & ADNEXA PROC FOR NON-MALIGNANCY W/O CC/MCC	0.9079	35
744	No	No	13	SURG	D&C, CONIZATION, LAPAROSCOPY & TUBAL INTERRUPTION W CC/MCC	1.5151	14
745	No	No	13	SURG	D&C, CONIZATION, LAPAROSCOPY & TUBAL INTERRUPTION W/O CC/MCC	0.8045	12
746	No	No	13	SURG	VAGINA, CERVIX & VULVA PROCEDURES W CC/MCC	1.3373	13
747	No	No	13	SURG	VAGINA, CERVIX & VULVA PROCEDURES W/O CC/MCC	0.8852	6
748	No	No	13	SURG	FEMALE REPRODUCTIVE SYSTEM RECONSTRUCTIVE PROCEDURES	0.9169	4
749	No	No	13	SURG	OTHER FEMALE REPRODUCTIVE SYSTEM O.R. PROCEDURES W CC/MCC	2.5275	3
750	No	No	13	SURG	OTHER FEMALE REPRODUCTIVE SYSTEM O.R. PROCEDURES W/O CC/MCC	0.9368	12
754	No	No	13	MED	MALIGNANCY, FEMALE REPRODUCTIVE SYSTEM W MCC	2.0295	18
755	No	No	13	MED	MALIGNANCY, FEMALE REPRODUCTIVE SYSTEM W CC	1.1444	22
756	No	No	13	MED	MALIGNANCY, FEMALE REPRODUCTIVE SYSTEM W/O CC/MCC	0.6361	21
757	No	No	13	MED	INFECTIONS, FEMALE REPRODUCTIVE SYSTEM W MCC	1.6565	35
758	No	No	13	MED	INFECTIONS, FEMALE REPRODUCTIVE SYSTEM W CC	1.0963	12
759	No	No	13	MED	INFECTIONS, FEMALE REPRODUCTIVE SYSTEM W/O CC/MCC	0.7368	21
760	No	No	13	MED	MENSTRUAL & OTHER FEMALE REPRODUCTIVE SYSTEM DISORDERS W CC/MCC	0.8388	25

761	13	MED	No	No	MENSTRUAL & OTHER FEMALE REPRODUCTIVE SYSTEM DISORDERS W/O CC/MCC	0.5219	4
765	14	SURG	No	No	CESAREAN SECTION W CC/MCC	1.1269	265
766	14	SURG	No	No	CESAREAN SECTION W/O CC/MCC	0.7995	351
767	14	SURG	No	No	VAGINAL DELIVERY W STERILIZATION &/OR D&C	0.9111	654
768	14	SURG	No	No	VAGINAL DELIVERY W O.R. PROC EXCEPT STERIL &/OR D&C	1.8112	651
769	14	SURG	No	No	POSTPARTUM & POST ABORTION DIAGNOSES W O.R. PROCEDURE	2.0631	4
770	14	SURG	No	No	ABORTION W D&C, ASPIRATION CURETTAGE OR HYSTEROTOMY	0.7017	3
774	14	MED	No	No	VAGINAL DELIVERY W COMPLICATING DIAGNOSES	0.6848	235
775	14	MED	No	No	VAGINAL DELIVERY W/O COMPLICATING DIAGNOSES	0.5256	354
776	14	MED	No	No	POSTPARTUM & POST ABORTION DIAGNOSES W/O O.R. PROCEDURE	0.6513	53
777	14	MED	No	No	ECTOPIC PREGNANCY	0.7406	14
778	14	MED	No	No	THREATENED ABORTION	0.4942	65
779	14	MED	No	No	ABORTION W/O D&C	0.5311	21
780	14	MED	No	No	FALSE LABOR	0.2284	66
781	14	MED	No	No	OTHER ANTEPARTUM DIAGNOSES W MEDICAL COMPLICATIONS	0.6809	3
782	14	MED	No	No	OTHER ANTEPARTUM DIAGNOSES W/O MEDICAL COMPLICATIONS	0.4744	2
789	15	MED	No	No	NEONATES, DIED OR TRANSFERRED TO ANOTHER ACUTE CARE FACILITY	1.4877	15
790	15	MED	No	No	EXTREME IMMATURITY OR RESPIRATORY DISTRESS SYNDROME, NEONATE	4.9058	18
791	15	MED	No	No	PREMATURITY W MAJOR PROBLEMS	3.3505	15
792	15	MED	No	No	PREMATURITY W/O MAJOR PROBLEMS	2.0216	66
793	15	MED	No	No	FULL TERM NEONATE W MAJOR PROBLEMS	3.4417	74
794	15	MED	No	No	NEONATE W OTHER SIGNIFICANT PROBLEMS	1.2181	45
795	15	MED	No	No	NORMAL NEWBORN	0.1649	645
799	16	SURG	No	No	SPLENECTOMY W MCC	4.9434	4
800	16	SURG	No	No	SPLENECTOMY W CC	2.5874	2
801	16	SURG	No	No	SPLENECTOMY W/O CC/MCC	1.5586	3

(Continued)

Table 2-17 (Continued)

MS-DRG	FY 2011 Final Rule Post-Acute DRG	FY 2011 Final Rule Special Pay DRG	MDC	TYPE	MS-DRG Title	Weights	Discharges
802	No	No	16	SURG	OTHER O.R. PROC OF THE BLOOD & BLOOD FORMING ORGANS W MCC	3.6171	8
803	No	No	16	SURG	OTHER O.R. PROC OF THE BLOOD & BLOOD FORMING ORGANS W CC	1.8905	5
804	No	No	16	SURG	OTHER O.R. PROC OF THE BLOOD & BLOOD FORMING ORGANS W/O CC/MCC	1.0446	2
808	No	No	16	MED	MAJOR HEMATOL/IMMUN DIAG EXC SICKLE CELL CRISIS & COAGUL W MCC	2.1479	8
809	No	No	16	MED	MAJOR HEMATOL/IMMUN DIAG EXC SICKLE CELL CRISIS & COAGUL W CC	1.1951	0
810	No	No	16	MED	MAJOR HEMATOL/IMMUN DIAG EXC SICKLE CELL CRISIS & COAGUL W/O CC/MCC	0.9230	2
811	No	No	16	MED	RED BLOOD CELL DISORDERS W MCC	1.2544	6
812	No	No	16	MED	RED BLOOD CELL DISORDERS W/O MCC	0.7957	8
813	No	No	16	MED	COAGULATION DISORDERS	1.4372	12
814	No	No	16	MED	RETICULOENDOTHELIAL & IMMUNITY DISORDERS W MCC	1.6431	2
815	No	No	16	MED	RETICULOENDOTHELIAL & IMMUNITY DISORDERS W CC	1.0024	2
816	No	No	16	MED	RETICULOENDOTHELIAL & IMMUNITY DISORDERS W/O CC/MCC	0.6818	2
820	No	No	17	SURG	LYMPHOMA & LEUKEMIA W MAJOR O.R. PROCEDURE W MCC	5.7112	13
821	No	No	17	SURG	LYMPHOMA & LEUKEMIA W MAJOR O.R. PROCEDURE W CC	2.3998	15
822	No	No	17	SURG	LYMPHOMA & LEUKEMIA W MAJOR O.R. PROCEDURE W/O CC/MCC	1.2253	3
823	No	No	17	SURG	LYMPHOMA & NON-ACUTE LEUKEMIA W OTHER O.R. PROC W MCC	4.5640	7
824	No	No	17	SURG	LYMPHOMA & NON-ACUTE LEUKEMIA W OTHER O.R. PROC W CC	2.3055	1
825	No	No	17	SURG	LYMPHOMA & NON-ACUTE LEUKEMIA W OTHER O.R. PROC W/O CC/MCC	1.2418	3
826	No	No	17	SURG	MYELOPROLIF DISORD OR POORLY DIFF NEOPL W MAJ O.R. PROC W MCC	4.8666	7
827	No	No	17	SURG	MYELOPROLIF DISORD OR POORLY DIFF NEOPL W MAJ O.R. PROC W CC	2.1459	2
828	No	No	17	SURG	MYELOPROLIF DISORD OR POORLY DIFF NEOPL W MAJ O.R. PROC W/O CC/MCC	1.3861	3

DRG	Type				Description	Weight	Count
829	SURG	17	No	No	MYELOPROLIF DISORD OR POORLY DIFF NEOPL W OTHER O.R. PROC W CC/MCC	2.7093	7
830	SURG	17	No	No	MYELOPROLIF DISORD OR POORLY DIFF NEOPL W OTHER O.R. PROC W/O CC/MCC	1.0976	1
834	MED	17	No	No	ACUTE LEUKEMIA W/O MAJOR O.R. PROCEDURE W MCC	4.9277	14
835	MED	17	No	No	ACUTE LEUKEMIA W/O MAJOR O.R. PROCEDURE W CC	2.4284	8
836	MED	17	No	No	ACUTE LEUKEMIA W/O MAJOR O.R. PROCEDURE W/O CC/MCC	1.1386	4
837	MED	17	No	No	CHEMO W ACUTE LEUKEMIA AS SDX OR W HIGH DOSE CHEMO AGENT W MCC	6.6599	56
838	MED	17	No	No	CHEMO W ACUTE LEUKEMIA AS SDX W CC OR HIGH DOSE CHEMO AGENT	3.1428	54
839	MED	17	No	No	CHEMO W ACUTE LEUKEMIA AS SDX W/O CC/MCC	1.2823	32
840	MED	17	No	Yes	LYMPHOMA & NON-ACUTE LEUKEMIA W MCC	2.9317	8
841	MED	17	No	Yes	LYMPHOMA & NON-ACUTE LEUKEMIA W CC	1.6376	4
842	MED	17	No	Yes	LYMPHOMA & NON-ACUTE LEUKEMIA W/O CC/MCC	1.0389	17
843	MED	17	No	No	OTHER MYELOPROLIF DIS OR POORLY DIFF NEOPL DIAG W MCC	1.8363	0
844	MED	17	No	No	OTHER MYELOPROLIF DIS OR POORLY DIFF NEOPL DIAG W CC	1.1940	0
845	MED	17	No	No	OTHER MYELOPROLIF DIS OR POORLY DIFF NEOPL DIAG W/O CC/MCC	0.8029	1
846	MED	17	No	No	CHEMOTHERAPY W/O ACUTE LEUKEMIA AS SECONDARY DIAGNOSIS W MCC	2.1961	86
847	MED	17	No	No	CHEMOTHERAPY W/O ACUTE LEUKEMIA AS SECONDARY DIAGNOSIS W CC	0.9860	98
848	MED	17	No	No	CHEMOTHERAPY W/O ACUTE LEUKEMIA AS SECONDARY DIAGNOSIS W/O CC/MCC	0.8078	12
849	MED	17	No	No	RADIOTHERAPY	1.2627	58
853	SURG	18	No	Yes	INFECTIOUS & PARASITIC DISEASES W O.R. PROCEDURE W MCC	5.5237	12
854	SURG	18	No	Yes	INFECTIOUS & PARASITIC DISEASES W O.R. PROCEDURE W CC	2.7883	9
855	SURG	18	No	Yes	INFECTIOUS & PARASITIC DISEASES W O.R. PROCEDURE W/O CC/MCC	1.3797	4

(Continued)

Table 2-17 *(Continued)*

MS-DRG	FY 2011 Final Rule Post-Acute DRG	FY 2011 Final Rule Special Pay DRG	MDC	TYPE	MS-DRG Title	Weights	Discharges
856	Yes	No	18	SURG	POSTOPERATIVE OR POST-TRAUMATIC INFECTIONS W O.R. PROC W MCC	5.1296	14
857	Yes	No	18	SURG	POSTOPERATIVE OR POST-TRAUMATIC INFECTIONS W O.R. PROC W CC	2.0975	2
858	Yes	No	18	SURG	POSTOPERATIVE OR POST-TRAUMATIC INFECTIONS W O.R. PROC W/O CC/MCC	1.3050	1
862	Yes	No	18	MED	POSTOPERATIVE & POST-TRAUMATIC INFECTIONS W MCC	1.9511	4
863	Yes	No	18	MED	POSTOPERATIVE & POST-TRAUMATIC INFECTIONS W/O MCC	0.9790	2
864	No	No	18	MED	FEVER	0.8276	14
865	No	No	18	MED	VIRAL ILLNESS W MCC	1.5651	5
866	No	No	18	MED	VIRAL ILLNESS W/O MCC	0.7462	3
867	Yes	No	18	MED	OTHER INFECTIOUS & PARASITIC DISEASES DIAGNOSES W MCC	2.4708	7
868	Yes	No	18	MED	OTHER INFECTIOUS & PARASITIC DISEASES DIAGNOSES W CC	1.1614	4
869	Yes	No	18	MED	OTHER INFECTIOUS & PARASITIC DISEASES DIAGNOSES W/O CC/MCC	0.7207	3
870	Yes	No	18	MED	SEPTICEMIA OR SEVERE SEPSIS W MV 96+ HOURS	5.8305	13
871	Yes	No	18	MED	SEPTICEMIA OR SEVERE SEPSIS W/O MV 96+ HOURS W MCC	1.9074	7
872	Yes	No	18	MED	SEPTICEMIA OR SEVERE SEPSIS W/O MV 96+ HOURS W/O MCC	1.1545	17
876	No	No	19	SURG	O.R. PROCEDURE W PRINCIPAL DIAGNOSES OF MENTAL ILLNESS	2.8143	8
880	No	No	19	MED	ACUTE ADJUSTMENT REACTION & PSYCHOSOCIAL DYSFUNCTION	0.6161	14
881	No	No	19	MED	DEPRESSIVE NEUROSES	0.6178	0
882	No	No	19	MED	NEUROSES EXCEPT DEPRESSIVE	0.6276	0
883	No	No	19	MED	DISORDERS OF PERSONALITY & IMPULSE CONTROL	1.0694	0
884	Yes	No	19	MED	ORGANIC DISTURBANCES & MENTAL RETARDATION	0.9308	0
885	No	No	19	MED	PSYCHOSES	0.9041	0
886	No	No	19	MED	BEHAVIORAL & DEVELOPMENTAL DISORDERS	0.7903	0
887	No	No	19	MED	OTHER MENTAL DISORDER DIAGNOSES	0.7888	0
894	No	No	20	MED	ALCOHOL/DRUG ABUSE OR DEPENDENCE, LEFT AMA	0.4074	0
895	No	No	20	MED	ALCOHOL/DRUG ABUSE OR DEPENDENCE W REHABILITATION THERAPY	1.0275	0
896	Yes	No	20	MED	ALCOHOL/DRUG ABUSE OR DEPENDENCE W/O REHABILITATION THERAPY W MCC	1.4565	0

MS-DRG					Description	Weight	
897	Yes	No	20	MED	ALCOHOL/DRUG ABUSE OR DEPENDENCE W/O REHABILITATION THERAPY W/O MCC	0.6513	0
901	No	No	21	SURG	WOUND DEBRIDEMENTS FOR INJURIES W MCC	3.9042	4
902	No	No	21	SURG	WOUND DEBRIDEMENTS FOR INJURIES W CC	1.7922	2
903	No	No	21	SURG	WOUND DEBRIDEMENTS FOR INJURIES W/O CC/MCC	1.0624	1
904	No	No	21	SURG	SKIN GRAFTS FOR INJURIES W CC/MCC	2.9335	2
905	No	No	21	SURG	SKIN GRAFTS FOR INJURIES W/O CC/MCC	1.1714	1
906	No	No	21	SURG	HAND PROCEDURES FOR INJURIES	1.0356	5
907	Yes	No	21	SURG	OTHER O.R. PROCEDURES FOR INJURIES W MCC	3.8268	3
908	Yes	No	21	SURG	OTHER C.R. PROCEDURES FOR INJURIES W CC	1.9251	1
909	Yes	No	21	SURG	OTHER C.R. PROCEDURES FOR INJURIES W/O CC/MCC	1.1554	7
913	No	No	21	MED	TRAUMATIC INJURY W MCC	1.3444	15
914	No	No	21	MED	TRAUMATIC INJURY W/O MCC	0.6994	10
915	No	No	21	MED	ALLERGIC REACTIONS W MCC	1.4252	11
916	No	No	21	MED	ALLERGIC REACTIONS W/O MCC	0.4867	14
917	Yes	No	21	MED	POISONING & TOXIC EFFECTS OF DRUGS W MCC	1.4868	1
918	Yes	No	21	MED	POISONING & TOXIC EFFECTS OF DRUGS W/O MCC	0.6269	3
919	No	No	21	MED	COMPLICATIONS OF TREATMENT W MCC	1.5903	7
920	No	No	21	MED	COMPLICATIONS OF TREATMENT W CC	0.9785	2
921	No	No	21	MED	COMPLICATIONS OF TREATMENT W/O CC/MCC	0.6216	14
922	No	No	21	MED	OTHER INJURY, POISONING & TOXIC EFFECT DIAG W MCC	1.3478	35
923	No	No	21	MED	OTHER INJURY, POISONING & TOXIC EFFECT DIAG W/O MCC	0.6808	35
927	No	No	22	SURG	EXTENSIVE BURNS OR FULL THICKNESS BURNS W MV 96+ HRS W SKIN GRAFT	12.6651	0
928	No	No	22	SURG	FULL THICKNESS BURN W SKIN GRAFT OR INHAL INJ W CC/MCC	4.7724	0
929	No	No	22	SURG	FULL THICKNESS BURN W SKIN GRAFT OR INHAL INJ W/O CC/MCC	2.0557	0
933	No	No	22	MED	EXTENSIVE BURNS OR FULL THICKNESS BURNS W MV 96+ HRS W/O SKIN GRAFT	2.1979	0
934	No	No	22	MED	FULL THICKNESS BURN W/O SKIN GRFT OR INHAL INJ	1.3556	0
935	No	No	22	MED	NON-EXTENSIVE BURNS	1.2919	7

(Continued)

Table 2-17 *(Continued)*

MS-DRG	FY 2011 Final Rule Post-Acute DRG	FY 2011 Final Rule Special Pay DRG	MDC	TYPE	MS-DRG Title	Weights	Discharges
939	No	No	23	SURG	O.R. PROC W DIAGNOSES OF OTHER CONTACT W HEALTH SERVICES W MCC	2.8702	2
940	No	No	23	SURG	O.R. PROC W DIAGNOSES OF OTHER CONTACT W HEALTH SERVICES W CC	1.6797	1
941	No	No	23	SURG	O.R. PROC W DIAGNOSES OF OTHER CONTACT W HEALTH SERVICES W/O CC/MCC	1.1457	2
945	Yes	No	23	MED	REHABILITATION W CC/MCC	1.2795	0
946	Yes	No	23	MED	REHABILITATION W/O CC/MCC	1.1273	0
947	Yes	No	23	MED	SIGNS & SYMPTOMS W MCC	1.0952	5
948	Yes	No	23	MED	SIGNS & SYMPTOMS W/O MCC	0.6865	3
949	No	No	23	MED	AFTERCARE W CC/MCC	1.0006	0
950	No	No	23	MED	AFTERCARE W/O CC/MCC	0.5040	0
951	No	No	23	MED	OTHER FACTORS INFLUENCING HEALTH STATUS	0.6593	1
955	No	No	24	SURG	CRANIOTOMY FOR MULTIPLE SIGNIFICANT TRAUMA	5.5336	0
956	Yes	No	24	SURG	LIMB REATTACHMENT, HIP & FEMUR PROC FOR MULTIPLE SIGNIFICANT TRAUMA	3.3704	0
957	No	No	24	SURG	OTHER O.R. PROCEDURES FOR MULTIPLE SIGNIFICANT TRAUMA W MCC	6.2519	0
958	No	No	24	SURG	OTHER O.R. PROCEDURES FOR MULTIPLE SIGNIFICANT TRAUMA W CC	3.7692	0
959	No	No	24	SURG	OTHER O.R. PROCEDURES FOR MULTIPLE SIGNIFICANT TRAUMA W/O CC/MCC	2.3208	0
963	No	No	24	MED	OTHER MULTIPLE SIGNIFICANT TRAUMA W MCC	2.8123	0
964	No	No	24	MED	OTHER MULTIPLE SIGNIFICANT TRAUMA W CC	1.4901	0
965	No	No	24	MED	OTHER MULTIPLE SIGNIFICANT TRAUMA W/O CC/MCC	0.9386	0
969	No	No	25	SURG	HIV W EXTENSIVE O.R. PROCEDURE W MCC	5.5073	15
970	No	No	25	SURG	HIV W EXTENSIVE O.R. PROCEDURE W/O MCC	2.6755	18
974	No	No	25	MED	HIV W MAJOR RELATED CONDITION W MCC	2.5849	12
975	No	No	25	MED	HIV W MAJOR RELATED CONDITION W CC	1.3640	25
976	No	No	25	MED	HIV W MAJOR RELATED CONDITION W/O CC/MCC	0.8975	21
977	No	No	25	MED	HIV W OR W/O OTHER RELATED CONDITION	1.0486	21

981	Yes	No	SURG	EXTENSIVE O.R. PROCEDURE UNRELATED TO PRINCIPAL DIAGNOSIS W MCC	5.0634	12
982	Yes	No	SURG	EXTENSIVE O.R. PROCEDURE UNRELATED TO PRINCIPAL DIAGNOSIS W CC	2.9402	15
983	Yes	No	SURG	EXTENSIVE O.R. PROCEDURE UNRELATED TO PRINCIPAL DIAGNOSIS W/O CC/MCC	1.7767	15
984	No	No	SURG	PROSTATIC O.R. PROCEDURE UNRELATED TO PRINCIPAL DIAGNOSIS W MCC	3.3242	4
985	No	No	SURG	PROSTATIC O.R. PROCEDURE UNRELATED TO PRINCIPAL DIAGNOSIS W CC	2.1508	2
986	No	No	SURG	PROSTATIC O.R. PROCEDURE UNRELATED TO PRINCIPAL DIAGNOSIS W/O CC/MCC	1.1140	3
987	Yes	No	SURG	NON-EXTENSIVE O.R. PROC UNRELATED TO PRINCIPAL DIAGNOSIS W MCC	3.4495	4
988	Yes	No	SURG	NON-EXTENSIVE O.R. PROC UNRELATED TO PRINCIPAL DIAGNOSIS W CC	1.8739	4
989	Yes	No	SURG	NON-EXTENSIVE O.R. PROC UNRELATED TO PRINCIPAL DIAGNOSIS W/O CC/MCC	1.0589	8
998	No	No	**	PRINCIPAL DIAGNOSIS INVALID AS DISCHARGE DIAGNOSIS	0.0000	0
999	No	No	**	UNGROUPABLE	0.0000	0
				Total		28440

CASE 2-32

Case Mix Index (CMI) Analysis

You have been asked to speak at the local health information management program on the CMI. The instructor has asked you to talk about the CMI in general and then to discuss your facility's data to keep the presentation interesting and to show how the CMI is used. You think that it is a good idea because when you were in school, you preferred real-world examples. You decide to take it a step further and walk the students through your calculations so that they understand that process as well.

1. Use the data provided in Table 2-17 to calculate the CMI.

2. What does the CMI tell you about the facility?

3. You will need to give the students 6 ideas of what could be done to increase your CMI. Include facility and HIM-related activities.

CASE 2-33

Medicare Provider Analysis and Review (MEDPAR) Data Analysis

Based on the data in Tables 2-18 and 2-19, identify/answer the following:

1. The top 20 MS-DRGs by number of discharges

2. The top 10 MS-DRGs by patient days

3. The highest 5 MS-DRGs by ALOS

4. What state is the most efficient, based on ALOS?

5. What state is the most efficient, based on cost-of-stay average charge?

6. How can MEDPAR be used by a hospital?

Table 2-18 *Medicare Provider Analysis and Review (MEDPAR) Data 2010 by Diagnosis-Related Group Short Stay Inpatient by State*

Centers for Medicare & Medicaid Services
100% MEDPAR Inpatient Hospital Fiscal Year 2010
Short Stay Inpatient by State

State	Total Charges	Covered Charges	Medicare Reimbursement	Total Days	Number of Discharges	Avg Tot Days
ALABAMA	$10,147,574,758	$10,038,072,172	$1,871,880,274	1,510,549	282,003	5.4
ALASKA	$577,259,995	$566,639,626	$178,507,545	63,829	12,412	5.1
ARIZONA	$12,131,537,372	$12,004,545,106	$1,890,455,415	1,259,379	268,233	4.7
ARKANSAS	$4,650,893,942	$4,617,340,101	$1,198,753,807	859,328	163,926	5.2
CALIFORNIA	$76,320,204,015	$75,110,250,884	$11,191,656,553	5,991,233	1,159,833	5.2
COLORADO	$6,904,049,450	$6,859,514,264	$1,117,218,735	682,982	145,861	4.7
CONNECTICUT	$6,139,247,809	$6,046,063,110	$1,797,610,980	1,018,530	179,172	5.7
DELAWARE	$1,196,604,851	$1,188,116,227	$444,808,903	244,161	43,237	5.6
DISTRICT OF CO	$1,801,374,695	$1,758,124,064	$535,615,255	244,515	38,178	6.4
FLORIDA	$52,617,494,107	$52,293,923,852	$7,587,899,229	5,830,082	1,099,252	5.3
GEORGIA	$12,774,675,044	$12,670,647,571	$2,971,580,228	1,993,096	366,794	5.4
HAWAII	$1,155,327,643	$1,128,511,837	$303,609,640	210,869	32,879	6.4
IDAHO	$1,070,859,131	$1,068,209,787	$282,670,824	172,290	39,761	4.3
ILLINOIS	$23,220,247,028	$22,986,364,994	$5,506,557,400	3,167,766	616,325	5.1
INDIANA	$10,046,158,605	$9,974,718,544	$2,644,144,815	1,667,772	322,776	5.2
IOWA	$3,500,727,854	$3,471,430,275	$987,181,870	620,740	124,562	5
KANSAS	$4,298,673,428	$4,272,076,840	$967,292,484	596,333	118,347	5
KENTUCKY	$7,569,184,626	$7,505,177,124	$2,044,026,403	1,379,637	264,888	5.2
LOUISIANA	$8,235,304,586	$8,133,823,924	$1,647,692,129	1,279,408	231,488	5.5
MAINE	$1,447,797,039	$1,434,223,961	$533,523,616	304,584	61,257	5
MARYLAND	$3,946,237,184	$3,883,076,774	$3,223,158,908	1,367,904	276,931	4.9
MASSACHU-SETTS	$9,139,634,478	$9,036,823,618	$3,389,376,309	1,843,260	357,214	5.2
MICHIGAN	$15,619,449,714	$15,466,296,055	$4,996,125,348	2,958,671	555,665	5.3
MINNESOTA	$6,935,040,451	$6,873,436,755	$1,829,860,224	952,088	205,607	4.6
MISSISSIPPI	$5,382,816,252	$5,340,100,260	$1,317,180,432	957,191	169,249	5.7
MISSOURI	$11,736,910,838	$11,455,708,404	$2,690,755,303	1,782,840	344,361	5.2
MONTANA	$865,186,366	$858,204,690	$266,045,718	158,962	34,071	4.7
NEBRASKA	$2,758,111,247	$2,737,944,914	$670,223,142	380,521	74,966	5.1
NEVADA	$6,179,609,713	$6,115,884,991	$775,757,239	522,179	98,868	5.3
NEW HAMPSHIRE	$1,476,037,830	$1,467,436,682	$460,132,445	252,953	47,692	5.3
NEW JERSEY	$28,489,630,729	$28,080,939,035	$4,101,798,474	2,516,729	425,674	5.9
NEW MEXICO	$2,050,325,541	$2,036,148,735	$484,642,557	304,839	63,606	4.8
NEW YORK	$36,991,790,908	$36,109,494,617	$9,804,172,781	6,583,804	983,092	6.7
NORTH CAROLINA	$13,298,007,382	$13,194,616,158	$4,018,966,039	2,479,974	465,217	5.3
NORTH DAKOTA	$724,008,854	$716,854,958	$266,956,934	148,920	30,999	4.8

Table 2-18 *(Continued)*

Centers for Medicare & Medicaid Services
100% MEDPAR Inpatient Hospital Fiscal Year 2010
Short Stay Inpatient by State

State	Total Charges	Covered Charges	Medicare Reimbursement	Total Days	Number of Discharges	Avg Tot Days
OHIO	$21,264,776,632	$20,950,208,271	$4,548,391,978	3,306,485	647,345	5.1
OKLAHOMA	$6,358,089,969	$6,288,927,901	$1,464,254,308	992,113	192,253	5.2
OREGON	$3,968,392,976	$3,947,051,190	$858,307,627	594,065	128,713	4.6
PENNSYLVANIA	$37,410,926,656	$36,256,231,748	$5,280,683,810	4,378,798	787,788	5.6
PUERTO RICO	$603,859,499	$598,657,220	$177,973,749	432,535	63,620	6.8
RHODE ISLAND	$1,756,908,758	$1,729,754,707	$405,756,528	313,857	55,596	5.6
SOUTH CAROLINA	$8,807,688,270	$8,737,287,659	$1,858,440,523	1,228,448	218,321	5.6
SOUTH DAKOTA	$1,167,580,116	$1,155,116,775	$335,715,909	181,462	36,146	5
TENNESSEE	$12,746,772,706	$12,679,779,976	$2,742,276,783	2,041,124	383,981	5.3
TEXAS	$42,875,387,649	$41,971,787,681	$7,851,225,314	5,031,311	928,834	5.4
UTAH	$1,901,227,466	$1,883,723,968	$463,159,245	277,474	62,834	4.4
VERMONT	$420,145,959	$416,954,353	$217,601,470	93,556	17,870	5.2
VIRGIN ISLANDS	$39,501,740	$38,982,645	$18,577,125	15,343	1,957	7.8
VIRGINIA	$10,757,693,488	$10,689,967,199	$2,651,053,226	1,724,897	326,211	5.3
WASHINGTON	$8,468,518,610	$8,424,232,175	$1,933,437,855	1,009,585	217,781	4.6
WEST VIRGINIA	$2,628,845,839	$2,610,209,963	$819,069,756	648,423	118,769	5.5
WISCONSIN	$6,857,942,766	$6,804,514,268	$1,750,294,339	1,074,539	219,821	4.9
WYOMING	$418,561,455	$413,241,167	$150,892,761	65,075	14,116	4.6
UNKNOWN	$26,501,628	$25,960,389	$11,968,865	17,531	2,325	7.5
TOTAL LINE	**$559,877,318,647**	**$552,123,330,164**	**$117,536,919,129**	**75,734,539**	**14,128,677**	**5.4**

Courtesy of the Centers for Medicare and Medicaid Services.

Table 2-19 *Medicare Provider Analysis and Review (MEDPAR) Inpatient National Data by Short Stay Inpatient Diagnosis-Related Groups (DRGs)*

Centers for Medicare & Medicaid Services
100% MEDPAR Inpatient Hospital National Data for Fiscal Year 2010
Short Stay Inpatient Diagnosis Related Groups
Blank cells represent ten or less discharges in order to conform to CMS guidelines, zero means
no discharges, therefore, sum of columns will not equal total

Drg	Total Charges	Covered Charges	Medicare Reimbursement	Total Days	Number of Discharges	Avg Tot Days
1	$1,117,985,829	$1,090,743,161	$286,358,414	56,582	1,528	37
2	$140,502,546	$140,205,825	$32,065,545	6,165	340	18.1
3	$11,615,298,430	$11,376,271,614	$2,730,104,797	932,325	25,937	35.9
4	$6,883,608,321	$6,772,437,052	$1,644,116,325	700,736	26,334	26.6
5	$536,660,556	$523,614,813	$105,731,995	25,975	1,264	20.5
6	$81,182,083	$78,643,466	$12,279,994	3,048	354	8.6
7	$262,789,035	$255,603,053	$45,062,614	11,773	604	19.5
8	$175,972,939	$168,897,085	$22,564,644	6,887	574	12
9	$567,469,241	$552,460,131	$143,027,966	56,323	2,741	20.5
10	$30,143,942	$29,339,199	$4,450,723	1,444	147	9.8
11	$295,466,194	$291,834,258	$69,624,418	32,296	2,130	15.2
12	$220,515,688	$217,391,636	$49,339,587	24,976	2,495	10
13	$68,341,801	$67,433,386	$13,652,721	8,189	1,247	6.6
20	$368,647,928	$361,900,643	$82,162,628	24,660	1,470	16.8
21	$107,157,847	$106,458,732	$22,749,702	8,204	575	14.3
22	$20,739,902	$20,659,675	$4,041,955	1,365	177	7.7
23	$882,403,654	$870,985,336	$188,705,591	70,583	6,053	11.7
24	$211,292,564	$209,850,830	$41,041,146	16,299	2,212	7.4
25	$2,056,624,169	$2,041,667,831	$462,265,665	183,111	16,773	10.9
26	$1,037,741,879	$1,031,428,875	$215,109,592	92,916	13,338	7
27	$938,564,429	$931,288,046	$178,589,497	58,276	15,651	3.7
28	$360,938,746	$358,080,879	$77,931,794	32,524	2,481	13.1
29	$318,517,999	$316,380,961	$68,427,214	26,899	4,397	6.1
30	$184,224,557	$182,526,420	$36,746,483	13,956	4,341	3.2
31	$173,582,626	$171,584,124	$44,375,603	19,300	1,577	12.2
32	$156,840,627	$155,387,108	$33,741,779	16,172	3,121	5.2
33	$141,216,554	$140,686,167	$27,489,347	10,181	3,915	2.6
34	$118,484,660	$112,734,822	$22,045,991	8,889	1,246	7.1
35	$156,693,536	$153,558,341	$29,191,285	8,195	2,758	3
36	$318,194,476	$313,455,607	$57,042,777	11,487	7,291	1.6
37	$558,705,110	$541,710,113	$110,947,634	56,225	7,049	8
38	$663,459,914	$650,504,718	$113,810,384	54,956	16,362	3.4
39	$1,467,780,661	$1,445,653,303	$225,954,554	88,434	53,289	1.7
40	$675,720,893	$664,811,989	$159,007,555	81,513	7,032	11.6
41	$430,266,157	$426,250,341	$88,988,681	50,934	8,080	6.3
42	$196,761,257	$193,527,177	$37,239,920	14,329	4,321	3.3
52	$64,478,116	$64,288,652	$13,713,327	9,749	1,591	6.1
53	$13,912,886	$13,704,326	$2,374,719	2,002	593	3.4

Table 2-19 *(Continued)*

Centers for Medicare & Medicaid Services
100% MEDPAR Inpatient Hospital National Data for Fiscal Year 2010
Short Stay Inpatient Diagnosis Related Groups
Blank cells represent ten or less discharges in order to conform to CMS guidelines, zero means
no discharges, therefore, sum of columns will not equal total

Drg	Total Charges	Covered Charges	Medicare Reimbursement	Total Days	Number of Discharges	Avg Tot Days
54	$439,551,450	$436,952,029	$98,859,323	68,392	11,313	6
55	$400,739,058	$397,030,153	$76,306,161	63,288	14,148	4.5
56	$673,144,943	$661,893,296	$172,953,789	152,636	18,259	8.4
57	$1,762,289,022	$1,698,820,233	$479,004,212	594,899	74,367	8
58	$45,473,713	$45,059,972	$10,761,922	7,957	1,189	6.7
59	$95,925,712	$94,490,314	$18,579,888	17,903	3,637	4.9
60	$86,275,941	$85,352,841	$14,830,908	15,766	4,158	3.8
61	$303,534,322	$301,979,724	$62,785,937	30,852	3,938	7.8
62	$292,681,977	$290,401,883	$52,904,980	29,706	5,496	5.4
63	$93,631,735	$92,948,688	$15,017,877	7,915	2,091	3.8
64	$4,165,859,831	$4,130,693,605	$887,553,425	610,353	91,703	6.7
65	$3,739,821,756	$3,715,714,395	$709,881,578	597,729	130,125	4.6
66	$1,874,477,204	$1,861,269,708	$302,910,888	268,945	85,258	3.2
67	$91,666,056	$90,527,880	$17,218,443	12,986	2,490	5.2
68	$278,442,031	$274,768,848	$44,341,378	35,650	11,356	3.1
69	$2,270,920,888	$2,204,521,964	$351,122,407	305,759	114,296	2.7
70	$721,068,555	$716,136,757	$172,440,683	122,776	18,332	6.7
71	$360,513,934	$357,002,930	$79,997,297	72,164	14,273	5.1
72	$125,914,525	$122,942,941	$21,696,240	19,651	6,428	3.1
73	$459,906,672	$443,526,776	$104,529,023	79,799	14,916	5.3
74	$767,701,926	$751,178,923	$139,159,755	131,995	34,430	3.8
75	$81,220,873	$80,530,175	$15,665,469	11,834	1,730	6.8
76	$19,995,516	$19,939,781	$3,020,745	3,175	847	3.7
77	$98,962,837	$98,245,725	$22,289,287	14,426	2,392	6
78	$61,771,373	$61,499,474	$11,552,504	9,803	2,460	4
79	$20,579,935	$20,411,125	$3,250,367	3,063	1,048	2.9
80	$81,719,854	$80,803,237	$17,445,095	13,545	2,761	4.9
81	$123,771,316	$122,160,079	$23,030,351	22,293	6,505	3.4
82	$192,610,201	$189,635,866	$43,276,897	20,564	3,449	6
83	$116,508,233	$115,635,333	$23,117,464	14,834	3,161	4.7
84	$79,371,849	$78,724,245	$13,896,808	8,702	3,234	2.7
85	$602,495,271	$599,433,741	$135,603,700	81,601	11,637	7
86	$512,097,684	$508,595,175	$107,049,762	76,144	17,309	4.4
87	$353,029,120	$350,741,571	$63,635,135	48,146	16,995	2.8
88	$52,123,005	$51,653,662	$10,009,231	6,832	1,307	5.2
89	$92,022,041	$90,873,741	$15,145,663	12,051	3,487	3.5
90	$64,244,798	$63,194,789	$9,033,489	6,732	3,010	2.2
91	$546,743,309	$538,741,266	$120,226,771	82,538	14,241	5.8
92	$482,576,545	$474,718,229	$95,977,558	84,169	21,007	4

(Continued)

Table 2-19 *(Continued)*

Centers for Medicare & Medicaid Services
100% MEDPAR Inpatient Hospital National Data for Fiscal Year 2010
Short Stay Inpatient Diagnosis Related Groups
Blank cells represent ten or less discharges in order to conform to CMS guidelines, zero means
no discharges, therefore, sum of columns will not equal total

Drg	Total Charges	Covered Charges	Medicare Reimbursement	Total Days	Number of Discharges	Avg Tot Days
93	$287,305,154	$281,420,478	$47,719,708	43,392	15,681	2.8
94	$162,878,697	$161,386,841	$37,494,905	21,515	1,870	11.5
95	$80,816,719	$80,329,493	$15,291,728	9,744	1,286	7.6
96	$32,833,801	$32,704,454	$5,623,946	3,575	630	5.7
97	$139,767,442	$138,923,630	$30,010,680	18,748	1,701	11
98	$54,244,525	$53,637,349	$11,631,965	8,493	1,167	7.3
99	$19,197,976	$18,867,079	$3,382,557	3,067	580	5.3
100	$1,042,382,685	$1,029,639,675	$229,736,675	155,295	27,234	5.7
101	$1,309,231,621	$1,298,479,928	$249,514,325	210,895	64,450	3.3
102	$53,845,199	$53,078,191	$10,322,064	8,551	1,968	4.3
103	$287,876,714	$282,667,679	$43,453,447	44,864	15,676	2.9
113	$44,199,886	$43,975,117	$9,550,671	4,552	820	5.6
114	$13,314,633	$13,070,519	$2,309,893	1,299	481	2.7
115	$36,741,207	$36,210,753	$7,273,100	4,581	1,066	4.3
116	$22,334,037	$22,037,584	$4,550,527	2,669	645	4.1
117	$13,963,838	$13,760,670	$2,403,393	1,479	693	2.1
121	$24,204,277	$23,997,958	$5,499,582	4,948	943	5.2
122	$9,316,207	$9,290,432	$1,826,740	2,154	583	3.7
123	$78,974,117	$78,357,268	$11,813,644	9,683	3,672	2.6
124	$40,154,874	$39,906,521	$9,538,965	6,865	1,434	4.8
125	$89,190,669	$88,156,933	$15,697,255	15,463	4,978	3.1
129	$127,372,855	$125,980,332	$26,296,324	10,442	1,960	5.3
130	$50,086,953	$49,558,605	$9,128,562	3,905	1,371	2.8
131	$97,402,936	$95,473,068	$19,287,298	8,575	1,494	5.7
132	$34,484,428	$33,752,352	$6,152,445	2,546	948	2.7
133	$136,459,949	$134,346,800	$26,368,075	15,338	2,820	5.4
134	$79,903,514	$77,408,087	$12,894,042	6,678	3,137	2.1
135	$29,926,811	$29,723,602	$5,977,225	3,343	531	6.3
136	$13,630,402	$13,451,629	$2,139,710	1,080	452	2.4
137	$44,325,989	$43,357,312	$9,800,096	6,243	1,257	5
138	$20,483,067	$19,788,568	$3,372,745	2,219	937	2.4
139	$41,975,662	$41,413,561	$6,239,919	2,798	1,614	1.7
146	$51,784,219	$51,281,702	$13,176,019	8,459	1,036	8.2
147	$48,481,198	$47,428,742	$10,285,854	8,539	1,524	5.6
148	$14,442,276	$14,170,359	$2,589,196	2,177	704	3.1
149	$743,770,603	$734,564,391	$115,171,049	107,940	43,026	2.5
150	$61,943,914	$61,478,716	$15,634,487	10,602	2,149	4.9
151	$105,780,894	$105,032,624	$20,204,477	19,788	7,243	2.7
152	$124,781,537	$123,308,045	$24,212,896	19,994	4,451	4.5

Table 2-19 *(Continued)*

Centers for Medicare & Medicaid Services
100% MEDPAR Inpatient Hospital National Data for Fiscal Year 2010
Short Stay Inpatient Diagnosis Related Groups
Blank cells represent ten or less discharges in order to conform to CMS guidelines, zero means
no discharges, therefore, sum of columns will not equal total

Drg	Total Charges	Covered Charges	Medicare Reimbursement	Total Days	Number of Discharges	Avg Tot Days
153	$242,394,350	$240,096,842	$39,926,300	44,124	14,675	3
154	$130,848,670	$128,978,937	$29,369,840	21,473	3,864	5.6
155	$147,209,699	$145,683,468	$29,240,390	26,081	6,587	4
156	$68,118,583	$67,532,447	$11,549,067	11,793	4,232	2.8
157	$83,862,663	$82,933,469	$19,338,742	13,994	2,159	6.5
158	$105,030,831	$103,925,739	$22,495,262	18,960	4,691	4
159	$29,521,332	$28,923,064	$5,031,204	5,001	1,938	2.6
163	$2,148,988,542	$2,122,990,512	$467,990,473	239,050	17,620	13.6
164	$1,428,503,330	$1,416,187,936	$290,008,331	155,304	22,343	7
165	$635,065,976	$629,869,374	$121,650,158	58,546	13,737	4.3
166	$2,602,377,375	$2,558,347,321	$571,477,012	331,466	28,637	11.6
167	$986,753,487	$978,536,248	$198,578,496	134,123	19,833	6.8
168	$171,133,027	$169,729,606	$31,693,069	20,968	5,092	4.1
175	$908,434,177	$901,544,105	$187,762,074	155,868	23,706	6.6
176	$1,145,112,074	$1,135,932,979	$221,223,610	211,070	45,889	4.6
177	$4,457,215,315	$4,410,141,327	$1,026,870,149	769,347	93,710	8.2
178	$2,210,955,688	$2,191,984,480	$504,295,472	423,990	66,133	6.4
179	$416,452,790	$413,729,949	$88,940,008	85,851	18,001	4.8
180	$1,284,827,495	$1,275,227,770	$267,397,650	210,791	28,937	7.3
181	$900,643,038	$894,087,677	$174,525,389	149,223	28,809	5.2
182	$74,627,956	$73,946,822	$12,773,248	11,867	3,372	3.5
183	$133,995,790	$133,159,511	$26,866,618	22,577	3,724	6.1
184	$166,959,982	$165,241,033	$27,861,734	26,537	6,356	4.2
185	$47,847,724	$47,489,201	$7,097,912	7,651	2,591	3
186	$536,208,140	$531,832,943	$116,459,021	92,287	14,007	6.6
187	$312,622,387	$310,522,201	$61,692,027	53,418	11,674	4.6
188	$75,631,809	$75,038,645	$13,695,045	13,329	3,933	3.4
189	$3,590,091,019	$3,550,434,146	$781,915,284	616,572	115,177	5.4
190	$5,331,771,619	$5,289,374,429	$1,111,789,327	995,302	189,511	5.3
191	$3,689,361,712	$3,650,203,391	$729,422,772	711,098	162,090	4.4
192	$2,692,247,215	$2,660,353,427	$477,513,733	543,919	155,808	3.5
193	$6,243,397,348	$6,195,818,601	$1,322,133,496	1,123,406	181,973	6.2
194	$4,921,375,189	$4,883,990,900	$990,294,781	980,308	209,875	4.7
195	$1,758,688,273	$1,743,970,112	$312,650,422	367,395	103,594	3.5
196	$370,607,649	$368,183,979	$75,034,953	65,006	9,427	6.9
197	$183,324,916	$181,958,814	$36,158,386	32,771	6,957	4.7
198	$74,695,848	$73,872,183	$13,751,232	13,061	3,654	3.6
199	$234,239,513	$232,886,330	$51,398,777	41,391	5,382	7.7
200	$245,730,432	$243,776,253	$46,709,755	45,429	10,195	4.5

(Continued)

Table 2-19   *(Continued)*

Centers for Medicare & Medicaid Services
100% MEDPAR Inpatient Hospital National Data for Fiscal Year 2010
Short Stay Inpatient Diagnosis Related Groups
Blank cells represent ten or less discharges in order to conform to CMS guidelines, zero means
no discharges, therefore, sum of columns will not equal total

Drg	Total Charges	Covered Charges	Medicare Reimbursement	Total Days	Number of Discharges	Avg Tot Days
201	$65,104,991	$64,449,799	$12,042,391	13,097	3,801	3.4
202	$992,312,330	$981,557,749	$187,196,484	189,539	47,117	4
203	$518,293,194	$513,434,275	$85,833,193	105,622	34,348	3.1
204	$514,004,502	$504,954,010	$86,285,130	75,196	28,778	2.6
205	$336,993,851	$331,603,762	$69,630,226	52,310	10,130	5.2
206	$451,201,658	$443,573,581	$79,099,834	69,705	22,999	3
207	$5,702,119,183	$5,579,978,300	$1,254,886,214	633,080	42,918	14.8
208	$5,264,999,423	$5,213,278,590	$1,080,395,088	622,232	89,338	7
215	$61,906,042	$61,904,603	$16,289,873	2,283	174	13.1
216	$3,330,212,592	$3,308,675,457	$746,726,517	221,193	13,396	16.5
217	$1,187,916,590	$1,177,729,466	$249,437,008	73,142	7,137	10.2
218	$210,233,723	$209,394,595	$39,929,011	11,866	1,498	7.9
219	$3,987,383,021	$3,967,068,540	$901,413,865	244,055	19,726	12.4
220	$2,683,783,071	$2,671,122,329	$556,621,399	150,475	20,307	7.4
221	$646,800,897	$644,093,321	$126,057,893	34,213	5,777	5.9
222	$811,192,645	$807,397,813	$179,064,971	43,619	3,746	11.6
223	$587,022,770	$583,764,460	$124,946,036	20,797	3,773	5.5
224	$721,353,404	$716,034,555	$155,780,185	36,019	3,704	9.7
225	$733,128,582	$726,367,167	$149,196,830	23,896	4,925	4.9
226	$1,656,132,471	$1,641,666,802	$371,808,538	86,896	10,124	8.6
227	$4,035,699,852	$3,954,850,755	$856,394,315	90,993	33,030	2.8
228	$618,592,717	$614,674,857	$137,393,898	42,423	3,133	13.5
229	$358,705,703	$356,979,074	$71,860,245	23,628	2,954	8
230	$83,037,450	$82,577,817	$16,210,423	4,805	875	5.5
231	$398,652,372	$396,310,272	$79,354,500	23,829	1,896	12.6
232	$200,525,637	$199,131,757	$35,663,391	11,383	1,335	8.5
233	$3,842,777,812	$3,812,450,251	$746,416,238	285,786	21,817	13.1
234	$3,650,691,817	$3,621,451,085	$642,646,014	256,771	29,990	8.6
235	$1,977,345,263	$1,966,583,917	$407,384,819	144,929	13,746	10.5
236	$2,745,488,842	$2,732,094,916	$499,422,455	184,221	28,981	6.4
237	$4,303,532,591	$4,275,617,709	$923,429,349	308,910	31,163	9.9
238	$3,607,244,778	$3,591,024,121	$702,553,151	180,646	47,152	3.8
239	$1,474,534,842	$1,435,999,300	$360,819,184	205,246	14,360	14.3
240	$632,020,795	$627,316,204	$139,530,545	99,207	11,296	8.8
241	$65,740,454	$65,263,114	$14,047,673	11,389	1,911	6
242	$2,515,393,506	$2,500,122,270	$564,491,048	224,447	30,221	7.4
243	$2,539,964,225	$2,521,364,135	$533,810,848	184,404	40,943	4.5
244	$2,503,763,489	$2,463,796,482	$483,296,132	142,626	50,600	2.8
245	$491,284,046	$485,917,677	$104,733,081	18,236	4,758	3.8

Table 2-19 *(Continued)*

Centers for Medicare & Medicaid Services
100% MEDPAR Inpatient Hospital National Data for Fiscal Year 2010
Short Stay Inpatient Diagnosis Related Groups
Blank cells represent ten or less discharges in order to conform to CMS guidelines, zero means
no discharges, therefore, sum of columns will not equal total

Drg	Total Charges	Covered Charges	Medicare Reimbursement	Total Days	Number of Discharges	Avg Tot Days
246	$4,025,327,252	$4,000,624,351	$755,223,155	234,732	45,966	5.1
247	$9,653,692,665	$9,448,373,471	$1,482,828,905	374,698	168,099	2.2
248	$1,648,080,726	$1,637,690,703	$315,173,096	122,803	20,154	6.1
249	$2,568,258,357	$2,498,806,459	$381,070,979	131,374	48,671	2.7
250	$983,685,801	$974,727,474	$194,312,123	81,308	11,786	6.9
251	$2,298,034,095	$2,283,366,953	$350,055,848	113,779	40,632	2.8
252	$4,258,539,051	$4,191,951,486	$960,671,651	428,200	53,716	8
253	$3,003,481,089	$2,960,285,132	$583,151,731	273,367	48,656	5.6
254	$2,043,381,393	$1,972,815,067	$342,045,254	124,323	46,314	2.7
255	$201,329,717	$199,081,528	$48,996,197	31,757	3,493	9.1
256	$122,665,482	$121,875,255	$25,300,583	22,593	3,423	6.6
257	$11,337,078	$11,263,346	$2,379,221	2,157	522	4.1
258	$80,095,415	$79,616,493	$18,131,383	7,814	1,145	6.8
259	$200,007,138	$198,725,153	$41,446,406	13,877	1,622	3
260	$240,613,841	$235,964,740	$54,159,212	26,905	2,709	9.9
261	$181,179,153	$179,857,927	$34,724,212	17,774	4,397	4
262	$86,153,407	$85,255,083	$14,156,270	7,448	2,772	2.7
263	$24,954,936	$24,768,349	$5,380,338	2,910	585	5
264	$1,678,777,918	$1,645,994,042	$390,747,429	214,456	26,297	8.2
265	$113,741,490	$112,983,310	$23,324,183	6,602	1,876	3.5
280	$4,182,532,300	$4,151,826,471	$910,465,483	619,130	99,629	6.2
281	$1,367,838,891	$1,358,407,898	$264,624,536	192,510	49,942	3.9
282	$913,322,199	$907,508,778	$149,127,557	114,013	43,024	2.6
283	$725,724,752	$720,087,434	$155,701,590	81,373	16,614	4.9
284	$48,870,546	$48,692,104	$9,233,739	5,887	2,467	2.4
285	$22,547,075	$22,482,418	$3,565,242	2,635	1,524	1.7
286	$2,319,728,384	$2,301,139,077	$460,450,912	274,845	42,141	6.5
287	$4,779,233,034	$4,737,257,960	$725,895,240	452,240	154,375	2.9
288	$211,046,122	$208,207,866	$52,657,689	32,357	3,153	10.3
289	$50,207,446	$49,676,166	$10,883,051	8,554	1,207	7.1
290	$7,637,075	$7,568,760	$1,581,070	1,398	275	5.1
291	$10,261,290,755	$10,161,158,157	$2,259,454,810	1,789,510	297,355	6
292	$4,893,032,026	$4,850,705,902	$1,040,108,566	951,764	221,202	4.3
293	$2,214,551,174	$2,190,828,419	$420,029,203	427,782	134,846	3.2
294	$34,100,348	$33,565,196	$7,566,479	7,853	1,499	5.2
295	$11,053,196	$11,001,848	$2,146,042	3,119	771	4
296	$101,262,920	$99,340,215	$18,568,597	8,336	2,859	2.9
297	$13,341,211	$13,281,971	$2,418,978	1,182	753	1.6
298	$5,827,586	$5,770,307	$1,046,767	582	512	1.1

(Continued)

Table 2-19 *(Continued)*

Centers for Medicare & Medicaid Services
100% MEDPAR Inpatient Hospital National Data for Fiscal Year 2010
Short Stay Inpatient Diagnosis Related Groups
Blank cells represent ten or less discharges in order to conform to CMS guidelines, zero means
no discharges, therefore, sum of columns will not equal total

Drg	Total Charges	Covered Charges	Medicare Reimbursement	Total Days	Number of Discharges	Avg Tot Days
299	$1,070,703,050	$1,059,852,081	$241,671,594	193,434	33,028	5.9
300	$1,114,891,424	$1,106,131,723	$234,973,438	231,027	50,733	4.6
301	$546,985,150	$542,291,827	$99,076,381	116,441	34,739	3.4
302	$293,691,918	$287,738,340	$63,449,856	48,075	12,188	3.9
303	$827,516,223	$815,663,149	$139,430,321	131,293	56,145	2.3
304	$139,187,024	$138,180,706	$28,553,902	23,143	5,526	4.2
305	$659,223,540	$651,504,750	$106,060,063	106,095	41,320	2.6
306	$134,636,464	$134,124,509	$32,958,030	21,900	4,178	5.2
307	$126,145,305	$125,068,688	$25,546,211	21,216	6,672	3.2
308	$2,790,167,461	$2,766,019,392	$601,951,239	473,225	96,683	4.9
309	$2,236,544,463	$2,220,774,926	$436,230,294	393,137	114,041	3.4
310	$2,244,258,359	$2,225,399,506	$358,904,374	375,376	155,583	2.4
311	$248,607,883	$244,440,513	$38,173,393	40,637	18,604	2.2
312	$3,869,813,110	$3,778,856,547	$667,777,908	587,277	206,679	2.8
313	$3,291,940,587	$3,190,271,003	$474,177,576	424,184	212,665	2
314	$3,371,555,455	$3,269,461,747	$777,178,561	511,275	77,443	6.6
315	$697,430,337	$685,579,490	$142,951,179	117,743	29,870	3.9
316	$199,804,251	$195,406,387	$34,389,563	31,175	12,373	2.5
326	$2,128,530,892	$2,098,521,468	$483,646,657	233,887	15,158	15.4
327	$883,491,938	$871,252,864	$186,820,717	107,100	12,631	8.5
328	$444,930,740	$441,380,249	$82,024,425	43,108	11,967	3.6
329	$7,695,865,800	$7,618,956,223	$1,721,830,798	917,360	61,736	14.9
330	$4,210,440,418	$4,177,495,220	$864,556,050	598,647	69,406	8.6
331	$1,263,303,530	$1,255,786,713	$232,598,117	163,798	32,103	5.1
332	$254,731,810	$252,648,216	$57,063,566	30,422	2,320	13.1
333	$362,188,265	$359,868,328	$72,221,028	47,470	6,154	7.7
334	$162,726,564	$161,545,332	$30,698,447	19,594	4,075	4.8
335	$1,062,241,705	$1,052,186,106	$238,507,045	140,374	10,665	13.2
336	$834,941,793	$829,027,122	$169,518,732	124,360	14,997	8.3
337	$357,364,454	$354,255,984	$65,076,376	48,063	9,588	5
338	$166,605,454	$165,374,982	$34,794,859	20,284	2,132	9.5
339	$163,897,021	$163,178,365	$30,304,539	22,183	3,613	6.1
340	$128,637,996	$127,827,435	$21,215,218	15,026	4,054	3.7
341	$81,830,438	$81,474,081	$16,078,266	9,026	1,375	6.6
342	$117,762,494	$116,706,911	$20,256,081	11,834	3,354	3.5
343	$212,873,170	$210,968,854	$31,633,904	16,006	8,178	2
344	$104,227,028	$102,080,370	$23,702,255	14,413	1,308	11
345	$153,738,145	$152,329,384	$31,276,979	24,447	3,765	6.5
346	$94,845,323	$94,338,645	$18,490,772	15,100	3,346	4.5

Table 2-19 *(Continued)*

Centers for Medicare & Medicaid Services
100% MEDPAR Inpatient Hospital National Data for Fiscal Year 2010
Short Stay Inpatient Diagnosis Related Groups
Blank cells represent ten or less discharges in order to conform to CMS guidelines, zero means
no discharges, therefore, sum of columns will not equal total

Drg	Total Charges	Covered Charges	Medicare Reimbursement	Total Days	Number of Discharges	Avg Tot Days
347	$142,222,073	$140,524,350	$31,844,887	20,322	2,353	8.6
348	$163,753,826	$162,509,066	$32,699,361	24,711	4,841	5.1
349	$101,279,261	$99,405,608	$16,139,817	13,395	4,849	2.8
350	$158,579,416	$157,593,815	$32,942,543	19,996	2,642	7.6
351	$173,638,775	$172,466,023	$31,856,738	21,854	5,160	4.2
352	$175,929,064	$173,747,152	$27,530,382	18,000	7,729	2.3
353	$351,049,616	$348,673,665	$71,893,441	41,449	5,094	8.1
354	$442,521,173	$439,168,572	$81,730,678	54,537	11,474	4.8
355	$438,034,464	$434,316,805	$71,770,837	44,916	16,258	2.8
356	$1,044,850,966	$1,022,965,816	$248,183,374	130,287	10,977	11.9
357	$434,192,085	$430,928,643	$91,069,407	56,883	8,317	6.8
358	$84,783,760	$83,915,342	$15,011,879	9,643	2,461	3.9
368	$227,183,973	$224,958,725	$49,828,480	33,164	5,302	6.3
369	$151,177,547	$153,017,897	$29,479,592	24,464	5,781	4.2
370	$40,728,020	$40,405,368	$6,959,563	6,379	2,085	3.1
371	$1,639,762,413	$1,621,627,705	$389,627,525	302,067	37,702	8
372	$905,574,555	$897,225,924	$201,766,769	188,237	31,301	6
373	$270,443,075	$268,241,979	$54,870,752	59,476	13,574	4.4
374	$664,479,920	$659,114,446	$151,080,177	105,841	13,002	8.1
375	$614,624,537	$609,064,550	$127,749,109	105,473	19,415	5.4
376	$71,375,858	$70,789,473	$13,335,648	10,999	3,078	3.6
377	$3,444,376,345	$3,410,692,885	$763,903,482	516,269	88,901	5.8
378	$3,486,836,395	$3,463,383,214	$682,558,931	575,379	146,401	3.9
379	$1,030,739,153	$1,021,762,951	$180,611,569	170,211	58,273	2.9
380	$210,643,150	$208,508,609	$44,646,433	32,191	4,819	6.7
381	$178,512,818	$176,780,430	$33,966,874	29,033	6,400	4.5
382	$65,466,164	$65,004,798	$10,866,031	10,187	3,112	3.3
383	$70,127,520	$69,745,181	$14,135,372	11,317	2,273	5
384	$196,177,716	$194,512,186	$31,694,478	30,526	8,804	3.5
385	$169,393,926	$166,104,748	$37,893,418	29,754	4,051	7.3
386	$247,816,251	$244,904,711	$47,927,490	47,715	9,364	5.1
387	$104,234,041	$102,867,200	$18,733,859	20,224	5,169	3.9
388	$1,219,040,698	$1,204,280,848	$268,309,803	220,591	33,745	6.5
389	$1,317,950,444	$1,306,095,605	$255,826,183	260,546	57,473	4.5
390	$852,355,568	$845,801,527	$135,833,422	168,754	51,333	3.3
391	$2,411,091,606	$2,370,901,621	$496,714,443	420,679	87,286	4.8
392	$5,558,221,441	$5,494,374,195	$914,551,214	980,026	296,684	3.3
393	$1,409,245,924	$1,383,521,648	$311,331,138	224,351	34,935	6.4
394	$1,311,348,601	$1,297,825,883	$259,688,337	235,161	53,838	4.4

(Continued)

Table 2-19   *(Continued)*

Centers for Medicare & Medicaid Services
100% MEDPAR Inpatient Hospital National Data for Fiscal Year 2010
Short Stay Inpatient Diagnosis Related Groups
Blank cells represent ten or less discharges in order to conform to CMS guidelines, zero means
no discharges, therefore, sum of columns will not equal total

Drg	Total Charges	Covered Charges	Medicare Reimbursement	Total Days	Number of Discharges	Avg Tot Days
395	$441,896,957	$436,680,442	$74,729,601	75,793	25,249	3
405	$894,134,894	$885,009,932	$206,380,013	90,726	5,875	15.4
406	$490,824,062	$486,035,139	$108,050,864	51,788	6,638	7.8
407	$146,769,090	$145,700,851	$29,646,348	14,266	2,779	5.1
408	$222,067,170	$219,734,979	$51,722,340	26,988	2,087	12.9
409	$96,476,435	$95,957,567	$20,496,110	12,718	1,623	7.8
410	$25,663,178	$25,490,775	$5,024,393	3,495	630	5.5
411	$87,288,983	$86,025,982	$19,842,635	11,042	948	11.6
412	$50,898,024	$50,575,544	$10,261,064	6,473	854	7.6
413	$28,261,755	$28,007,197	$4,498,766	3,205	619	5.2
414	$561,447,729	$557,378,563	$121,333,020	67,962	6,296	10.8
415	$325,670,254	$323,944,597	$61,928,612	43,554	6,361	6.8
416	$169,125,487	$168,160,463	$29,071,973	21,483	4,924	4.4
417	$1,684,130,867	$1,670,518,139	$325,890,754	200,614	26,228	7.6
418	$1,355,462,539	$1,344,828,490	$239,672,285	156,934	31,393	5
419	$1,112,583,985	$1,096,720,980	$171,263,408	106,527	35,275	3
420	$96,974,079	$95,673,487	$22,581,797	11,056	943	11.7
421	$51,450,026	$50,672,630	$9,892,560	6,566	1,055	6.2
422	$11,077,988	$10,942,913	$1,675,108	1,198	319	3.8
423	$229,629,734	$223,666,848	$54,622,553	27,607	2,029	13.6
424	$47,883,102	$46,898,540	$9,813,891	6,480	790	8.2
425	$5,560,025	$5,468,152	$1,020,329	573	117	4.9
432	$646,741,014	$640,956,618	$144,044,938	95,219	15,036	6.3
433	$192,261,157	$190,248,234	$38,472,568	34,398	8,311	4.1
434	$7,743,347	$7,694,970	$1,351,663	1,347	455	3
435	$823,950,800	$817,435,406	$172,691,106	124,752	17,714	7
436	$404,853,167	$400,839,620	$79,331,505	66,499	13,205	5
437	$70,784,994	$70,118,857	$11,686,452	9,678	2,758	3.5
438	$1,083,388,127	$1,070,861,723	$241,802,342	172,787	25,167	6.9
439	$735,039,817	$728,335,449	$142,729,390	135,819	29,196	4.7
440	$476,443,519	$472,410,871	$76,645,598	88,254	26,068	3.4
441	$1,173,382,006	$1,152,479,435	$265,519,684	175,139	25,681	6.8
442	$446,466,036	$442,221,622	$94,790,270	81,983	19,162	4.3
443	$103,916,474	$102,864,516	$18,936,977	19,072	5,847	3.3
444	$776,411,138	$768,409,558	$155,110,431	114,972	18,879	6.1
445	$596,126,821	$591,728,602	$110,175,312	89,861	21,239	4.2
446	$316,506,341	$313,339,926	$49,869,566	46,237	15,556	3
453	$467,725,968	$464,541,182	$109,811,821	22,078	1,740	12.7
454	$713,571,907	$708,094,851	$159,326,931	24,828	3,950	6.3

Table 2-19 *(Continued)*

Centers for Medicare & Medicaid Services
100% MEDPAR Inpatient Hospital National Data for Fiscal Year 2010
Short Stay Inpatient Diagnosis Related Groups
Blank cells represent ten or less discharges in order to conform to CMS guidelines, zero means
no discharges, therefore, sum of columns will not equal total

Drg	Total Charges	Covered Charges	Medicare Reimbursement	Total Days	Number of Discharges	Avg Tot Days
455	$495,337,361	$493,578,044	$101,036,393	13,407	3,689	3.6
456	$412,128,152	$408,226,028	$93,381,429	21,809	1,687	12.9
457	$638,373,417	$636,116,682	$146,081,341	27,470	4,099	6.7
458	$223,528,102	$221,960,094	$51,495,461	7,443	1,882	4
459	$904,710,042	$901,173,644	$201,771,856	53,930	6,408	8.4
460	$7,163,615,714	$7,131,101,754	$1,516,517,563	302,506	81,132	3.7
461	$138,252,809	$136,708,223	$28,974,855	9,118	1,225	7.4
462	$1,014,935,730	$1,010,101,506	$208,720,537	53,099	13,445	3.9
463	$759,964,626	$746,990,423	$193,565,073	99,348	6,831	14.5
464	$631,106,460	$622,487,077	$136,764,315	78,207	9,326	8.4
465	$138,355,858	$137,561,106	$28,866,822	15,580	3,115	5
466	$646,686,667	$641,710,579	$143,642,419	49,868	6,086	8.2
467	$1,807,937,263	$1,798,735,698	$380,518,156	114,911	24,638	4.7
468	$1,198,466,379	$1,191,880,654	$244,949,053	68,435	19,810	3.5
469	$3,258,967,687	$3,241,580,967	$715,199,404	323,331	45,442	7.1
470	$25,210,434,893	$25,048,195,227	$5,068,979,380	1,883,957	536,271	3.5
471	$464,301,533	$461,568,945	$107,369,276	35,735	3,960	9
472	$802,446,517	$798,467,656	$166,813,202	42,961	11,523	3.7
473	$1,680,814,767	$1,673,490,245	$314,429,920	60,399	33,073	1.8
474	$324,340,601	$319,988,709	$77,599,523	47,180	3,980	11.9
475	$186,231,411	$184,496,475	$39,933,061	30,251	4,229	7.2
476	$39,553,945	$39,042,454	$7,778,232	6,019	1,460	4.1
477	$327,804,922	$323,850,004	$71,675,265	44,321	4,121	10.8
478	$501,829,869	$498,024,196	$99,045,310	60,796	9,056	6.7
479	$210,961,972	$208,252,654	$37,884,675	19,636	5,120	3.8
480	$2,655,008,191	$2,638,267,482	$590,281,254	321,649	39,260	8.2
481	$4,020,676,653	$3,999,192,860	$818,921,112	482,629	90,612	5.3
482	$1,462,492,008	$1,453,177,338	$278,448,302	171,561	39,267	4.4
483	$845,334,037	$842,316,052	$170,239,628	52,707	14,882	3.5
484	$1,184,969,118	$1,179,053,164	$220,121,951	53,562	25,502	2.1
485	$128,385,556	$127,509,627	$29,047,350	17,575	1,700	10.3
486	$133,944,656	$133,021,577	$28,380,733	18,527	2,727	6.8
487	$46,339,940	$46,078,806	$8,857,655	6,376	1,276	5
488	$170,234,601	$168,664,330	$33,610,973	18,514	4,100	4.5
489	$174,080,306	$172,352,996	$31,287,090	16,311	5,866	2.8
490	$1,237,423,605	$1,228,483,126	$244,628,766	115,212	26,834	4.3
491	$1,417,353,061	$1,404,795,406	$222,437,680	108,755	52,810	2.1
492	$613,219,180	$610,659,066	$133,730,360	68,964	8,777	7.9
493	$1,105,472,805	$1,097,262,547	$213,332,142	113,503	24,108	4.7

(Continued)

Table 2-19 *(Continued)*

Centers for Medicare & Medicaid Services
100% MEDPAR Inpatient Hospital National Data for Fiscal Year 2010
Short Stay Inpatient Diagnosis Related Groups
Blank cells represent ten or less discharges in order to conform to CMS guidelines, zero means
no discharges, therefore, sum of columns will not equal total

Drg	Total Charges	Covered Charges	Medicare Reimbursement	Total Days	Number of Discharges	Avg Tot Days
494	$1,056,677,316	$1,047,779,581	$183,263,938	95,916	31,539	3
495	$177,783,789	$174,706,302	$40,669,003	24,632	2,494	9.9
496	$243,359,652	$240,675,614	$50,206,862	30,302	5,927	5.1
497	$175,758,083	$173,924,706	$30,701,277	15,184	6,201	2.4
498	$90,479,730	$89,681,013	$19,838,968	12,005	1,691	7.1
499	$23,751,609	$23,609,018	$4,222,807	2,573	975	2.6
500	$243,038,150	$239,239,168	$57,091,507	33,404	3,195	10.5
501	$239,790,263	$237,227,278	$48,431,942	34,616	6,273	5.5
502	$184,184,008	$180,428,645	$32,192,820	19,419	7,001	2.8
503	$86,372,499	$85,366,535	$19,345,179	12,859	1,520	8.5
504	$123,714,450	$122,871,246	$25,236,215	19,512	3,289	5.9
505	$80,255,324	$78,959,189	$13,548,723	8,971	2,842	3.2
506	$27,020,053	$26,749,474	$5,202,026	3,201	896	3.6
507	$39,908,885	$39,597,065	$8,060,365	4,446	848	5.2
508	$40,269,113	$39,788,332	$7,791,164	2,772	1,320	2.1
509	$12,857,668	$12,686,912	$2,178,468	1,321	365	3.6
510	$92,019,717	$91,676,611	$20,058,301	10,268	1,666	6.2
511	$187,507,192	$185,927,609	$33,187,340	18,589	5,029	3.7
512	$257,669,657	$254,710,209	$42,738,084	20,242	9,406	2.2
513	$58,234,317	$57,621,109	$10,982,533	8,075	1,695	4.8
514	$25,530,958	$25,130,295	$4,094,262	3,100	1,184	2.6
515	$440,667,948	$434,469,213	$99,620,946	55,238	5,916	9.3
516	$583,994,930	$579,876,648	$113,896,892	68,103	12,129	5.6
517	$430,880,621	$423,195,577	$74,311,060	38,323	11,281	3.4
533	$44,463,134	$43,804,803	$10,890,484	7,955	1,319	6
534	$60,675,902	$60,059,722	$12,414,832	13,795	3,716	3.7
535	$338,214,255	$336,214,743	$74,749,174	61,422	11,423	5.4
536	$598,700,536	$593,834,224	$117,848,370	133,986	37,045	3.6
537	$22,269,532	$22,020,725	$4,507,859	4,391	1,065	4.1
538	$12,478,439	$12,332,187	$2,044,234	2,459	806	3.1
539	$192,592,293	$187,720,391	$51,920,278	37,158	4,287	8.7
540	$133,565,119	$131,710,596	$30,650,650	28,174	4,431	6.4
541	$29,778,010	$29,553,496	$6,527,435	7,119	1,423	5
542	$399,172,654	$394,591,290	$91,676,657	68,431	8,643	7.9
543	$491,362,797	$486,651,098	$100,116,240	93,610	17,516	5.3
544	$126,644,099	$125,075,799	$24,370,931	26,648	6,897	3.9
545	$331,734,373	$327,872,694	$80,198,158	46,654	5,677	8.2
546	$169,538,962	$167,372,808	$34,345,785	30,024	6,100	4.9
547	$75,574,265	$74,579,155	$14,453,692	13,559	3,892	3.5

Table 2-19 *(Continued)*

Centers for Medicare & Medicaid Services
100% MEDPAR Inpatient Hospital National Data for Fiscal Year 2010
Short Stay Inpatient Diagnosis Related Groups
Blank cells represent ten or less discharges in order to conform to CMS guidelines, zero means
no discharges, therefore, sum of columns will not equal total

Drg	Total Charges	Covered Charges	Medicare Reimbursement	Total Days	Number of Discharges	Avg Tot Days
548	$42,549,670	$40,088,633	$9,937,117	7,744	904	8.6
549	$37,802,207	$37,382,874	$7,809,957	7,620	1,324	5.8
550	$11,368,835	$11,301,670	$2,088,055	2,521	643	3.9
551	$706,800,884	$697,077,425	$149,161,535	121,485	19,180	6.3
552	$1,754,455,323	$1,710,500,400	$306,044,051	328,495	86,784	3.8
553	$159,731,583	$158,377,604	$36,513,843	31,239	6,069	5.1
554	$315,563,123	$311,124,704	$59,747,160	68,068	19,650	3.5
555	$129,762,082	$128,293,438	$25,166,105	22,111	4,594	4.8
556	$364,856,597	$358,502,199	$59,791,630	65,821	21,601	3
557	$295,107,183	$292,198,157	$65,105,834	54,198	9,122	5.9
558	$367,231,830	$363,280,685	$68,787,903	71,928	17,851	4
559	$118,024,924	$116,603,299	$27,593,012	20,132	2,841	7.1
560	$135,505,867	$133,901,169	$29,703,145	27,268	5,814	4.7
561	$95,214,679	$93,718,349	$18,398,011	16,785	6,288	2.7
562	$301,252,516	$299,025,061	$67,894,334	53,504	9,711	5.5
563	$608,503,338	$601,358,887	$109,539,889	120,721	35,637	3.4
564	$106,433,569	$104,623,546	$26,017,959	18,875	2,994	6.3
565	$100,566,774	$99,364,527	$20,635,392	20,109	4,437	4.5
566	$32,185,304	$31,444,952	$6,160,729	6,548	2,013	3.3
573	$431,670,884	$419,078,498	$114,147,507	75,835	6,279	12.1
574	$405,852,161	$399,969,993	$94,709,650	80,075	9,767	8.2
575	$104,162,814	$103,347,972	$21,874,071	21,166	4,151	5.1
576	$82,615,929	$80,566,468	$20,909,642	10,712	976	11
577	$127,676,166	$125,974,245	$28,079,181	16,038	2,819	5.7
578	$86,574,408	$84,583,461	$15,845,509	9,513	3,029	3.1
579	$414,031,061	$405,742,150	$96,014,609	62,818	6,206	10.1
580	$487,736,790	$480,077,811	$93,887,557	68,427	13,645	5
581	$352,019,544	$342,117,701	$51,981,694	32,291	13,672	2.4
582	$173,152,209	$171,207,155	$27,755,264	15,437	5,762	2.7
583	$204,140,647	$201,029,412	$28,851,452	14,575	8,687	1.7
584	$47,620,490	$45,775,983	$8,331,378	5,605	1,089	5.1
585	$57,750,876	$53,755,854	$7,137,514	4,019	1,915	2.1
592	$216,934,008	$212,098,959	$56,594,124	44,845	5,899	7.6
593	$252,327,507	$248,753,927	$59,135,182	61,002	11,032	5.5
594	$28,327,019	$28,143,385	$6,169,713	7,568	1,734	4.4
595	$104,717,035	$104,015,936	$24,646,048	16,132	2,195	7.3
596	$112,823,403	$112,063,060	$23,330,584	23,741	5,493	4.3
597	$39,189,676	$39,005,400	$8,304,723	6,815	895	7.6
598	$46,482,881	$45,867,745	$9,550,040	8,851	1,690	5.2

(Continued)

Table 2-19 *(Continued)*

Centers for Medicare & Medicaid Services
100% MEDPAR Inpatient Hospital National Data for Fiscal Year 2010
Short Stay Inpatient Diagnosis Related Groups
Blank cells represent ten or less discharges in order to conform to CMS guidelines, zero means
no discharges, therefore, sum of columns will not equal total

Drg	Total Charges	Covered Charges	Medicare Reimbursement	Total Days	Number of Discharges	Avg Tot Days
599	$4,564,166	$4,505,309	$793,998	863	258	3.3
600	$31,535,397	$31,173,423	$6,853,379	6,421	1,318	4.9
601	$14,470,270	$14,301,163	$2,643,381	3,434	1,004	3.4
602	$1,461,908,430	$1,446,805,373	$340,627,601	291,466	46,491	6.3
603	$2,925,170,247	$2,897,971,799	$601,983,398	679,615	159,317	4.3
604	$144,901,290	$143,424,925	$30,033,178	23,938	4,731	5.1
605	$400,450,104	$394,141,512	$68,689,375	68,253	21,825	3.1
606	$84,886,603	$83,997,264	$19,893,924	15,520	2,807	5.5
607	$126,091,556	$124,978,723	$25,134,421	27,033	7,871	3.4
614	$158,118,508	$156,600,703	$34,734,523	13,641	2,257	6
615	$84,825,059	$84,159,185	$14,063,518	5,633	1,990	2.8
616	$207,140,971	$204,169,559	$50,545,974	30,391	2,101	14.5
617	$432,040,660	$427,828,417	$90,900,137	69,994	9,117	7.7
618	$4,772,993	$4,675,171	$913,783	864	168	5.1
619	$102,309,310	$93,401,332	$25,314,868	8,414	1,227	6.9
620	$176,160,558	$160,745,835	$33,349,252	11,192	3,677	3
621	$549,105,806	$509,688,005	$97,242,447	26,343	14,268	1.8
622	$136,583,238	$132,790,842	$37,218,419	22,522	1,621	13.9
623	$140,913,143	$139,728,655	$33,709,708	25,351	3,298	7.7
624	$5,376,142	$5,357,594	$1,291,707	1,137	247	4.6
625	$101,627,640	$101,018,756	$22,681,214	11,202	1,642	6.8
626	$113,769,021	$112,534,968	$20,334,424	9,252	3,537	2.6
627	$343,031,990	$338,531,984	$48,959,053	21,148	15,033	1.4
628	$394,469,316	$384,700,304	$96,784,283	48,725	4,833	10.1
629	$317,068,536	$312,906,619	$70,879,740	46,283	5,978	7.7
630	$17,074,332	$16,309,987	$3,189,913	2,049	477	4.3
637	$1,101,294,737	$1,081,999,384	$247,729,877	186,894	35,530	5.3
638	$1,146,698,087	$1,131,542,790	$233,751,386	223,605	57,852	3.9
639	$425,189,351	$418,936,498	$73,802,081	81,466	30,498	2.7
640	$2,598,060,322	$2,560,580,232	$611,209,757	476,670	105,030	4.5
641	$2,854,889,937	$2,822,791,219	$556,489,450	581,971	172,586	3.4
642	$52,059,299	$50,132,728	$10,210,458	8,297	1,753	4.7
643	$379,759,416	$376,603,965	$86,636,163	66,378	9,863	6.7
644	$368,584,588	$365,277,983	$75,528,410	70,222	14,250	4.9
645	$146,919,328	$145,698,910	$26,491,201	26,854	7,817	3.4
652	$1,891,737,348	$1,870,381,844	$261,733,765	78,323	11,115	7
653	$378,622,378	$373,028,070	$86,303,059	42,659	2,715	15.7
654	$355,392,727	$349,665,328	$74,100,953	41,322	4,615	9
655	$97,448,820	$95,322,255	$18,024,825	9,675	1,737	5.6

Table 2-19 *(Continued)*

Centers for Medicare & Medicaid Services
100% MEDPAR Inpatient Hospital National Data for Fiscal Year 2010
Short Stay Inpatient Diagnosis Related Groups
Blank cells represent ten or less discharges in order to conform to CMS guidelines, zero means
no discharges, therefore, sum of columns will not equal total

Drg	Total Charges	Covered Charges	Medicare Reimbursement	Total Days	Number of Discharges	Avg Tot Days
656	$561,024,454	$556,382,536	$125,566,397	60,368	6,595	9.2
657	$447,858,544	$443,553,503	$86,533,790	46,382	9,004	5.2
658	$350,114,385	$346,625,220	$58,944,520	29,629	9,028	3.3
659	$564,028,194	$556,329,633	$143,936,750	70,229	6,968	10.1
660	$413,945,505	$410,756,960	$86,021,281	47,830	8,782	5.4
661	$183,638,711	$180,171,316	$32,152,977	14,718	5,247	2.8
662	$88,721,801	$87,681,814	$21,339,656	12,734	1,280	9.9
663	$74,119,423	$73,453,208	$14,899,422	9,778	2,133	4.6
664	$105,677,438	$101,071,171	$17,348,662	6,854	3,720	1.8
665	$79,899,996	$78,201,290	$16,931,996	12,220	1,070	11.4
666	$77,213,996	$76,782,492	$16,233,120	11,886	2,119	5.6
667	$61,341,496	$60,172,044	$9,276,213	6,851	2,949	2.3
668	$392,330,886	$389,473,754	$89,330,558	55,174	7,448	7.4
669	$463,824,456	$458,048,124	$86,817,045	59,324	15,319	3.9
670	$209,307,917	$204,661,329	$33,428,693	22,920	10,287	2.2
671	$38,559,013	$38,319,317	$8,404,918	5,340	998	5.4
672	$20,457,800	$20,273,584	$3,350,339	1,986	848	2.3
673	$1,130,087,297	$1,109,126,303	$261,791,744	144,041	14,919	9.7
674	$524,689,350	$518,137,431	$110,390,010	64,645	9,768	6.6
675	$111,637,381	$102,137,543	$18,376,336	7,067	3,077	2.3
682	$4,899,385,111	$4,833,818,722	$1,107,894,423	829,360	124,245	6.7
683	$3,214,539,792	$3,185,470,425	$674,833,893	629,159	131,444	4.8
684	$555,878,329	$548,244,266	$102,318,347	110,265	34,869	3.2
685	$78,542,388	$76,847,718	$17,346,817	12,716	3,671	3.5
686	$99,496,497	$98,699,031	$23,258,429	17,173	2,505	6.9
687	$80,230,452	$79,132,579	$16,752,316	14,532	3,207	4.5
688	$15,141,763	$14,920,826	$2,752,606	2,270	840	2.7
689	$3,090,954,344	$3,053,280,153	$718,100,482	622,839	117,783	5.3
690	$4,123,772,969	$4,088,799,520	$810,722,798	863,318	225,199	3.8
691	$42,722,604	$42,444,224	$7,829,089	4,625	1,161	4
692	$10,959,758	$10,892,920	$2,170,077	869	451	1.9
693	$181,507,643	$179,632,616	$34,761,211	25,859	6,275	4.1
694	$353,337,430	$346,887,306	$51,894,875	45,059	19,495	2.3
695	$64,712,955	$64,216,215	$15,038,569	11,855	2,236	5.3
696	$204,588,570	$202,399,105	$39,536,529	39,939	13,193	3
697	$15,338,904	$15,029,525	$2,958,063	2,418	750	3.2
698	$1,545,615,120	$1,523,329,694	$367,805,103	259,900	41,958	6.2
699	$638,108,305	$630,650,721	$138,365,493	118,309	27,328	4.3
700	$156,250,409	$154,831,595	$29,499,439	28,553	9,110	3.1

(Continued)

Table 2-19 *(Continued)*

Centers for Medicare & Medicaid Services
100% MEDPAR Inpatient Hospital National Data for Fiscal Year 2010
Short Stay Inpatient Diagnosis Related Groups
Blank cells represent ten or less discharges in order to conform to CMS guidelines, zero means
no discharges, therefore, sum of columns will not equal total

Drg	Total Charges	Covered Charges	Medicare Reimbursement	Total Days	Number of Discharges	Avg Tot Days
707	$332,603,079	$329,565,650	$55,297,606	28,966	6,815	4.3
708	$757,132,128	$750,775,291	$108,774,504	38,363	21,374	1.8
709	$51,675,628	$51,333,499	$11,494,858	5,987	1,033	5.8
710	$62,895,481	$57,791,214	$11,697,828	3,017	1,894	1.6
711	$44,968,927	$44,707,101	$9,343,928	6,631	895	7.4
712	$10,653,416	$10,577,370	$1,705,154	1,387	499	2.8
713	$344,569,404	$341,602,480	$63,480,006	46,101	11,476	4
714	$456,682,445	$450,514,968	$66,938,361	47,446	26,555	1.8
715	$30,398,332	$30,122,847	$6,156,784	3,869	641	6
716	$24,861,976	$24,594,975	$3,625,903	1,169	870	1.3
717	$42,455,229	$41,756,723	$9,215,284	6,399	1,029	6.2
718	$12,026,557	$11,924,551	$2,127,454	1,454	592	2.5
722	$44,649,728	$44,422,184	$10,326,881	8,066	1,212	6.7
723	$41,023,388	$40,796,180	$8,281,302	7,894	1,666	4.7
724	$5,262,626	$5,124,126	$998,559	919	336	2.7
725	$54,654,781	$54,142,412	$12,388,570	10,831	2,350	4.6
726	$68,286,474	$67,654,467	$12,906,756	13,168	4,012	3.3
727	$97,705,435	$96,773,139	$21,477,543	18,160	3,037	6
728	$123,632,961	$122,785,225	$22,371,200	26,235	6,807	3.9
729	$27,489,466	$27,116,031	$5,821,216	4,968	1,011	4.9
730	$5,718,158	$5,688,539	$994,676	1,039	377	2.8
734	$137,127,623	$136,176,140	$30,141,664	14,049	2,039	6.9
735	$52,106,149	$51,669,374	$8,147,951	3,827	1,488	2.6
736	$148,534,049	$146,664,660	$33,402,802	16,710	1,285	13
737	$213,607,421	$211,524,948	$42,698,050	25,359	3,979	6.4
738	$32,031,029	$31,938,763	$5,568,317	3,341	943	3.5
739	$118,182,719	$117,758,489	$26,558,141	13,252	1,385	9.6
740	$228,913,925	$227,053,722	$43,006,999	23,241	5,500	4.2
741	$229,051,157	$226,431,257	$35,950,408	16,972	7,296	2.3
742	$495,831,081	$491,786,945	$89,864,224	52,069	13,011	4
743	$850,493,102	$842,755,735	$126,459,906	67,678	34,191	2
744	$82,074,740	$81,672,779	$17,518,967	11,202	2,057	5.4
745	$33,448,238	$33,190,246	$5,402,199	3,230	1,419	2.3
746	$110,076,649	$108,477,175	$20,850,166	12,779	3,209	4
747	$208,421,863	$201,087,837	$30,214,547	15,180	8,862	1.7
748	$493,496,294	$479,030,916	$72,808,418	33,916	20,572	1.6
749	$87,851,676	$87,231,022	$18,871,401	11,155	1,291	8.6
750	$12,034,176	$11,977,934	$2,079,899	1,114	404	2.8
754	$97,582,010	$96,292,833	$22,753,171	16,671	2,058	8.1

Table 2-19 *(Continued)*

Centers for Medicare & Medicaid Services
100% MEDPAR Inpatient Hospital National Data for Fiscal Year 2010
Short Stay Inpatient Diagnosis Related Groups
Blank cells represent ten or less discharges in order to conform to CMS guidelines, zero means
no discharges, therefore, sum of columns will not equal total

Drg	Total Charges	Covered Charges	Medicare Reimbursement	Total Days	Number of Discharges	Avg Tot Days
755	$105,988,811	$105,209,685	$22,321,774	18,666	3,680	5.1
756	$9,224,325	$9,096,288	$1,579,577	1,616	534	3
757	$85,206,153	$84,482,662	$22,721,264	16,501	2,290	7.2
758	$56,025,130	$55,316,768	$12,435,034	11,474	2,127	5.4
759	$21,496,912	$21,350,004	$4,576,481	4,673	1,193	3.9
760	$54,651,367	$54,174,345	$11,330,933	9,546	2,620	3.6
761	$18,206,995	$17,844,206	$3,132,417	3,035	1,342	2.3
765	$105,417,393	$103,816,465	$27,897,134	21,116	4,040	5.2
766	$51,670,077	$51,159,855	$11,950,152	9,641	3,147	3.1
767	$8,555,220	$8,284,192	$2,282,516	1,345	505	2.7
768						
769	$5,018,788	$4,963,629	$1,404,223	604	111	5.4
770	$3,756,248	$3,398,719	$546,199	407	199	2
774	$29,388,427	$29,228,603	$7,591,957	6,176	1,852	3.3
775	$65,073,998	$64,816,114	$14,866,351	14,631	6,421	2.3
776	$14,166,223	$14,018,989	$3,769,107	3,394	769	4.4
777	$4,766,311	$4,732,089	$911,526	435	214	2
778	$5,651,734	$5,573,732	$1,153,077	1,462	520	2.8
779	$2,025,532	$1,756,147	$282,278	290	134	2.2
780	$216,074	$213,965	$38,944	56	45	1.2
781	$68,058,435	$66,831,488	$16,802,074	18,084	4,061	4.5
782	$1,418,755	$1,404,038	$408,113	340	169	2
790						
793						
799	$89,855,565	$88,877,242	$21,830,989	8,991	692	13
800	$46,380,122	$46,303,589	$10,092,878	5,118	743	6.9
801	$18,575,363	$18,351,240	$3,719,189	1,853	470	3.9
802	$126,648,622	$124,309,524	$30,296,379	15,738	1,402	11.2
803	$50,472,801	$49,587,318	$11,477,402	6,563	1,225	5.4
804	$23,092,321	$22,606,374	$3,829,157	2,356	798	3
808	$641,372,646	$632,188,105	$146,244,756	93,869	11,884	7.9
809	$480,316,987	$476,019,633	$102,790,932	78,245	15,891	4.9
810	$61,870,666	$61,281,639	$11,396,949	9,493	2,605	3.6
811	$1,500,096,780	$1,463,466,400	$331,518,968	247,766	49,973	5
812	$2,167,672,994	$2,084,727,983	$420,804,847	388,623	113,717	3.4
813	$583,952,034	$575,228,705	$125,061,972	65,142	13,056	5
814	$101,948,871	$100,624,438	$21,780,688	16,244	2,498	6.5
815	$93,673,634	$92,582,729	$18,420,603	16,346	3,747	4.4
816	$34,556,091	$34,336,200	$5,792,377	5,759	1,804	3.2

(Continued)

Table 2-19 *(Continued)*

Centers for Medicare & Medicaid Services
100% MEDPAR Inpatient Hospital National Data for Fiscal Year 2010
Short Stay Inpatient Diagnosis Related Groups
Blank cells represent ten or less discharges in order to conform to CMS guidelines, zero means
no discharges, therefore, sum of columns will not equal total

Drg	Total Charges	Covered Charges	Medicare Reimbursement	Total Days	Number of Discharges	Avg Tot Days
820	$273,072,998	$270,786,191	$57,899,675	28,624	1,690	16.9
821	$154,223,212	$153,072,904	$32,585,646	16,891	2,488	6.8
822	$72,302,926	$71,674,908	$13,018,867	6,410	2,168	3
823	$328,330,077	$324,836,390	$72,957,901	42,885	3,040	14.1
824	$182,445,000	$181,386,297	$37,574,735	23,697	3,047	7.8
825	$61,205,602	$60,283,897	$10,244,641	6,832	1,722	4
826	$121,895,974	$121,003,419	$26,496,946	12,313	894	13.8
827	$101,357,190	$100,093,965	$20,261,997	11,855	1,690	7
828	$42,990,851	$42,546,445	$7,736,790	4,053	1,151	3.5
829	$149,320,536	$147,613,970	$33,203,068	18,150	1,911	9.5
830	$16,949,342	$16,623,086	$2,695,452	1,626	535	3
834	$745,821,933	$737,024,871	$174,763,804	88,853	5,453	16.3
835	$204,456,395	$201,347,429	$53,287,119	29,528	3,164	9.3
836	$39,968,020	$39,331,329	$9,807,605	6,222	1,426	4.4
837	$336,217,850	$331,326,556	$87,880,167	42,628	1,940	22
838	$177,069,028	$173,061,755	$44,022,958	23,612	1,995	11.8
839	$65,728,523	$64,346,193	$15,194,703	10,456	1,828	5.7
840	$884,785,809	$874,711,608	$206,544,787	126,164	12,474	10.1
841	$419,662,993	$415,359,313	$88,323,095	64,639	10,199	6.3
842	$119,411,633	$118,213,826	$21,737,322	17,633	4,272	4.1
843	$108,860,453	$108,074,905	$23,373,061	17,640	2,362	7.5
844	$95,304,445	$94,433,121	$20,496,145	17,093	3,202	5.3
845	$17,605,662	$17,239,991	$3,275,024	3,030	846	3.6
846	$232,078,144	$229,374,000	$56,583,921	29,888	3,756	8
847	$797,319,036	$786,880,558	$157,607,946	90,922	26,915	3.4
848	$33,413,140	$33,131,340	$7,540,634	4,373	1,521	2.9
849	$43,253,160	$43,059,225	$9,358,731	6,658	1,121	5.9
853	$7,150,624,099	$6,971,531,312	$1,675,827,160	812,084	54,594	14.9
854	$412,898,043	$409,087,070	$92,454,905	60,746	7,024	8.6
855	$15,868,960	$15,806,718	$3,780,106	2,173	384	5.7
856	$917,085,238	$897,266,560	$219,311,844	116,410	8,111	14.4
857	$530,897,366	$525,172,181	$119,552,095	82,988	11,204	7.4
858	$86,908,768	$86,000,622	$18,301,141	13,750	2,757	5
862	$625,155,401	$618,826,419	$141,005,508	102,013	13,609	7.5
863	$589,259,110	$583,439,162	$128,305,038	121,566	25,813	4.7
864	$481,408,908	$475,227,581	$93,462,634	83,139	22,639	3.7
865	$134,841,413	$133,463,841	$28,847,465	20,445	3,483	5.9
866	$143,541,286	$141,562,511	$23,802,477	26,198	7,881	3.3
867	$427,609,531	$422,210,477	$99,104,715	61,847	6,633	9.3
868	$67,292,753	$66,539,656	$14,627,229	12,887	2,630	4.9

Table 2-19 *(Continued)*

Centers for Medicare & Medicaid Services
100% MEDPAR Inpatient Hospital National Data for Fiscal Year 2010
Short Stay Inpatient Diagnosis Related Groups
Blank cells represent ten or less discharges in order to conform to CMS guidelines, zero means
no discharges, therefore, sum of columns will not equal total

Drg	Total Charges	Covered Charges	Medicare Reimbursement	Total Days	Number of Discharges	Avg Tot Days
869	$13,669,240	$13,607,771	$2,758,049	2,920	819	3.6
870	$5,143,134,773	$4,998,778,956	$1,168,166,966	511,096	33,952	15.1
871	$17,488,769,570	$17,285,101,695	$3,843,731,887	2,634,743	383,410	6.9
872	$2,395,785,824	$2,375,232,542	$504,105,554	462,617	93,891	4.9
876	$84,561,035	$78,668,715	$21,714,053	20,689	1,318	15.7
880	$213,865,682	$208,161,572	$43,078,268	49,059	12,769	3.8
881	$252,698,120	$237,014,721	$66,067,596	101,129	17,238	5.9
882	$78,626,523	$74,306,042	$21,888,313	32,386	5,716	5.7
883	$57,718,580	$53,571,351	$16,606,772	23,301	2,497	9.3
884	$1,119,073,418	$1,077,654,580	$318,105,020	409,333	46,396	8.8
885	$8,031,805,295	$7,412,308,398	$2,307,836,361	3,459,268	340,621	10.2
886	$53,563,617	$48,288,400	$14,937,397	23,123	2,361	9.8
887	$12,897,094	$12,551,633	$3,173,997	3,325	648	5.1
894	$57,000,189	$54,744,740	$13,466,974	17,761	6,133	2.9
895	$171,049,630	$167,274,815	$65,297,880	111,888	10,673	10.5
896	$377,785,996	$373,265,336	$89,932,885	72,811	11,761	6.2
897	$770,408,902	$748,500,938	$175,903,628	232,342	53,874	4.3
901	$103,370,822	$101,110,232	$28,319,389	14,772	1,058	14
902	$80,491,456	$79,724,978	$19,969,659	13,776	1,901	7.2
903	$27,182,277	$26,934,991	$5,537,613	4,223	1,009	4.2
904	$191,777,217	$187,617,874	$45,945,286	25,534	2,374	10.8
905	$32,196,773	$31,774,284	$6,580,739	4,751	1,076	4.4
906	$30,064,752	$29,858,027	$5,208,307	3,262	1,010	3.2
907	$1,098,198,488	$1,076,502,950	$261,488,422	126,862	11,226	11.3
908	$516,537,961	$510,858,074	$109,322,623	65,549	11,138	5.9
909	$176,986,846	$174,880,731	$32,522,585	19,704	5,971	3.3
913	$49,107,505	$48,707,348	$12,061,870	8,207	1,612	5.1
914	$116,518,203	$114,866,206	$20,484,027	20,001	6,551	3.1
915	$88,060,277	$87,529,313	$18,013,134	11,783	2,605	4.5
916	$85,556,333	$84,770,425	$13,173,084	14,537	7,448	2
917	$1,123,258,937	$1,112,537,673	$242,035,172	152,095	31,115	4.9
918	$639,378,819	$630,845,119	$113,456,612	108,631	41,274	2.6
919	$599,061,004	$590,626,067	$141,554,025	89,112	14,786	6
920	$406,736,443	$400,953,742	$84,366,572	68,889	17,314	4
921	$140,446,463	$138,440,691	$25,901,624	24,551	8,877	2.8
922	$70,339,286	$68,450,058	$16,056,981	10,983	2,206	5
923	$67,590,272	$66,587,867	$12,689,438	11,409	3,896	2.9
927	$86,098,606	$81,688,047	$24,549,557	6,216	228	27.3
928	$156,942,077	$155,167,146	$47,280,050	18,507	1,187	15.6
929	$28,367,142	$27,860,219	$6,440,633	3,749	505	7.4

(Continued)

Table 2-19 *(Continued)*

Centers for Medicare & Medicaid Services
100% MEDPAR Inpatient Hospital National Data for Fiscal Year 2010
Short Stay Inpatient Diagnosis Related Groups
Blank cells represent ten or less discharges in order to conform to CMS guidelines, zero means
no discharges, therefore, sum of columns will not equal total

Drg	Total Charges	Covered Charges	Medicare Reimbursement	Total Days	Number of Discharges	Avg Tot Days
933	$14,255,525	$14,243,700	$3,808,589	1,094	189	5.8
934	$27,427,706	$27,278,279	$6,438,134	4,500	780	5.8
935	$90,255,958	$88,723,135	$22,118,574	13,576	2,753	4.9
939	$210,658,611	$201,324,664	$56,127,336	39,314	2,603	15.1
940	$172,055,471	$166,505,614	$42,891,711	31,733	3,191	9.9
941	$54,617,346	$52,656,817	$11,669,910	6,171	1,729	3.6
945	$8,013,417,772	$7,615,671,144	$2,906,325,725	2,520,920	191,491	13.2
946	$1,453,353,896	$1,370,122,535	$578,473,442	512,038	49,420	10.4
947	$591,386,348	$581,924,448	$132,315,386	106,206	22,433	4.7
948	$1,143,347,629	$1,132,019,817	$213,157,717	219,618	66,984	3.3
949	$23,154,512	$20,735,343	$5,646,979	4,572	815	5.6
950	$5,245,174	$5,159,077	$1,255,117	1,376	345	4
951	$26,518,930	$22,937,405	$7,870,883	6,892	1,381	5
955	$90,406,813	$89,072,472	$21,282,335	6,875	590	11.7
956	$483,804,047	$480,800,605	$105,855,219	47,182	5,575	8.5
957	$367,700,816	$361,696,033	$84,402,090	28,646	2,002	14.3
958	$159,698,874	$157,472,358	$33,415,249	13,880	1,512	9.2
959	$18,436,452	$18,306,430	$3,289,408	1,493	261	5.7
963	$196,992,546	$195,678,867	$44,315,625	22,045	2,639	8.4
964	$140,625,007	$139,191,713	$27,261,540	18,987	3,508	5.4
965	$30,163,394	$29,819,809	$5,373,037	4,140	1,092	3.8
969	$109,664,627	$108,164,972	$29,763,135	11,334	658	17.2
970	$5,552,472	$5,491,936	$1,361,289	686	89	7.7
974	$489,965,217	$480,644,913	$125,952,359	64,426	6,716	9.6
975	$146,096,390	$142,728,150	$35,869,387	24,681	3,831	6.4
976	$41,356,442	$40,950,353	$9,951,850	7,376	1,619	4.6
977	$113,875,008	$112,111,036	$26,523,997	18,654	3,802	4.9
981	$4,096,191,823	$4,033,649,122	$939,400,727	456,265	33,529	13.6
982	$1,352,866,584	$1,336,291,117	$294,153,719	153,043	19,508	7.8
983	$282,889,389	$273,631,356	$54,392,586	25,321	6,159	4.1
984	$70,564,367	$69,187,616	$15,711,159	11,515	868	13.3
985	$37,984,147	$37,803,298	$8,400,112	6,368	844	7.5
986	$15,629,401	$15,565,839	$3,180,175	2,136	560	3.8
987	$887,136,152	$869,358,436	$208,867,693	128,647	11,123	11.6
988	$478,257,667	$472,437,373	$98,115,688	72,461	10,810	6.7
989	$122,569,572	$120,730,914	$22,160,419	14,842	4,509	3.3
999	$30,565,273	$30,344,031	$6,083,758	4,017	623	6.4
TOTALS	$559,876,462,562	$552,122,474,079	$117,536,754,242	75,734,416	**14,128,664**	**5.4**

Courtesy of the Centers for Medicare and Medicaid Services.

CASE 2-34

Explanation of Benefits (EOB)

As patient advocate, you frequently receive questions from patients regarding their bills. A patient called today and asked you to explain a form that she received from her insurance company. She said the form was called an Explanation of Benefits. She said that it provided the information shown in the table below.

Table 2-20 *Information Found in Patient's Explanation of Benefits*

Provider:	Dr. Theodore Simmons
Date:	11/11/2012
Type of service:	Office visit
Amount submitted:	$82.00
Amount allowed:	$74.00
Coinsurance:	$14.80
Deductible:	$300.00
Copay:	$20.00

1. What would you say to explain what an Explanation of Benefits form is?

2. What would you say to explain the difference between the amount submitted and the amount allowed?

3. After you explain the difference between the amount submitted and the amount allowed to her, the patient gets irate and exclaims, "How dare Dr. Simmons overcharge me by $8.00!" She then says that she is going to call his office and give him a piece of her mind. What will you say in response?

CASE 2-35

Qualification for Insurance

You are working with a new graduate who comments that she never did understand the various types of insurance and who they typically insure. She asks you to help her understand. Review the patients described in Table 2-21. Explain to her which one of these insurance plans they are most likely enrolled in:

1. Medicare

2. Medicaid

3. Commercial Insurance

4. TRICARE

5. Worker's compensation

Table 2-21 *Patient Situations and Probable Insurer*

Patient Situation and Probable Insurer	
Patient	Probable Insurer
A 72-year-old male with diabetes	
A 45-year-old female with end-stage renal disease (ESRD)	
A newborn born to a mother on Medicaid	
A 24-year-old female who works at Metro Hospital who was admitted for delivery	
A 33-year-old single mother who makes $8,000.00 per year	
A 26-year-old construction worker who fell off a ladder and broke his arm at work	
A 54-year-old male with urticaria; his wife is in the military	
A 64-year-old female with clinical depression; her husband is a coal miner	

CASE 2-36

Medicare Part D

You are a patient advocate. A patient comes to you with questions regarding Medicare Part D. She wants to know whether or not she should enroll when she becomes eligible next month. You are not familiar with all of the pertinent details on this program, so you go to http://www.medicare.gov to learn more information.

The patient is currently spending $250.00 per month on prescription drugs for a total of 4 medications.

1. Would you recommend she enroll in Medicare Part D?

2. Justify your recommendation.

CASE 2-37

Medicare Coverage

You are a student who is trying to understand the various Medicare programs. Your clinical site supervisor has asked you to determine whether Medicare A, Medicare B, Medicare C, and/or Medicare D cover(s) each of the services in Table 2-22.

Table 2-22 *Medicare Services*

Service	Medicare Part
Prescriptions	
Physician office visit	
Hospice	
Eye examination	
Lab tests	
Physical therapy	
Long-term care hospitalization	
Inpatient hospitalization	
Dental services	
Same-day surgery hospital charges (OP surgery)	
Durable medical equipment	

CASE 2-38

Local Care Determination (LCD)

You are a compliance coordinator. Part of your job is to assist the admissions clerk in determining if Medicare will cover services ordered or if an advanced beneficiary notice needs to be given. You are developing a table for the admission clerks to cross-reference when admitting patients.

To accomplish this, look up the local care determination (LCD) for each procedure identified in Table 2-23; fill in the table with the information you find. LCDs can be found online at http://www.cms .hhs.gov. You can also find a direct link to LCDs in the web links section of the student companion website.

If there are multiple LCDs, use the first one listed.

Table 2-23   *Local Care Determination (LCD)*

Local Care Determination (LCD)				
Procedure	Medicare Coverage?	Limitations (Summarize)	Last Date Reviewed	LCD Number
Blepharoplasty				
Debridement of mycotic nails				
B-scan				
Sleep disorders testing				
Blood glucose testing				
Skin substitutes				
Walkers				
Nail avulsion				
Group psychotherapy				

CASE 2-39

National Coverage Determination (NCD)

You are a compliance coordinator. Part of your job is to assist the admissions clerk in determining if Medicare will cover services ordered or if an advanced beneficiary notice needs to be given. You are developing a table for the admission clerks to cross-reference when admitting patients. To accomplish this, you need to look up the national coverage determination (NCD) for each procedure identified in Table 2-24 and fill in the rest of the table. NCDs can be found on the Internet at http://www.cms.hhs .gov. You can also find a direct link to NCDs in the web links section of the student companion website.

Table 2-24 *National Coverage Determination (NCD) Table*

National Coverage Determination (NCD)				
Procedure	Medicare Coverage?	Limitations?	Implementation Date	NCD Section
Prosthetic shoe				
Cytogenetic studies				
Treatment of actinic keratosis				
PET for perfusion of the heart				
Colonic irrigation				
Vitrectomy				
Gastric freezing				
Ambulatory EEG monitoring				

CASE 2-40

Calculating Medicare Inpatient Psychiatric Reimbursement

Your facility is considering opening an inpatient psychiatric unit. As part of the cost–benefit analysis, you have been given case studies and asked to calculate the reimbursement you would receive if you used the Medicare Inpatient Psychiatric reimbursement system. This is a very complicated reimbursement system, so you will need some help with the calculations.

Locate the most recent Inpatient Psychiatric Facility Prospective Payment System (IPF PPS) payment calculator at http://www/cms/hhs.gov. Many of the fields have a dropdown box. You may not see the button to click until you have selected the cell in the Microsoft Excel spreadsheet. You can also find a direct link to IPF PPS in the web links section of the student companion website.

Determine the reimbursement for the discharges shown in Tables 2-25 through 2-29.

Table 2-25 *Case 1: Calculating Medicare Inpatient Psychiatric Reimbursement for MS-DRG 56*

Calculating Medicare Inpatient Psychiatric Reimbursement for MS-DRG 56	
MS-DRG	56
Electroconvulsive shock therapy (ECTs)	2
LOS	24
Age	88
Geographic location	Rural
Emergency department	No
Residents	0
Wage area	Washington
Blended year	3
Federal payment	

Table 2-26 *Case 2: Calculating Medicare Inpatient Psychiatric Reimbursement for MS-DRG 880*

Calculating Medicare Inpatient Psychiatric Reimbursement for MS-DRG 880

MS-DRG	880
ECTs	0
LOS	12
Age	42
Geographic location	rural
Emergency department	No
Residents	0
Wage area	Alabama
Blended year	2

Federal payment

Table 2-27 *Case 3: Calculating Medicare Inpatient Psychiatric Reimbursement for MS-DRG 884*

Calculating Medicare Inpatient Psychiatric Reimbursement for DRG-MSD 884

MS-DRG	884
ECTs	4
LOS	7
Age	72
Geographic location	Urban
Emergency department	Yes
Residents	0
Wage area	Hawaii
Comorbidity	Cardiac complication
Blended year	1

Federal payment

Table 2-28 *Case 4: Calculating Medicare Inpatient Psychiatric Reimbursement for MS-DRG 890*

Calculating Medicare Inpatient Psychiatric Reimbursement for MS-DRG 890

MS-DRG	890
ECTs	12
LOS	5
Age	68
Geographic location	Urban
Emergency department	Yes
Residents	0
Wage area	New York
Blended year	3

Federal payment

Table 2-29 *Case 5: Calculating Medicare Inpatient Psychiatric Reimbursement for MS-DRG 882*

Calculating Medicare Inpatient Psychiatric Reimbursement for MS-DRG 882	
MS-DRG	882
ECTs	3
LOS	8
Age	66
Geographic location	Rural
Emergency department	No
Residents	0
Wage area	Alaska
Comorbidity	
Blended year	2
Federal payment	

CASE 2-41

Medical Necessity

Part of your job is reviewing the denial letters that the hospital receives. After review of the denial letter and the patient's medical record, you determine if an appeal is warranted. If an appeal is warranted, you are responsible for ensuring that the appeal is processed in a timely manner. In today's mail, you received the letter shown in Figure 2-11 from your QIO.

If the denial stands, your hospital stands to lose a MS-DRG payment of $7,324.44.

1. After a review of the denial, do you believe an appeal is warranted? Why or why not?

2. If an appeal is warranted, write the appeal letter.

3. If an appeal is not warranted, write a letter to the Chief Compliance Officer justifying your decision.

Sarah James   January 12, 2013
HIM Director
Pinehurst Hospital
100 Hospital Drive
Pinehurst, MS 32488

Re: Thomas Avery   Beneficiary number: 123456789A

                                              Encounter number: 1234567

Dear Ms. James:

This claim has been denied. The reason for denial is:

• Lack of medical necessity

If you disagree with this decision, you have 10 days from the date of this letter to respond.
Rebuttals must be received within 14 days of the date on this letter.

Submit all rebuttals to:

   Peer Review
   Delaware QIO
   123 Elm Street
   Dover, DE 54555

Sincerely,
Peer Review Services

Figure 2-11   *Denial Letter*

CASE 2-42

Calculating Commercial Insurance Reimbursement

You work for a billing service. You have been assigned the duty of calculating what the patient owes and what the insurance company owes, so that you can determine what revenue to expect for these services. You have the charge and the usual, customary, and reasonable (UCR) amount. The reimbursement will be calculated on the 80/20 distribution. The deductibles for each of these patients have been met. Under this insurance plan, $20.00 copays are due for physician office visits but not for other services. Use the data in Table 2-30 to calculate the coinsurance; amount insurance will pay; and how much the patient owes, including any copays.

Table 2-30 *Calculating Commercial Insurance Reimbursement*

Calculating Commercial Insurance Reimbursement					
Service	Charge	UCR	Copay	Coinsurance	Insurance Pays
Physician Visit	$120.00	$120.00			
Physical Therapy	$150.00	$97.00			
X-ray	$76.00	$43.00			
MRI	$1,245.00	$1,047.00			
Physician Visit	$65.00	$70.00			
Physician Visit	$75.00	$70.00			

CASE 2-43

Ambulatory Payment Classification (APC)

Julio, a student from the local Bachelor of Science in Health Information Management Program, is working on a clinical assignment at your facility. The assignment that you gave Julio required that he do some calculation of your ambulatory payment classification (APC) reimbursement, working with the other coders.

He went back to his workstation to begin but returned about 30 minutes later. He was at a complete loss. Julio knew the basics of the APC system—for example, that it was a hospital outpatient reimbursement system for Medicare and that a patient could have multiple APCs—but he was having trouble with the details that he needed to know for the project, especially the concept of discounting. So you decided to give Julio an additional assignment to help prepare him for the clinical assignment.

You provide Julio with a list of APCs to investigate. He is to identify the status indicator for the APC and determine if discounting applies to the APC. He is instructed to go to the CMS website (www.cms.gov) to research the APCs in Table 2-31. You can also find a direct link to this information in the web links section of the student companion website.

For each APC in Table 2-31, identify the status indicator for the APC and indicate if discounting applies to the APC.

Table 2-31 *Ambulatory Payment Classification (APCs) with the Status Indicator and Discounting Status*

Ambulatory Payment Classification (APC) with the Status Indicator and Discounting Status		
APC	Status Indicator	Subject to Discounting
0001		
0077		
0171		
0236		
0429		
0617		
0891		
1011		
1555		
1820		

CASE 2-44

Discharged Not Final Billed (DNFB) Reduction

You are the coding supervisor with a DNFB report that is staying significantly over the limit that administration desires. You have been given the mandate to determine what needs to be done to significantly reduce the amount of claims not billed and bring the DNFB down. Your CFO expects immediate results.

Table 2-32 shows a portion of the DNFB Report and is representative of the entire report.

1. Where would you begin to give your CFO the quick fix that he wants?

2. What problems can you identify that got you into this situation?

3. What are some possible solutions for these problems?

Table 2-32 *Discharged Not Final Billed Report*

Discharged Not Final Billed Report

Account Number	Discharge Date	Total Charges	Reason
1234567	2/7/13	$23,456.87	02
1234569	2/7/13	$12,564.88	02
1235712	2/12/13	$2,458.99	01
1238932	3/6/13	$1,345.77	01
1239999	3/12/13	$57,764.22	06
1305790	4/17/13	$39,652.13	05
1317267	5/15/13	$23,731.80	03
1419000	7/16/13	$2,653.44	02
1489001	8/15/13	$5,457.39	01
1506389	10/13/13	$7,987.33	01
1521111	10/31/13	$9,564.44	01
1529387	11/2/13	$10,536.63	01
1679835	12/16/13	$8,745.19	02

Legend for Reason Record Is Discharged Not Final Billed (DNFB)

01   Missing Codes
02   Missing Discharge Disposition
03   Missing Admitting Diagnosis
04   Billers Hold
05   Other—HIM
06   Other—Business Office

CASE 2-45

Chargemaster Updates

The chargemaster at your facility has had only limited updates over the past 3 years. The updates are only made when someone has a few minutes to work on it, as no one has the responsibility to keep it current. As you would expect, the facility is receiving many denials due to invalid codes and other errors in the system.

You have been asked to develop the process that will clean up the chargemaster as well as the process that will keep the chargemaster current on an ongoing basis. Include your recommendations for staffing in your plan.

CASE 2-46

Monitoring Revenue Cycle

You are the revenue cycle manager for Joplin Hospice. You have only been in this position for 4 months. One of the things you have learned is that there has been no system in place to monitor the revenue cycle. You have decided to identify 20 indicators that you will monitor on a routine basis.

1. What are the 20 indicators you recommend?

2. What threshold do you recommend that the organization should strive to meet?

3. Justify your recommendations.

CASE 2-47

Corrective Action Plan

You are the new chief compliance officer for Alabama Medical Center. In your monitoring of the facility's compliance activities, you realize that your organization has a problem with denials for medical necessity. Alabama Medical Center has received 100 denials for medical necessity from Medicare in the past 6 months. Your staff has reviewed the health records as well as the appeal letters that were submitted to Medicare in response to the denials. Your findings on the cause of the denials are presented in Table 2-33.

Of these 100 cases, 56 of the denials were overturned on appeal. There are 2 physicians that stand out, as they have 15 of the 100 cases. The remainder of the denials come from a variety of physicians. Many different services are represented.

Write a corrective action plan to decrease the number of denials received due to medical necessity.

Table 2-33   *Cause of Medical Necessity Denials*

Medical Necessity Denials	
Cause of Medical Necessity Denial	Number of Cases
Inadequate documentation	39
Failure to issue Advanced Beneficiary Notice	3
Patient admitted to inpatient status rather than observation	9
Lack of medical necessity	49

Statistics
and Quality
Improvement

CASE 3-1

Inpatient Service Days

As a health information management (HIM) manager of a small county hospital, you oversee the statistical reporting. You are in the process of cross-training a back-up HI clerk II. You are showing her how to calculate the inpatient service days.

The hospital daily census reports show that the inpatient census at midnight was 67. Two patients were admitted yesterday morning. One of these patients died 2 hours later; the second patient was discharged and transferred to another facility yesterday afternoon.

What would the inpatient service days for yesterday be?

CASE 3-2

Average Daily Census

You have been given an external report from Navaho Hospital administration requesting completion of a couple of statistical fields. Navaho Hospital has 275 adult beds, 30 pediatric beds, and 40 bassinets. Last year's (a non-leap year) inpatient service days were as shown in Table 3-1.

Table 3-1   *Navaho Hospital Inpatient Service Days for Year*

Navaho Hospital Inpatient Service Days for Year	
Type of Service	Number of Patients
Adult	75,860
Newborn	7,100
Pediatric	11,800

1. What was the average daily census of adults and children for the year? (Round to a whole number.)

2. What was the average daily census of newborns for the year? (Round to a whole number.)

CASE 3-3

Length of Stay (LOS)

As the education coordinator for HIM services, you have noted errors in the calculated length of stays (LOS) written on the discharge record facesheets by the new chart analyst. Your goal is to provide further training to him in calculating healthcare statistics to help alleviate this problem.

- Discharge record MR# 010362 is of a patient who was admitted to the hospital on March 24 and discharged on April 9.
- The second discharge record, MR# 120431, is of a patient admitted on the morning of July 12 who subsequently died at 11:10 p.m. on the same day.

Calculate the length of stay for each of these 2 patients.

CASE 3-4

Average Length of Stay (ALOS)

South Houston General Hospital has 500 beds and 55 bassinets. As the HIM manager, you report monthly statistical data of hospital operations to administration and departmental managers. Use the statistics reported in Table 3-2 for February (a non-leap year) to calculate the following statistics.

1. What is February's average length of stay for adults and children? (Round to 1 decimal place.)

2. What is February's average daily census for adults and children? (Round to a whole number.)

3. What is February's average length of stay for newborns? (Round to 1 decimal place.)

4. What is February's average daily census for newborns? (Round to a whole number.)

Table 3-2 *South Houston General Hospital Inpatient Activity*

South Houston General Hospital Inpatient Activity February	
Inpatient Activity	Number of Patients
Inpatient Service Days	
Adult and pediatric	12,345
Newborn	553
Discharges:	
Adult and pediatric	1,351
Newborn	93
Discharge days:	
Adult and pediatric	9,457
Newborn	231

CASE 3-5

Percentage of Occupancy for Month

Royal Palm Hospital has 500 beds and 55 bassinets. As the HIM manager, you report monthly statistical data of hospital operations to administration and departmental managers.

Use the information in Table 3-3 to calculate the percentage of occupancy for adults and pediatrics in the month of March. (Round to a whole number.)

Table 3-3 *Royal Palm Hospital Inpatient Service Days*

Royal Palm Hospital
March 2013

Inpatient Activity	Number of Patients
Inpatient Service Days	
Adult and pediatric	12,345
Newborn	565
Discharges.	
Adult and pediatric	1,351
Newborn	77
Discharge days:	
Adult and pediatric	9,457
Newborn	231

Percentage of Occupancy for Year

Table 3-4 shows the statistics for bed count and inpatient service days that Manatee Bay Health Center reported for last year (a non-leap year). The hospital's chief operations officer (COO) is meeting with the board of directors next Tuesday for a quarterly meeting. He asked you to figure the hospital's occupancy ratio for the past year.

Use the statistics in Table 3-4 to calculate the annual percentage of occupancy for the past year's operations.

Table 3-4 *Manatee Bay Health Center Hospital Bed Count and Inpatient Service Days*

Manatee Bay Health Center
Hospital Bed Count and Inpatient Service Days

Time Period Bed Count	Bed Count	Inpatient Service Days
January 1–May 31	200	28,690
June 1–October 15	250	27,400
October 16–December 31	275	19,250

CASE 3-7

Consultation Rate

Canyon Medical, a tertiary-care hospital, is participating in answering an external questionnaire requesting statistical information.

The hospital statistical data reported for the 300-bed hospital last year reflect:

20,932 discharges
136,651 discharge days
3,699 consultations performed

The chief medical officer (CMO) has requested that you calculate the consultation rate, rounded to 1 decimal place.

CASE 3-8

Nosocomial and Community-Acquired Infection Rate

You are the HIM manager at Blue Glacier Hospital. You are responsible for reporting hospital monthly statistics. The hospital reports 1,652 discharges for September, and the infection control report documents that there were 21 nosocomial infections and 27 community-acquired infections for the same month.

You need to calculate both the nosocomial and community-acquired infection rates (rounded to 2 decimal places) and report them to the hospital Quality Improvement (QI) Council.

CASE 3-9

Incidence Rate

The incidence of bird flu has been a concern on the coast. As the HIM manager of the Washington County health department, you have been asked to report the month's cases. Twelve new cases of bird flu occurred during the month of August. There were 4,000 people in the community who were at risk.

Calculate the incidence rate for the month.

CASE 3-10

Comparative Health Data: Hospital Mortality Statistics

Bob and Pat are trying to decide where to spend their retirement. They have narrowed the field to 4 retirement centers. Their decision will be based largely upon the quality of care offered at the hospitals local to each of the retirement communities. They are researching the closest vicinity hospital to each of the retirement centers, and they want to know each hospital's mortality rate.

Use the statistics listed in Table 3-5 to calculate the gross mortality rate (rounded to 1 decimal place) for each retirement center.

Table 3-5 *Hospital Mortality Statistics*

	Hospital Mortality Statistics		
Hospital Name	Discharged Patients	Inpatient Deaths	Mortality Rates
Sea Breeze Center	223	23	
Rocky Hills Homes	418	28	
San Diego Seniors	215	32	
Sunny Beach Cove	319	29	

1. Based on these data, where will Bob and Pat choose to live? Explain why.

2. Which is the least desired location? Explain why.

CASE 3-11

Joint Commission Hospital Quality Check

You are a health information practitioner, and personal issues require you and your family to relocate for your spouse's job transfer. As you seek hospital employment opportunities for yourself, you research Joint Commission accreditation status of the area hospitals.

1. Select 3 hospitals closest to your affiliated school to research. For help in selecting the hospitals, visit www.jointcommission.org and search under the Quality Check icon.

2. Develop a critique of each of your chosen hospital's most current surveys.
   - Comment on significant areas of achievement and/or deficiency.
   - Include the date of the most recent hospital survey and the accreditation decision awarded.

CASE 3-12

Nursing Home Comparative Data

You have an aging loved one who needs skilled nursing care on a daily basis, and the inevitable time has come for nursing home placement. So that you may visit on a weekly basis, you want a nursing home within close proximity of your residence.

1. Research the quality of at least 3 nursing homes within your geographic region, comparing the outcomes of the "quality measures." Visit the web links section of the student companion website for access to the Centers for Medicare and Medicaid Services (CMS) nursing home database.

2. Complete the search parameters to locate nursing homes within your geographical area and execute to deliver outcomes data on each nursing home.

3. Build a table of the quality measures and demonstrate the percentage that each nursing home shows in meeting the outcomes measurement.

4. Based on your comparison, which would be your top choice in which to place your loved one?

CASE 3-13

Residential Care Facilities in Long-Term Care (LTC)

As an independent health information consultant of nursing homes, you are developing some marketing material regarding common characteristics of the residential care facilities in the United States. You will be using information from the website for the Centers for for Disease Control and Prevention (CDC).

Access the CDC website at http://www.cdc.gov/nchs/ to research data from the 2010 National Survey of Residential Care Facilities National Health Survey report. Utilize the CDC database for national statistics to review the report and the graphs presented.

The graphs reflected should include the following:

Figure 1 – Residential Care Facilities and Residents, by Facility Size
Figure 2 – Selected Characteristics of Residential Care Facilities, by Facility Size
Figure 3 – Residential Care Facilities, by Region and Facility Size
Figure 4 – Residential Care Beds per 1,000 Persons Age 85 and over by Region
Figure 5 – Residential Care Facilities Serving Any Resident Receiving LTC Services Paid by Medicaid
Figure 6 – Provision of Selected Services, by Facility Size

Review the 6 graphs presented and select 3 to recreate using Microsoft Excel, in order to develop a different type of graph to display the information.

CASE 3-14

Relative Risk Comparison

As a data collection specialist at the National Institutes of Health (NIH), you have been involved in a research study conducted over the past year. The study found that liver cancer rates per 100,000 males among cigarette smokers versus nonsmokers, in a major U.S. city, were 48.0 to 25.4, respectively.

In view of these data, what would be the relative risk of males in developing liver cancer, for smokers as compared to nonsmokers? (Round to 2 decimal places.)

CASE 3-15

Determining Appropriate Formulas: Ratios

You are helping the nursing department write evaluation criteria for an upcoming quality improvement study. You need to determine appropriate formulas for ratios and set data collection time frames.

One important aspect of care is the documentation of education of patients. Specifically, the nursing department would like to assess its documentation compliance in education on colostomy care for patients receiving new colostomies.

You will help the nursing department decide what factors to use for the numerator and denominator of the equation in order to gather the necessary information.

CASE 3-16

Calculating Obstetrics (OB) Statistics

You are the HIM manager overseeing the state requirement for birth certificate reporting. Table 3-6 reflects the OB unit discharges for the month of January.

Calculate the monthly obstetric cesarean section rate and the neonatal death rate for January. (Round to 2 decimal places.)

Table 3-6 *January Discharge Data for the Obstetric Unit*

		Obstetric Unit Newborn Discharge Data January	
MR#	Deliveries	Cesarean Section Delivery Indicated (Y)	Neonatal Death (Y)
001	1-1-13	Y	
002	1-1-13		
003	1-2-13	Y	
004	1-3-13		
005	1-3-13		
006	1-4-13		
007	1-4-13		
008	1-5-13		
009	1-6-13		
010	1-7-13	Y	
011	1-7-13		
012	1-8-13		
013	1-9-13	Y	Y
014	1-9-13	Y	
015	1-10-13		
016	1-12-13		
017	1-13-13	Y	
018	1-13-13		
019	1-14-13		
020	1-14-13		
021	1-15-13		

Table 3-6 *(Continued)*

		Obstetric Unit Newborn Discharge Data January	
MR#	Deliveries	Cesarean Section Delivery Indicated (Y)	Neonatal Death (Y)
022	1-15-13	Y	
023	1-15-13		
024	1-16-13		
025	1-16-13		
026	1-17-13	Y	
027	1-17-13		
028	1-18-13		
029	1-18-13		
030	1-20-13		
031	1-21-13		
032	1-22-13		
033	1-22-13		
034	1-23-13		
035	1-24-13	Y	
036	1-24-13		
037	1-26-13		
038	1-27-13		
039	1-28-13	Y	
040	1-28-13		
041	1-29-13		
042	1-29-12		
043	1-30-13	Y	
044	1-31-13	Y	
045	1-31-13	Y	

CASE 3-17

Research Cesarean Section Trend

As a data specialist in the research department at your home town medical center, you are investigating the prevalence of cesarean section (CS) rates. Dr. Jenkins chairs the surgical committee and has been asked to research and benchmark CS rates for the state in comparison with the national trend. He has asked you to access the "Recent Trends in Cesarean Delivery in the United States" from the CDC website. (Visit the web links section of the student companion website for access to this report.)

Dr. Jenkins has asked you to review the national data comparing the years 1996 and 2007 and develop presentation graphs for the next meeting.

Create 2 different graphs containing the CS trends from 1996 and 2007.

1. Graph 1: Create a line graph of your home state reflecting the trend of the CS rate from 1996 in comparison to the rate from 2007.

2. Graph 2: Calculate the average national percent of change in the CS rates from 1996 and 2007. Then create a bar graph reflecting your home state's percent of change in comparison to the national average percent of change for the same time period.

3. Did your home state trend within 2% of the national average rate? If not, why do you think your home state varies from the national trend?

CASE 3-18

Hospital Statistics Spreadsheet

The HIM Department of Jenkins County Hospital is responsible for reporting monthly statistics to administration, utilizing discharge data from the previous month. Jenkins County is a rural hospital with limited automation for reporting statistics. As the HIM director of this small-town hospital, you need to develop a discharge analysis spreadsheet to simplify calculations at month-end.

1. Utilize the student companion website to access an Excel spreadsheet for the daily census discharge data for January. Table 3-7 below provides a key to the various discharge services.

2. Modify the companion website spreadsheet with formulas to automate the task of calculating month-end statistics for administrative reporting. The purpose here is to make the statistics function more efficiently and effectively in a template that can be used each month.

3. Submit or e-mail your rebuilt Excel spreadsheet reflecting formulas created and January statistics calculated.

Table 3-7 *Key to Discharge Services*

Key to Discharge Services	
Med	Medicine
Sur	Surgery
Orth	Orthopedic
Neur	Neurology
OB/Gyn	Obstetrics & Gynecology

Table 3-8 *Requested Monthly Statistics to Report*

Requested Monthly Statistics to Report	
1. Total number of discharges	
2. LOS (for each patent)	
3. Total LOS (for all patients)	
4. ALOS (for all patients) rounded to 2 decimal points	
5. Gross Death Rate (round to 1 decimal place)	
6. Net Death Rate (round to 1 decimal place)	

Benchmarks for Leading Causes of Death

The QI Committee is reviewing mortality data for the hospital in comparison to national mortalities. The QI coordinator will present a graph on the top 10 causes of death for the hospital. As the HIM director, you have been asked to prepare a graph showing the top 10 causes of death in the United States for the year 2010 and to present it to the committee at the next quarterly meeting. To gather the information, you will need to utilize data from the National Center for Health Statistics (NCHS) published listing the Ten Leading Causes of Death and Injury by Age Group: United States, preliminary 2010. Visit the web links section of the student companion website for access to these data.

Create a graph to report the top 10 causes of death in the United States for 2010.

CASE 3-20

Death Trends for Heart and Malignant Neoplasms

You work for NCHS as a data specialist. You have been chosen to work on a mortality research project. As a data analyst you are to analyze the mortality data of the top 2 causes of death in the United States from the National Vital Statistic Reports on Deaths, Final Data for 2009. Your preliminary research reflects that diseases of the heart and malignant neoplasms are the leading causes of death to report from the CDC data.

Visit the web links section of the student companion website to access the CDC data to complete your research.

Develop 2 line graphs for the top 2 most common causes of death from an age category of your interest, and report the "age adjusted rate" trend of death occurrences for the time period of 2005 through 2009.

CASE 3-21

Principal Diagnoses and Principal Procedures for U.S. Hospitalizations

The research department at your facility is conducting a study on principal diagnoses and principal procedures of U.S. hospitalizations for strategic planning. You are the data specialist instructed to gather statistics on stays in U.S. hospitals by principal diagnoses. You are able to access information from the Agency for Healthcare Research and Quality (AHRQ) national statistics database for 2009. ["Healthcare Cost and Utilization Project (HCUP) Facts and Figures 2009 – Section 2, Inpatient Hospital Stays by Diagnosis (PDF) and Section 3: Inpatient Hospital Stays by Procedures" (PDF)]

Visit the web links section of the student companion website to access the data required to complete your research.

1. Review Exhibit 2.2 from the HCUP report on Most Frequent Principal Diagnoses. Develop a pareto chart graph reflecting the 5 most frequent principal diagnoses for hospital stays in 2009.

2. Review Exhibit 3.1 from the HCUP report on Most Frequent All Listed Procedures. Develop a pareto chart graph indicating the top 5 procedures reflecting the number of hospital stays that involved each of the top 5 procedures in 2009.

CASE 3-22

Diagnosis-Related Groups (DRGs) and Revenue

Rocky Top Hospital collected the data displayed in Table 3-9 concerning its 4 highest volume DRGs.

Table 3-9 *Rocky Top Hospital's Highest Volume DRGs*

Rocky Top Hospital Highest Volume DRGs			
DRG A	DRG B	DRG C	DRG D
Number of patients with this DRG 323	Number of patients with this DRG 489	Number of patients with this DRG 402	Number of patients with this DRG 386
CMS WEIGHT 2.0230	CMS WEIGHT 0.9870	CMS WEIGHT 1.9250	CMS WEIGHT 1.2430

1. Which of the DRGs listed in Table 3-9 generated the most revenue for Rocky Top Hospital?

2. CMS has increased the weight for DRG A by 14% and for DRG B by 20%. The weight for DRG D was decreased by 10%. Given these DRG weight changes, which DRG generated the most revenue for Rocky Top Hospital?

CASE 3-23

DRG 110 versus DRG 111 Cost Analysis (DRG version 10)

As a health information consultant, you need some financial data on cardiovascular procedures. Visit the web links section of the student companion website to access 1994 historical discharge data presented by the Agency for Healthcare Research and Quality (AHRQ).

Utilizing the historical DRG data given in the table, what are the financial implications in cost between DRG 111, Major cardiovascular procedures without cc, as compared to DRG 110, Major cardiovascular procedures with cc, if 10% more of the discharges had complications or comorbidity conditions diagnosed?

CASE 3-24

Calculating Physician Service Statistics

You are on the Chargemaster committee at Pike's Peak Clinic. An annual review of services and charges is being conducted for necessary revisions. Table 3-10 shows some statistics reported on the physicians' services at Pike's Peak Clinic last Tuesday.

Table 3-10 *Pike's Peak Clinic Physician Services Statistics for Tuesday*

Pike's Peak Clinic Physician Service Statistics for Tuesday			
Physician	Service A	Service B	Service C
Truba	10	18	14
Wooley	14	22	9
Howe	18	5	6
Masters	12	20	7

It takes twice as long to perform Service C, so the physicians are proposing that Service C should count as 2 services for the purpose of calculating workload.

If Service C counts twice as much as Service A or Service B, which physician provided the most services on Tuesday?

CASE 3-25

Determining the Percentage of Patients with Unacceptable Waiting Time

You serve as the operations manager as well as HIM director at a community health clinic. Customer service indicators are tracked on an ongoing basis at your community health clinic. Currently, you are reviewing the data relative to wait times for patients to see their physicians.

Use the information in Table 3-11 to calculate the average percentage of patients for the entire year who were delayed longer than an acceptable amount of waiting time. The sample size for each month's data is 100 (round to 1 decimal place).

Table 3-11 *Percentage of Patients with Unacceptable Waiting Time*

Patients with Unacceptable Waiting Time	
Month	Percent
January	5%
February	4%
March	3%
April	5%
May	3%
June	10%
July	5%
August	2%
September	1%
October	2%
November	1%
December	3%

CASE 3-26

Systems Analysis of Health Information Management (HIM) Function from Clinical Experience

In your clinical experience, you will be rotating through various services performed within health information management. There are common functions that you will observe and participate in during your clinical experience. Perform a systems analysis of a selected function (system) within a hospital HIM department. If necessary, interview the area staff to acquire a more thorough knowledge of the process. Select a function of 1 of the following systems for analysis, some of which are pertinent to the paper record and others to electronic health record (EHR) environments.

- Record Assembly and Analysis (quantitative analysis and incomplete record control)
- Filing and/or Storage and Retrieval of Patient Record
- Preparation of Record for Image Scanning and Indexing
- Processing a Request for Patient Records in ROI (release of information)
- Serving as Editor of either Transcription or Coding (CAC) Function
- Review of Record for Coding Diagnosis and Procedures (Concurrent or Discharge)
- Processing Record Completion from Time of Admission to after Discharge
- Abstracting Clinical Data for Core Measure Reporting

Develop a flowchart. You may choose to use Microsoft Word or Visio software, which has a flowchart application, in completing your flowchart. (You may want to visit the Microsoft Office website to search for tips or training material on flowcharting.)

Access Microsoft Office website at:
http://office.microsoft.com/training

A written procedure of the process should accompany your flowchart.

CASE 3-27

Clinical Quality Improvement Literature Research

Perform a literature search on clinical quality management (clinical quality improvement or clinical performance improvement) for articles presenting actual quality studies performed in a healthcare facility.

Select an article about a QI study performed to present and discuss the problem or process the study sought to improve. In your presentation, include as many of the following elements regarding the QI study performed:

- The problem or risk identified
- Why the topic was chosen for study
- Current method or process of performance
- Alternative methods of improvement considered
- Selected alternative to implement
- Implementation
- Monitoring or follow-up of the results

CASE 3-28

Quality Improvement (QI)/Performance Improvement (PI) Interview Project

As an HIM student, contact a QI department at a healthcare facility to interview a staff representative of a QI/PI project performed by the facility. Identify what department/unit team members were represented (i.e., hospital, managed care organization, ambulatory surgery center) in the study performed within the facility. Obtain data regarding identification of the PI opportunity, findings, recommendations, and any follow-up made. The project will include a storyboard display and an oral presentation reflecting the steps in the PI process.

1. Develop a storyboard display of QI/PI study project.

2. Present an oral presentation describing the QI/PI project conducted and overview, reflecting the mission, vision, customers and expectations, findings, and recommendations. The presentation should last approximately 10 minutes; allow a maximum of 5 additional minutes for questions and answers.

CASE 3-29

Research Report Utilizing NCHS Public Database

You work for a large teaching hospital affiliated with a college that has Masters and Baccalaureate degree programs in Health Information Management and Informatics (HIM). You have been asked to speak with the HIM students about your role in assisting the physicians and medical students intern about conducting research utilizing patient record data. Often, the research projects lead to accessing benchmark data for comparison. As part of your presentation, you offer the students access to the vital statistics in the public database with the National Center for Health Statistics (NCHS) as a resource for benchmark data. Visit the web links section of the student companion website for access to the database.

1. Select a topic of interest from the tables offered in the database and customize your search to obtain findings of your selected group population.

2. Print a chart diagram (graph) of the customized report you create.

3. Write a paragraph that briefly summarizes your graphed findings.

CASE 3-30

Septicemic Hospitalizations as Principal Diagnosis vs. Secondary Diagnosis

As a data analyst, you are researching prevalence of septicemia as the principal diagnosis in hospitalized patients in comparison to septicemia occurrence as the secondary diagnosis. You need to retrieve benchmark data for comparison and choose to utilize the Agency for Healthcare Research and Quality (AHRQ) data.

Visit the web links section of the student companion website to access the AHRQ Septicemia in U.S. Hospitalizations, 2009, Statistical Brief Report #122, to complete your research.

1. Determine the top 4 septicemia infections by specific organism.

2. Develop a graph of the top 4 septicemia infectious organisms as principal diagnosis in comparison to the same organism as secondary diagnosis from 2009 hospitalizations.

CASE 3-31

Pain Assessment Study

As the QI Director of General Hospital, you are assisting the Department of Nursing with a Pain Assessment Study. Review the established pain classification system in Table 3-12 and respond to the questions presented.

1. What type of data does the table represent?

2. Explain why these data differ from other categorical data and why the data are appropriate to use with this Pain Assessment Study.

Table 3-12 *Pain Assessment Study*

Pain Level Scale	
Documented Pain Level Range	Pain Description
01–02	None or Occasional
03–04	Little or Minimal
05–06	Moderate
07–08	Heavy
09–10	Severe

CASE 3-32

Coronary Artery Bypass Graft Postoperative LOS

The hospital reviewed the postoperative length of stay (PLOS) for patients who have had a coronary artery bypass graft (CABG) procedure over the past year's third quarter. The results from this review can be found in Table 3-13. You are preparing a report of the study to present at the Cardiology Department meeting next week.

1. What is the mean postoperative length of stay (PLOS) for the CABG cases from the third quarter?

2. What is the median PLOS for the CABG cases from the third quarter?

3. Is there a LOS outlier that skewed the mean LOS from the third quarter?

4. Plot each LOS on a line graph, with the LOS represented on the Y axis.

5. What conclusion can you draw regarding the graph?

Table 3-13 *Coronary Artery Bypass Graft Postoperative LOS*

Third-Quarter CABG Procedures	
MR #	LOS
068922	6
101877	8
097562	7
107955	25
109500	7
072391	7
069284	4
011892	8
054390	9
049299	6
068271	8
042091	7
023956	9
039581	8
092027	7
104921	6
058411	9
089255	14
064280	7

CASE 3-33

Skyview Hospital Monthly Statistical Report

Skyview Hospital reports the following activity for the month of May, as found in Table 3-14. Calculate the following statistics, knowing that the bed count is 225 and the bassinet count is 30 for the period.

1. What is May's Average Length of Stay (ALOS)?

2. What is the ALOS for each hospital service for May?
   a. Medicine
   b. Obstetric
   c. Gynecology
   d. Urology
   e. Newborns

3. What is the Percentage of Occupancy:
   a. For adults and children
   b. For newborns

Table 3-14 *Skyview Monthly Statistical Report*

Skyview Monthly Statistical Report					
Service	Admits	Live Discharges	Deaths	Inpatient Service Days	Discharge Days
Medicine	325	315	18	1,950	1,915
Surgery	146	143	5	730	718
Obstetric	130	132	2	290	278
Gynecology	105	102	1	408	401
Urology	98	92	3	774	761
Newborn	122	126	1	396	405

Healthcare Privacy, Confidentiality, Legal, and Ethical Issues

CASE 4-1

Notice of Privacy Practices

The Health Insurance Portability and Accountability Act (HIPAA) Privacy Rule requires each covered entity to provide patients with a clear written explanation of how the covered entity may use and disclose their health information. The privacy rule gives specific content that must be included in a Notice of Privacy Practice.

Review the Notice of Privacy Practices shown in Figure 4-1.

What problems do you identify with this Notice of Privacy Practices?

Georgia State Hospital

Notice of Privacy Practices

THIS NOTICE DESCRIBES HOW INFORMATION ABOUT YOU MAY BE USED AND DISCLOSED AND HOW YOU CAN GET ACCESS TO THIS INFORMATION. PLEASE REVIEW IT CAREFULLY.

A healthcare facility may use your medical information to make treatment, payment, and healthcare operations decisions. Georgia State Hospital may also use your medical information without your consent as required by law. For any other usage, your written authorization is required. You may revoke your authorization at anytime prior to the actual release of the health information.

Georgia State Hospital may also use PHI to contact you with appointment reminders, treatment options, other services, and fund raising.

HIPAA gives you certain rights including:

- the right to request restrictions on the use of your PHI
- the right to confidential communications between you, your healthcare provider and the Hospital
- the right to review and obtain copies of PHI
- the right to obtain an accounting of disclosure once every five years
- the right to a copy of this notice upon request

Georgia State Hospital is required by law to protect the privacy of your PHI. This means that we cannot utilize your health information in anyway contrary to this notice. We are also responsible for providing you with our legal duties through the presentation of this document for your review.

Georgia State Hospital will conform to the guidelines outlined in this document as long as this document remains in effect. We do reserve the right to amend this form at any time. We will make any revised forms available to you via the website, when you return to our facility, or upon your written request. The new agreement will cover all PHI under the care of Georgia State Hospital.

If you believe that your privacy rights have been violated, you have the right to complain to:

Chief Privacy Officer
Georgia State Hospital
100 Main Street
Dublin, Georgia 12345
(912) 555-5689

If you would like more information about your privacy rights, please contact the Chief Privacy Officer as described above.

Effective: 12/1/09

Figure 4-1 *Notice of Privacy Practices*

CASE 4-2

Accounting for Disclosure of Protected Health Information (PHI) under the Health Insurance Portability and Accountability Act

A request for an accounting of disclosure of PHI has been received. This request has been assigned to you to process. The patient, John Austin, had also requested an accounting for disclosure 14 months ago. His last visit was April 1, 2011. He also had visits in 2005 and 2006. The routine charge for an accounting of disclosure is $150.00 for the first request and $300.00 for subsequent requests during a 12-month period.

1. What HIPAA issues apply to this case study?

2. What information would you include in the accounting of disclosure?

3. How will you handle this situation?

Table 4-1 *Disclosures of PHI*

Disclosures of PHI			
Released to	Date of Request	Authorized by	Evaluation
Attorney	3/7/06	Patient	
Attorney	3/2/06	TPO	
Physician	2/15/05	Patient	
Physician	1/13/05	TPO	
Blue Cross	2/11/11	TPO	
Patient	12/17/05	Patient	
Health Department	7/12/04	Law	
Subpoena	1/19/05	Law	
Researcher	12/28/05	Patient	
Prison official	11/19/05	Law	

CASE 4-3

Legal Issues in Accounting for Disclosure of Protected Health Information (PHI) to the Health Department

George recently requested a copy of his accounting of disclosures. He is appalled to see that his diagnosis of syphilis was reported to the state health department 3 months ago. In this state, syphilis is a reportable disease. He comes to the hospital administrator's office demanding that the report be retracted. The administrator listens to George's complaints and then advises him that the appropriate action would be to file a privacy complaint. George files the complaint with the hospital and with the OIG.

1. What are George's legal rights?

2. What are the hospital's legal responsibilities to the state health department and to George?

3. What response would you expect from the hospital and the OIG?

4. Was filing a privacy complaint the best suggestion the administrator could have given the patient to pursue?

CASE 4-4

Patient Right to Amend Record

Martha, a former patient at Talbotton Memorial Hospital, recently obtained a copy of her medical record. She saw on the discharge summary that her blood type was A+. Martha's blood type is actually B-. The lab test shows the correct blood type.

Martha went to the ROI coordinator, showed her the Red Cross card documenting her true blood type, and told the coordinator to change it.

The ROI coordinator refused, stating that the medical record is a legal document and cannot be changed. Martha was very angry by now.

She went to the HIM director, who told her that the records can only be amended if her attorney obtains a court order.

Critique the responses to her request for changing the hospital's medical record.

CASE 4-5

Institutional Process for Patient Request to Amend Record

You just had your first request for an amendment of the medical record. The process failed miserably. Lack of communication and documentation were identified as the root causes of the problem.

The request was not responded to within the appropriate time frame and the physician was not familiar with the process and did not know what to do. When the physician asked what to do, the HIM staff person coordinating the process could not explain it to him.

The privacy officer at the facility knew that they needed to fix the problem. The decision was made to revise the existing form, to improve communication, and to update the process.

You have been given the responsibility of revising the Request for Amendment Form to ensure that the request by patient for amending the record is addressed and the process is documented appropriately.

How would you revise the form shown in Figure 4-2 to ensure that you are compliant with all privacy regulations and have adequate communication via the form? Utilize good form design principles.

Request for Amendment Form

Seaside Hospital
1123 Bay Drive
Seaside, Florida 12345

Patient Name_____   MRN:_____

Error:_____

_____

Decision: _____Revise   _____Do not revise

Signature_____   Date_____

Figure 4-2   *Request for Amendment Form*

CASE 4-6

Alteration of Patient Record

A patient was admitted to the hospital's ambulatory surgery unit for surgical removal of 4 impacted wisdom teeth. As required, a staff internist did a history and physical (H&P) examination prior to admission.

The dental surgeon removed the wisdom teeth and administered penicillin intramuscularly as a prophylactic. The patient had an immediate and violent reaction. After an extensive stay in the intensive care unit (ICU), the patient was discharged.

On routine discharge analysis, the HIM clerk found several deficiencies requiring physician completion. During this analysis of the record, the clerk observed that the H&P stated "no known allergies." As she was filing the ambulatory surgery record in the patient's file folder, she noticed that the previous encounter had ALLERGIC TO PENICILLIN stamped in red letters on the visit cover sheet. She placed the record in the incomplete chart area for completion.

When reanalyzing the chart a few days later, she saw that the H&P had been altered to read "patient denies any drug allergies." She took the record to the HIM director, who called the hospital attorney. The patient filed a malpractice suit a few months later.

1. What issues are involved in this situation?

2. What process should be implemented to prevent this problem from happening again?

CASE 4-7

Investigating Privacy Violations

There have been several potential privacy incidents reported at your facility in the past week. Your job is to investigate these incidents to determine if they are truly privacy violations. If there are violations, decide what should be done.

Review each of the privacy incidents described in the following list. Determine which ones are privacy violations. Determine to whom the privacy violation should be reported and the timing required for the notifications.

Identify the specific action(s) appropriate to address each of the following situations.

1. Some alcohol and drug abuse records were inadvertently left accessible via the Internet. Fifty patients were affected.

2. A patient overheard a physician telling another patient's family that the cancer had spread to the surrounding lymph nodes. The physician was talking in a low voice in a corner of the hallway.

3. A hacker accessed the lab system and viewed multiple records.

4. A single form from a different patient was sent to the requesting patient.

5. A computer was not logged off and a visitor looked up his mother's PHI.

6. A monitor is turned toward the reception desk so that anyone who walks by can see it.

7. A patient complained that his ex-wife looked at his record and told his girlfriend that he had human immunodeficiency virus (HIV).

8. A patient's lab test was left lying out on the counter of the staff workroom. Staff were in and out of the room all day.

9. A patient's radiology report was left lying out on the counter of the nursing unit. Patients and their families walked by this counter and also came to the counter to talk to staff.

CASE 4-8

Investigation of Breach of Privacy

Margaret found herself facing a tough situation. Her babysitter called and cancelled 10 minutes before she needed to leave for work. She had a meeting with her manager that she could not miss. She brought her 12-year-old daughter, Molly, with her to work. Margaret sat Molly down in front of the computer in the office, telling her to play solitaire and surf the Internet until she returned. After the meeting, they went home.

Three days later, the chief privacy officer (CPO) confronted Margaret about her access of patient information. Several patients had received phone calls telling them that they had avian flu. The patients had all panicked.

Margaret was the only user who had access to all of the patient accounts. She denied the accusations, but then realized that her daughter had had access to her computer. She relayed the story to her CPO.

1. What actions should be taken?

2. What could have been done to prevent this situation from happening?

CASE 4-9

Privacy Violation by Former Employee

A patient has filed a privacy complaint with the physician office where you work. She says that her former sister-in-law, who works there, told her ex-husband that she was being treated for depression. Now he has taken her to court to challenge her custody of their children.

1. How would you investigate if this was a paper record?

2. How would you investigate if this was an electronic health record?

3. If you found evidence that the former sister-in-law did violate the privacy of the patient, what would you do?

4. If you found no evidence of any wrongdoing, what would you do?

CASE 4-10

Privacy and Security Training for New Staff

You have been given the responsibility of providing privacy training to new HIM staff when one is hired. The staff should receive privacy awareness training as part of the hospital's new employee orientation.

Your training plan for the HIM Department staff is as follows:

- Timing of training:
  - Training should be implemented within 3 working days of beginning work in the HIM department.
  - Training should be completed within 30 days of the employee's first day in the HIM department.
- Trainer: Assistant director of HIM or designee
- Method: Computer-assisted training and traditional classroom time.
- Handouts: None
- Records: Signature of attendees
- Retention of training records: Forever in employee file
- Testing: None
- Who should be included in training: All HIM staff
- Content of training
  - Requesters should provide photo identification and written authorization.
  - Employees should not access charts that they do not have a business reason to access.
  - Send transcribed reports only to the physician(s) listed on the report.
  - There should be enough of an overview of functions of department so the employee knows to whom to refer people when questions or requests arise.
  - Employees should log out of the computer when they leave.
  - Passwords should not be shared.
  - Physicians do not get access to PHI unless there is a treatment, payment, or healthcare operations (TPO) reason.
  - Hospital and departmental privacy policies are maintained by the secretary and are maintained in each functional area of the department for easy access.
  - Privacy problems in the department can be reported to your supervisor or the chief privacy officer.
  - PHI should only be released by authorized staff.

1. Is the content appropriate for HIM department new employee training? Justify your response.

2. Is this plan compliant with privacy regulations?

3. How can this plan be improved?

CASE 4-11

Release of Information (ROI) Staff Privacy and Privacy Rule Training Test

The staff of the release of information section (ROI) frequently receive patient questions regarding the Notice of Privacy Practices and other privacy rule–related issues. The staff have to be well versed in patient rights and ROI regulations to answer these patients' questions.

The department supervisor has just developed a list of questions that will be used in training new ROI staff. The plan is to review each of the situations provided and have the new employee take a test. He or she will be instructed to place an X beside the situations that violate privacy regulations.

Create an answer key for each of the questions presented in the new employee quiz shown in Figure 4-3 and give an explanation for your decision about what was the correct answer.

Privacy and HIPAA Training Quiz for Release of Information

Instructions: Place an "X" beside the each of the following situations that violate HIPAA requirements.

_____a. Marjorie just processed a request for PHI. It was dated 60 days ago.

_____b. Mark, a HIM clerk, denied a request by Sarah, a patient, to obtain a copy of her pathology report from a hysterectomy.

_____c. The authorization does not have a Social Security number on it, so the HIM Coordinator returned it stating that it does not meet HIPAA requirements.

_____d. Natalie just requested a list of people who have reviewed her record. This is her second request of the year. The hospital is charging her $150.00.

_____e. Bob just refused to sign the notice of privacy practice, but the hospital treated him anyway.

_____f. The hospital received a request to amend a patient record. They refused to accept it.

_____g. The hospital received a request to amend a patient record. They reviewed the request and denied the request.

_____h. The request for an amendment of the medical record was processed in 28 days.

_____i. The notice of privacy practices gives an example of treatment, payment, and healthcare operations.

Figure 4-3 *Release of Information (ROI) Staff Privacy and Health Insurance Portability and Accountability Act (HIPAA) Training Quiz*

CASE 4-12

Compliance with Privacy Training

The new CPO was reviewing privacy policies and was horrified when she learned that training occurred only every 2 or 3 years and that new employees only received minimal training on hire. She immediately brought a committee together to develop a plan to get in compliance with the training requirements of the privacy rule and best practices.

1. What needs to be done to meet privacy rules requirements and best practices in privacy training?

2. What needs to be done from a training plan and management standpoint?

CASE 4-13

Privacy Plan Gap Analysis

The CPO was walking around the hospital one day conducting a privacy gap analysis. He just happened to hear an admissions clerk tell a patient that she needed the patient to sign an acknowledgment of receipt of a Notice of Privacy Practices. The patient asked what the Notice of Privacy Practices was and why she needed to sign an acknowledgement that she had received it. The admissions clerk said, "I don't know what the Notice of Privacy Practices is. I was just told to provide it to each patient and have the patient sign the form." The admissions clerk also told the patient that she could not be seen by the physician unless she signed the acknowledgment of receipt of the Notice of Privacy Practices. The patient reluctantly signed the form.

The CPO started investigating and asking other admission clerks about the Notice of Privacy Practices and got similar responses from other admissions clerks.

1. What would your response be if you were the admissions clerk?

2. What would you do if you were the CPO?

CASE 4-14

Security Measures for Access to Protected Health Information

Your facility recently had a privacy violation.

Terry, a former employee, was terminated 6 weeks ago. Apparently, Terry had a grudge against the hospital, so he went into the radiology information system, downloaded PHI from 1,000 patients, and then posted the information on his personal website.

One of the current employees, Sean, who knew Terry, just happened to visit Terry's website to see if it said what he was doing now. Sean saw an inflammatory story about the hospital and some PHI posted on Terry's website. Sean immediately reported the breach to the privacy and security officers.

1. What legal issues are involved in this situation?

2. What steps would this facility need to take during its investigation?

3. What happens after you complete the investigation?

CASE 4-15

Breach Notification

A laptop was stolen from the car of an employee. The laptop contained PHI on 4,300 patients and included Social Security numbers. The employee who left the laptop in the car notified you immediately when the breach occurred. The data were not encrypted but the laptop is password protected.

1. What privacy and security violations have occurred?

2. What should the facility do now?

3. Who should be notified of the breach?

4. What method(s) of notification should be used?

CASE 4-16

Breach of Information at Business Associate

You received a call from a patient today whose identity has been stolen. He blames your facility for the breach. You researched his complaint and do not find any indication that there has been a breach of the patient's data. You decide to call your business associates to see what they can find. When you call Coding Consulting, they admit that they had a security breach several months ago due to a hacker, and patient information was accessed. This patient information included Social Security numbers. They had not notified you of their breach.

1. What privacy and security violations have occurred?

2. What should Coding Consulting have done?

3. What should your facility do now?

CASE 4-17

Access to Health Information for Treatment

Lakeside Hospital takes patient privacy seriously. The hospital policy states that only healthcare professionals directly involved in patient care should have access to patient data. The hospital has had several incidents in which a patient had an adverse outcome because the nurse who had access was at lunch and the nurse covering did not have all of the information that was required to provide care.

1. What options does the hospital have?

2. What would you recommend? Justify your recommendation.

CASE 4-18

Monitoring Regulations Affecting Healthcare (Federal Register)

You are responsible for identifying and monitoring the status of proposed regulations that may affect your organization. You are also responsible for submitting comments on these proposed regulations to the federal government when appropriate.

Conduct a search of the recent issues of the *Federal Register*. This publication can be accessed at http://www.federalregister.gov. Regulations are sorted by agency. Examples of agencies that may have proposed regulations affecting healthcare are:

- Centers for Medicare and Medicaid Services
- Food and Drug Administration
- National Center for Health Statistics
- Centers for Disease Control and Prevention

1. Identify a proposed regulation that is related to healthcare. Provide your instructor with a copy of the regulation or an Internet link to this proposed regulation along with the following information on that proposed regulation.
   a. Name of the regulation
   b. Regulation number
   c. What agency has submitted this regulation?
   d. Summary of regulation
   e. How does your proposed regulation apply to HIM?
   f. What changes would this regulation cause in healthcare and HIM?
   g. What comments would you submit to the agency proposing the regulation?
   h. What deadline is there for submitting comments?

2. If you were to write a letter of comments back to the agency who submitted this regulation, what points would you want to make?

CASE 4-19

Monitoring Legislation Affecting Healthcare (Thomas)

In your job as government relations coordinator for the Southwestern Health Information Management Association, you are responsible for monitoring legislation under consideration in Congress. Your best tool is Thomas. Thomas is the Library of Congress search engine for the database of legislation under consideration in the U.S. Congress. You may locate Thomas at http://thomas.loc.gov/home/thomas.php.

Identify a current piece of healthcare legislation in Congress and provide the following information on the bill:

1. Name of the bill

2. Number of the bill

3. What is the current status of the bill?

4. Give an overview of the bill

5. Who proposed the bill?

6. How does it apply to HIM?

Responsibilities in Release of Information (ROI)

Margaret was the ROI supervisor. She overheard Susan, a ROI coordinator, explaining the content of a medical record to a patient. Specifically, Susan was explaining what the patient's diagnosis was and what the treatment usually was; she was also giving the patient advice on what she would do. Margaret was very concerned about Susan's actions, but decided to wait until the patient left to confront Susan.

1. Why would Margaret be concerned?

2. How would you have handled this situation? Justify your position.

CASE 4-21

Release of Information and the "Legal Health Record"

Our facility has a hybrid medical record. We implemented an EHR 6 months ago. We store paper records in hard copy for 2 years. We store microfilm for 50 years. We currently keep copies of records from other facilities in with our paper records. The radiology reports, lab reports, nurse's notes, orders, dictated reports, and pharmacy systems feed the EHR. Our physicians will not let us eliminate the hard copy record, so we print out everything in the EHR and file it in the chart. We have received a subpoena for any and all records in a sensitive medical malpractice case. Since the case is so sensitive, we want to make doubly sure that we provide the appropriate documentation. The patient has been to the facility multiple times beginning 30 years ago, with the most recent visit being 6 weeks ago.

1. What is the legal record for this patient?

2. How should the facility respond to the "any and all" statement?

CASE 4-22

Authorization for Release of Information (ROI)

You are the ROI coordinator. You have just received the following 9 authorizations. Before you pull the charts, you will evaluate the authorizations to determine if they are valid.

Review the 9 authorizations shown in Figures 4-4 through 4-12. Determine if the authorizations are compliant with privacy regulations.

If they are not compliant, identify the deficiencies.

AUTHORIZATION FOR RELEASE OF INFORMATION

Patient Name: Josiah Nix

DOB: 7-16-52

Social Security number: 123-45-6789

Phone number: (478) 555-8153 and (478) 555-3630

Josiah Nix requests Mountaintop Health Care Center to disclose the following protected health information to: Dr. Thomas Jones
123 Elm Street
Thomas, Georgia 12345

Information to be disclosed: Time period: November 5, 2010 to Present
ER record, path report, x-ray, discharge summary

This authorization expires 60 days from the date of the signature below. I may revoke this authorization in writing at any time by sending written notification to the Director of HIM. I understand that once the above information is disclosed, it may be redisclosed by the recipient and the information may not be protected by federal privacy laws or regulations.

Call when it is ready and I will pick up and take it to Dr. Jones.

Josiah Nix   *3/15/2013*

Signature of patient   Date

Figure 4-4 *Authorization for Release of Information Sample 1*

AUTHORIZATION FOR RELEASE OF INFORMATION

Patient Name: Josiah Nix

DOB: 7-16-52

Social Security number: 123-45-6789

Phone number: (478) 555-8153 and (478) 555-3630

Josiah Nix requests Mountaintop Health Care Center to disclose the following protected health
information to: Dr. Thomas Jones
123 Elm Street
Thomas, Georgia 12345

Information to be disclosed: Time period: November 5, 2010 to Present
ER record, path report, x-ray, discharge summary

This protected health information is being used or disclosed for the following purposes:

Personal reasons

This authorization expires 60 days from the date of the signature below. I may revoke this authorization in writing at any time by sending written notification to the Director of HIM. I understand that
once the above information is disclosed, it may be redisclosed by the recipient and the information
may not be protected by federal privacy laws or regulations.

Josiah Nix
_____

Signature of patient

Figure 4-5   *Authorization for Release of Information Sample 2*

AUTHORIZATION FOR RELEASE OF INFORMATION

Patient Name: Josiah Nix

DOB: 7-16-52

Social Security number: 123-45-6789

Phone number: (478) 555-8153 and (478) 555-3630

Josiah Nix requests Mountain Top Health Care Center to disclose the following protected health information to: Dr. Jones

Information to be disclosed: Time period: November 5, 2010 to Present
                                                          ER record, path report, x-ray, discharge summary

This protected health information is being used or disclosed for the following purposes:

   Personal reasons

This authorization expires 60 days from the date of the signature below. I may revoke this authorization in writing at any time by sending written notification to the Director of HIM. I understand that once the above information is disclosed, it may be redisclosed by the recipient and the information may not be protected by federal privacy laws or regulations.

Josiah Nix   *3/15/2013*

Signature of patient   Date

Figure 4-6   *Authorization for Release of Information Sample 3*

AUTHORIZATION FOR RELEASE OF INFORMATION

Patient Name: Josiah Nix

DOB: 7-16-52

Social Security number: 123-45-6789

Phone number: (478) 555-8153 and (478) 555-3630

Josiah Nix requests Mountain Top Health Care Center to disclose the following protected health information to: Dr. Thomas Jones
                                                                                                                              123 Elm Street
                                                                                                                              Thomas, Georgia 12345

Information to be disclosed: Time period: November 5, 2010

This protected health information is being used or disclosed for the following purposes:

   Personal reasons

This authorization expires 60 days from the date of the signature below. I may revoke this authorization in writing at any time by sending written notification to the Director of HIM. I understand that once the above information is disclosed, it may be redisclosed by the recipient and the information may not be protected by federal privacy laws or regulations.

Josiah Nix   *3/15/2013*
_____   _____

Signature of patient   Date

Figure 4-7   *Authorization for Release of Information Sample 4*

This authorizes General Hospital to release a copy of my discharge summary and lab reports for my August hospitalization to Dr. John Doe. His address is:

1213 Main Street
Macon, GA 22255

My name is Jane S. Jones and my birth date is 11-2-54.

This release is valid for 60 days from the date signed.

Please release a copy of my medical records to James Jones, M.D.

Sally Smith

Figure 4-8   *Authorization for Release of Information Sample 5*

To Community Hospital Medical Record Department:

Please release a copy of my daughter's discharge summary from her April admission to me. Her name is Marsha Brodie and her date of birth is 10-21-1963. Thank you.

Carolyn Brodie
123 Elm St.
Macon, GA 54695

This authorization is valid for 60 days from date signed.

Carolyn Brodie

Figure 4-9 *Authorization for Release of Information Sample 6*

To General Hospital Health Information Management Department:

Please release a copy of my daughter's prenatal records to me. Her name is Cindy Smith and her date of birth is 5-4-1987. Thank you.

This authorization is valid for 60 days from date of signature.

Naomi Johnson

Figure 4-10 *Authorization for Release of Information Sample 7*

This authorizes General Hospital to release A copy of my discharge summary and lab reports for my August hospitalization to Dr. John Doe. His address is:
        1213 Main Street
        Macon, GA 22255

My name is Jane S. Jones and my birth date is 11-2-54.

Jane Jones

Figure 4-11 *Authorization for Release of Information Sample 8*

This authorizes General Hospital to release A copy of my discharge summary and lab reports for my August hospitalization to Dr. John Doe. His address is:

1213 Main Street
Macon, GA 22255

My name is Jane S. Jones and my birth date is 11-2-54.

This release is valid for 60 days from the date signed.

Jane Jones

Figure 4-12 *Authorization for Release of Information Sample 9*

CASE 4-23

Processing a Request for Release of Information (ROI)

You are the ROI coordinator. You are having a busy day today and are facing a variety of ROI situations. How should you handle the situations described below and what, if any, additional information will you need? If you will need to provide copies of the medical record, explain which forms (information) you would provide. Include dates if appropriate.

1. A patient just called. The patient has an appointment at her doctor's office in 1 hour and wants copies of records to take to the office. The hospital has a policy that requires a 48-hour notice except in medical emergencies. The patient did not specify what records she needs.

2. A patient has requested that his charts be sent to Disability Determination 3 times and that department has not received them. Your records show that they have been sent twice. The patient is very upset.

3. An FBI agent shows up and flashes a badge at you. He demands that you release a patient's chart to him immediately.

4. Dr. Lawrence calls and requests a copy of the medical record on Stephanie Smith. The records show that Dr. Jones was the patient's physician. Dr. Jones and Dr. Lawrence are not partners.

5. You receive a subpoena requesting your presence in court. You do not want to appear, so you talk to the court clerk. The subpoena specifies all charts for a patient for the period of June 2004 to September 2011. The hospital has records for the period of April 1975 to the present.

6. You receive a subpoena requesting the entire medical record for the 3/2/12 admission of Mary Taylor.

7. You receive a subpoena to appear in court and to bring a specific medical record. You are scheduled to testify tomorrow. How will you prepare? What guidelines will you follow in testifying?

8. You receive a subpoena for Mary Taylor's medical record. When the record is pulled and reviewed, you realize that she is HIV positive.

9. Today a patient requested a copy of all of his records to take to his attorney. Your policy prohibits records from being released without a 24-hour notice, except for patient care. You explain the situation and the patient becomes extremely hostile.

10. A mother requests a discharge summary of her daughter's record (6/6/12 discharge). The daughter's record shows that she delivered a baby during this admission.

11. Dr. Smith requests his wife's medical record.

CASE 4-24

Reporting Communicable Diseases

One of the responsibilities of your job is to report communicable diseases. You have been asked by an HIM student about what diagnoses you report to the state. You start listing the names of diseases that must be reported to the state.

1. Which of the cases in Table 4-2 would you list for your state?

2. If the disease is reportable, how soon after diagnosis should it be reported?

Table 4-2 *Reportable Diseases*

Reportable Diseases		
Disease	Yes/Reporting Deadline	No
Herpes zoster		
Cholera		
Hantavirus pulmonary syndrome		
Varicella		
Hepatitis A		
AIDS		
Cancer		
Gonorrhea		
Tetanus		
Rubella		
Malaria		
Poliomyelitis		
Whooping cough		
Diphtheria		
Mononucleosis		
Coxsackie		
Pneumococcal septicemia		
Spirillum fever		
Whipple disease		
Influenza		
Streptococcus pneumoniae		
Shingles		
Legionnaires disease		
Bacterial meningitis		
Lyme disease		

CASE 4-25

Disclosure of Information from a Psychiatric Record

Dr. Little is a psychiatrist. One of his patients threatened to harm his ex-wife. Dr. Little documented the following:

> "Patient expresses anger against ex-wife and talked about how happy he would be if she were dead. He talked about how easy it would be to break into her house and kill her. I don't believe these threats are anything more than fantasies."

Two weeks later, the patient is shown on the evening news as a murder suspect in the death of his ex-wife.

What legal principles apply in this situation?

CASE 4-26

Processing a Request for Information from an Attorney

You have just processed an attorney request for copies of records. There were 634 pages copied. Use the information in Table 4-3 to complete the invoice for this service (excluding postage). The following are some additional notes:

- Copies to healthcare providers for patient care are at no charge.
- Copies to patients: First 10 pages are free. The per-page fee applies after that. There is no retrieval fee.
- State law limits worker's comp to $0.25 per page.

Table 4-3 *Invoice for Retrieval Fees for Copies to Attorney*

Invoice for Retrieval Fees for Copies to Attorney			
Service	Charge (See notes below)	Quantity	Charges
Retrieval fee	$20.00		
Per page	$0.75 1–25 pages		
	$0.65 26–75 pages		
	$0.50 >75 pages		
Microfilm per page	$1.00		
Certification fee	$7.50		
Total charges (excluding postage)			

CASE 4-27

Processing a Request for Health Information from a Patient

You have just processed a patient request for information. There were 43 pages of hard copy and 39 pages of microfilm. Use the information in Table 4-4 and complete the invoice (excluding postage).

The following are some additional notes:

- Copies to healthcare providers for patient care: no charge.
- Copies to patients: First 10 pages are free. The per-page fee applies after that. There is no retrieval fee.
- State law limits worker's comp to $0.25 per page.

Table 4-4 *Invoice for Retrieval Fees for Copies to Patient*

Invoice for Retrieval Fees for Copies to Patient			
Service	Charge (See notes below)	Quantity	Charges
Retrieval fee	$20.00	0	
Per page	$0.75 1–25 pages	25	
	$0.65 26–75 pages	8	
	$0.50 >75 pages	0	
Microfilm per page	$1.00	0	
Certification fee	$7.50	0	
Total charges			

CASE 4-28

Processing a Request for Certified Copy of Health Information

You have just processed a request for information from a subpoena. There were 423 pages of hard copy, 345 pages of microfilm copies. The authorization requests that the records be certified. Use the information in Table 4-5 and complete the invoice (excluding postage).

The following are some additional notes:

- Copies to healthcare providers for patient care: no charge.
- Copies to patients: First 10 pages are free. The per-page fee applies after that. There is no retrieval fee.
- State law limits worker's comp to $0.25 per page.

Table 4-5 *Invoice for Retrieval Fees for Certified Copies*

Invoice for Retrieval Fees for Certified Copies			
Service	Charge (See notes below)	Quantity	Charges
Retrieval fee	$20.00	1	
Per page	$0.75 1–25 pages	25	
	$0.65 26–75 pages	50	
	$0.50 >75 pages	348	
Microfilm per page	$1.00	345	
Certification fee	$7.50	1	
Total charges (excluding postage)			

CASE 4-29

Processing a Request for Health Information for Worker's Compensation

You have just processed a worker's compensation request for information. There were 179 pages of hard copy. Use the information in Table 4-6 and complete the invoice excluding postage.

The following are some additional notes:

- Copies to healthcare providers for patient care: no charge.
- Copies to patients: First 10 pages are free. The per-page fee applies after that. There is no retrieval fee.
- State law limits worker's comp to $0.25 per page.

Table 4-6 *Invoice for Retrieval Fees for Worker's Compensation Request*

Invoice for Retrieval Fees for Worker's Compensation Request			
Service	Charge (See notes below)	Quantity	Charges
Retrieval fee	$20.00		
Per page	$0.75 1–25 pages		
	$0.65 26–75 pages		
	$0.50 >75 pages		
Microfilm per page	$1.00		
Certification fee	$7.50		
Total charges (excluding postage)			

CASE 4-30

Valid Authorization for Requests for Release of Information (ROI)

You are the supervisor of release of information. You have hired a new graduate from the local HIT program. She will need extensive training. The first task is ensuring that she knows who should sign the authorization. To test her knowledge, you give her a stack of authorizations that you have received. Table 4-7 shows a summary of release of information requests that were received today. You have asked her to identify who should sign the authorization and why. The age of majority in this state is 18.

Table 4-7 *Information Requests*

Information Requests	
Description of Patient	Who Should Sign Authorization and Why?
17-year-old with laceration	
14 year old with gonorrhea	
26-year-old mentally retarded male	
43-year-old surgery patient	
83-year-old surgery patient	
63-year-old Alzheimer's patient	

CASE 4-31

Health Information Management (HIM) Department Process for Subpoenas for Release of Information (ROI)

The director received a phone call from the circuit court clerk earlier today. She immediately contacted the ROI section and called a mandatory meeting for that afternoon. She gave a synopsis of the phone call. She explained that the circuit court clerk was relaying a message from the judge. The message was, "If one more chart is late or does not contain the requested information, then someone is going to have to explain it to me in court! Then, if there is not a good reason, I will hold you in contempt of court!"

How should the director handle this? Include quality improvement, training, and other issues, as appropriate.

CASE 4-32

Validate Subpoenas for Release of Information

You are the ROI coordinator and have been charged with processing all subpoenas received by the department. The first thing that you will need to do when you receive a subpoena from the appropriate authorities is to review it to ensure that the subpoena is valid.

Review the subpoenas shown in Figure 4-13 through Figure 4-16.

Determine if they are valid. If they are not valid, identify the deficiencies.

Subpoena

Issued by the United States District Court

Subpoena in a Civil Case: 12165486464   *Thomas Smith vs. Jeff Jefferson*

To: Custodian of Records
       General Hospital
       1551 Elm Street
       Macon, GA 22448

You are commanded to produce copies of any and all records regarding treatment for:
Linda Fields, DOB 11/5/52, dated April 11, 2009 or after.
These records are to be released to the Court Clerk by 9:00 a.m. January 5, 2013.

Requesting Attorney:
Sam Wallace, Attorney at Law
431 Main Street
Macon, GA 24886
(912)554-5548

Signed: *Sally Thompson,*

         Court Clerk

Figure 4-13   *Subpoena 1*

Subpoena

Issued by the United States District Court

Subpoena in a Civil Case *Thomas Smith vs. Jeff Jefferson*

To: Custodian of Records
       General Hospital
       1551 Elm Street
       Macon, GA 22448

You are commanded to produce copies of any and all records regarding treatment for:
Linda Fields, DOB 11/5/52, dated April 11, 2009 or after.
These records are to be released to the Court Clerk by 9:00 a.m. January 5, 2013,

Requesting Attorney:
Sam Wallace, Attorney at Law
431 Main Street
Macon, GA 24886
(912)554-5548

Signed: *Sally Thompson*

Sally Thompson, Court Clerk

Figure 4-14   *Subpoena 2*

Subpoena

Issued by the United States District Court

Subpoena in a Civil Case: 12165486464

To: Custodian of Records
      General Hospital
      1551 Elm Street
      Macon, GA 22448

You are commanded to produce copies of any and all records regarding treatment for Linda Fields, DOB 11/5/52, dated April 11, 2009 or after.

Requesting Attorney:
Sam Wallace, Attorney at Law
431 Main Street
Macon, GA 24886
(912)554-5548

Signed: *Sally Thompson*

Sally Thompson, Court Clerk

Figure 4-15   *Subpoena 3*

Subpoena

Subpoena in a Civil Case: 12165486464 *Thomas Smith vs. Jeff Jefferson*

To: Custodian of Records
     General Hospital
     1551 Elm Street
     Macon, GA 22448

You are commanded to produce copies of any and all records regarding treatment for Linda Fields, DOB 11/5/52, dated April 11, 2009 or after.

These records are to be released to the Court Clerk by 9:00 a.m. January 5, 2013.

Requesting Attorney:

Sam Wallace, Attorney at Law

431 Main Street

Macon, GA 24886

(912)554-5548

Signed: *Sally Thompson*

Sally Thompson, Court Clerk

Figure 4-16 *Subpoena 4*

CASE 4-33

Quality and Performance Improvement in Release of Information (ROI) Turnaround Time

Your ROI area is having some problems with quality and turnaround times. You have been given the responsibility of determining how you will solve the problems. Your options are:

- Hire a consultant to come in and clean it up.
- Clean it up yourself.
- Outsource the services to a copy service.

1. What are the benefits and disadvantages of each option?

2. What facts would you want to have available in order to make your decision?

3. Which option would you choose? Justify your decision.

CASE 4-34

Updating the Retention and Destruction Policy for Healthcare Records

You work for a 575-bed acute care Level I research trauma center. This hospital is also a teaching hospital that is connected to a university. The medical center brings in many millions of dollars in grants each year. This facility's maternity ward delivers the most babies in the city. They have an active heart surgery center.

There are 6 months' worth of data in the new EHR. There are 2 years' worth of paper on the shelf. The 2 years of paper records include the contents of the EHR, since administration does not trust the EHR yet. All older records are maintained on microfilm. You have just run out of storage space. Because of this, you have been asked to evaluate the current retention policy, which is to retain records forever.

1. What should the minimum retention policy be based on?

2. What are your options?

3. Which option would you recommend? Justify your response.

Evaluating Records for Destruction

You are conducting your annual purge of records. Based on your retention policy, charts are retained for 10 years after the last visit. It is your responsibility to determine which records should be destroyed.

Assume that today's date is June 2, 2013. Which of the records in Table 4-8 should be destroyed?

Table 4-8   *Retention Decisions*

Retention Decisions		
Record Number	Dates of Service	Retention Decision (Yes/No)
123456	12/6/11 4/16/05 4/16/06	
145321	1/14/07 3/6/00	
237621	7/6/02 9/1/01	
179341	2/25/09 7/16/09	
180072	10/19/04	

CASE 4-36

Developing a Documentation Destruction Plan

You have been given the responsibility of developing the documentation destruction plan for your facility. Your plan is as follows:

- The health center is dedicated to meeting the needs of its customers as well as complying with state and federal laws.

- Patient information will be retained as per the criteria below:
  - MPI data will be retained 20 years.
  - Medical records will be retained for 5 years after the patient's last visit.
  - Registers and indices will be retained for 10 years.
  - Paper records will be destroyed by fire.

1. Critique the above plan.

2. Rewrite the plan so that it complies with federal laws (including privacy regulations), your state laws, and recommended HIM practices. In your plan, correct any errors and make the necessary changes so that the plan meets the needs of not only the HIM department, but also the entire enterprise.

CASE 4-37

Research Studies and Ethics

One of the physicians on staff is telling you about a study that he is doing on his patients. He hopes to have the study published and to receive a grant to expand his research. He offers to hire you to help him with the data collection during your off hours. You accept and begin helping him.

You start collecting data. When you access the file the next day, you realize that he has removed a number of patients from the study. You suspect that they were removed intentionally, but you cannot be sure. You put your suspicions aside and proceed with your work and add more patients to the database. A few days later, more patients have been removed from the database.

When you do some investigation, you discover that the patients who were removed were sicker and/or had a poor outcome.

1. What should you do?

2. What issues are involved in this situation?

CASE 4-38

Identity Theft

Larry was having abdominal pains and went to the emergency room. When asked his name, he gave them his brother's name, Bob, because Bob had insurance and Larry did not. Larry's family was in on the conspiracy, but they accidentally called him Larry in front of the nurse, Sandra.

Sandra quizzed the family and they admitted the switch in identity, but they begged Sandra not to tell. They even offered her $500 to keep silent.

What should Sandra do?

CASE 4-39

American Health Information Management Association (AHIMA) Code of Ethics

You have a learner in your department who has asked you how you as an HIM professional can exhibit ethical behavior. You tell the learner about the AHIMA Code of Ethics and walk her through each of the standards of the code.

1. Document how you as an HIM professional can comply with each standard.

2. Why is a code of ethics important?

3. What does the AHIMA Code of Ethics mean to you and your career?

Information Technology and Systems

CASE 5-1

System Conversion

Your facility is getting a new master patient index (MPI). You are replacing an existing computerized MPI that no longer meets the needs of the organization. Most of the staff is excited about the new functionality that will be available. The problem you find is that there are some differences in the structure of the data fields between the 2 systems. Use Table 5-1 to review the differences between them. Determine if the data in the old system need to be converted to meet the character requirements in the data dictionary of the new system. If any of the fields need to be converted, specify exactly what needs to be done (add leading zeroes, delete characters, convert data to new valid entries and so forth). Precision is important, since the programmers will be using this information to write the conversion software code. If appropriate, provide the programmers with examples so that there will not be any confusion. Identify any mapping that may be needed and document your findings in the comments column in Table 5-1.

Table 5-1 *Field Analysis for System Conversion*

Field Analysis for System Conversion			
Field	Old System	New System	Comments
Date of Birth (DOB)	mmddyyyy	mmddyyyy	
Last Name	25 characters	30 characters	
First Name	20 characters	18 characters	
Middle Initial	1 character	1 character	
Service	Medical Newborn OB/Gyn Pediatrics Surgery	Cardiology Cardiovascular Surgery Dermatology Endocrinology Family Practice Gastroenterology General Surgery Gynecology Internal Medicine Neonatology Neurology Neurosurgery Newborn Obstetrics Oncology Orthopedics Pediatrics Pulmonary	
Patient Types	Inpatient ER Outpatient	Inpatient Cardiac Rehab ER Outpatient Surgery Outpatient	
Physician Number	4 digit	5 digit	
MRN	7 digit	10 digit	
Social Security Number	11 characters	9 characters	
City	20 characters	15 characters	
State	20 characters	2 characters	

CASE 5-2

Web Page Design

You are the information systems liaison for the Health Information Management (HIM) Department. You have been asked to design and develop the web page for the HIM Department. You are a Registered Health Information Administrator (RHIA) with information systems experience, but you are not an expert web page designer, so the pages will be simple. The HIM Department is constantly getting requests for the same information, so the HIM director decided that basic information about the department should be provided on the hospital website and/or intranet. This availability of basic information about the department should cut down on the phone calls received in the department and improve customer service as well. The director has told you to create 3 simple web pages for the HIM Department at Island Palms General Hospital. These pages should link together and include, at a minimum, the following content:

• Name of the hospital
• Name of department
• Hours of operation
• Pictures of HIM Department and Director
• Services provided by HIM Department
• Phone numbers for services
• HIM administration names and contact information
• Information on how to request information
• Location of department
• Information for physicians (pulling charts, research, incomplete charts, etc.)
• Other information, as appropriate

The director also specified that the web pages should utilize:

• Hyperlinks
• Pictures
• Tables
• Background design
• Color font to accentuate key content
• Other tools as appropriate

The pages should all have the same look and feel, complementing each other in color, structure, and the like. They should not contain redundant information; however, the hospital and department name should be on each page as well as a link to the department home page and hospital home page. The director has asked that you make recommendations on whether these pages should be on the Internet or intranet.

CASE 5-3

Policy and Procedure Development

You have been given the responsibility to write a policy and procedure on how to abstract data into the quality indicator systems. The basic demographic information is already in the system due to an interface with the hospital information system, so the abstractors will only abstract clinical data. Use proper policy and procedure formatting. Write the policy as if the reader knew nothing about the system or the policies and procedures. Take into consideration what the user would want and need to know if using this system for the first time. Remember that policies and procedures should connect the technology and the manual processes. Assume that log-in instructions are spelled out in another policy and procedure.

CASE 5-4

Database Design

You are an RHIA who works in the information systems department. You have extensive HIM experience as well as information systems experience. You tend to get projects related to HIM. Your next assignment is to create a data dictionary that will be used for data collection in the new MPI at your hospital. Your HIM background kicks in when you see the data quality issues in the instructions that you are provided. Administration has told you that the data elements collected in Table 5-2 will be used to manage data collection in your new computerized MPI. Each row indicates one field; the format column tells how the data should be formatted and the number field is the number of characters the field should allow.

Analyze this information and identify possible problems with the way the fields would be entered into the system. Make recommendations on how to improve the information, including missing data elements, inappropriate data elements, ways to build quality into the system, ways to improve data collection, and so on. You have also been instructed to ensure that the data elements meet Uniform Hospital Discharge Data Set (UHDDS), Uniform Ambulatory Care Data Set (UACDS), and Data Elements for Emergency Department Systems (DEEDS) requirements.

Table 5-2 *Field Properties*

Field Properties

Field	Format	Number of Characters
Name	FN MI LN (alpha)	25
Address	Alpha	25
City, State, Zip	Alphanumeric	25
Discharge Date	Numeric	6
Admission Date	Numeric	6
Discharge Disposition	01, 02, 03, 04, 05, 06, 07, 20	2
Service	Alpha	3
Date of Birth	Numeric	6
Race	b, w, h	2
Gender	m, f, u	1
Ethnicity	Hispanic/Non-Hispanic	1

CASE 5-5

Database Development

You are a HIM subject-matter expert for a vendor who has just entered the Ambulatory EHR business arena. You have been assigned the responsibility of developing data entry screens for the programmer to use in the development of the system. Your instructions are to use Microsoft Access to develop 3 data entry computer screens for an EHR. You must use sound user interface principles. Each form should use different types of data entry skills and should build in data quality principles. In other words, you need to use different types of entry, such as free text, radio buttons, check boxes, drop-down boxes, and the like. Because all of the screens will be part of the same EHR, they need to use the same colors, have the same look and feel, and so on. Each screen should contain at least 8 data elements. All screens should have at least 1 drop-down box with data populated.

Write narratives to describe each of the 3 screens that you developed. In each narrative, answer the following questions:

1. What is the purpose of the screen?

2. Why is each data element important to this screen?

3. Why is the type of data entry appropriate for the data element?

4. How did you design data quality into the screen?

CASE 5-6

System Selection

Triad Hospital System comprises 6 hospitals. Corporate has asked the 6 HIM directors to select the electronic document management system (EDMS) that will be used by all 6 of the hospitals. Three of the hospitals want EDMS Plus, and the other three want HIM EDMS. No evaluation methods were established during the planning stage of this system selection. The HIM directors looked at demonstrations and the responses to the requests for proposals (RFPs) before voting; none of the directors are willing to change their votes.

1. What evaluation criteria could have been in place to prevent this stalemate from occurring?

2. Who else should have been involved in the decision-making process?

3. What lessons should the facility learn from this experience?

CASE 5-7

System Life Cycle

You recently heard about the concept of system life cycle in your HIM course. You really do not understand what it is. You know that it has something to do with the different stages of the information system, but you do not understand what those stages are and what would be included in each of the stages.

Perform some research to find the following information about system life cycle and write up your findings.

1. What are the stages of the life cycle?

2. How can you tell what stage an information system is in?

3. Cite at least 2 specific examples of how information systems could fall into each of the categories.

4. What is the HIM role in each of the stages?

5. How can you plan for the obsolescence of the information system?

CASE 5-8

Data Collection Questionnaire and Interview Questions for Systems Analysis

The HIM director has asked you, the assistant director, to represent the department on the EDMS Steering Committee. At the first meeting, you were asked to develop a questionnaire and the interview questions that will be used to collect information from users about the functionality they need in an EDMS. You know how important this system is to the hospital, and that administration is anxiously awaiting the findings, so you want to make sure that you use good form design principles and good questionnaire/interview design principles. You also want the questionnaire and interview questions to be comprehensive.

Develop the questionnaire and the interview questions to be used. Include both open and closed questions. Write 2 paragraphs to describe why you chose the questions you selected for the questionnaire and for the interviews.

CASE 5-9

Developing a Data Collection Plan for Systems Analysis

Your facility has decided to purchase an EDMS. You have just developed a survey instrument with interview questions to be used in determining the functional requirements of the system. Determine who should be included in the survey and interviews. Your facility has 1,800 employees and 500 physicians on medical staff. With your resources, there is no way that you can include everyone. You want to include as many people as possible, but you do not have a lot of time and personnel to do the data collection and analysis. You also want to include clinical and nonclinical users throughout the facility. At this time, you do not have to specify the number of surveys and interviews to conduct; the committee as a whole will make that decision.

1. Who should be interviewed as part of the project (provide titles and/or categories of employees, not names)?

2. Who should be administered a questionnaire as part of this process (provide titles and/or categories of employees, not names)?

3. Why did you choose these job titles?

4. How would you choose the specific individuals in each job category who should be included?

5. Would you recommend paper or web-based surveys? Explain your decision.

CASE 5-10

Information System Project Steering Committee

The Information System Steering Committee in conjunction with administration has decided to implement a computerized physician order entry (CPOE) system. A separate CPOE committee is being created to control the implementation of the CPOE with the Information System Steering Committee providing guidance.

As project manager, you have been given the responsibility for selecting the appropriate individuals—those with a vested interest in the CPOE—for inclusion on this committee.

1. What departments would you want represented on the CPOE committee?

2. Who should the CPOE committee report to?

3. How frequently would you recommend that the CPOE committee report to the Information System Steering Committee?

4. What responsibilities should the CPOE committee have?

CASE 5-11

Developing a System Selection Plan

Your facility does not have an existing voice recognition system. You are part of the 5-member team responsible for selecting a voice recognition system for your facility. The functional requirements and the request for proposal have been developed. The RFP is due back from the vendors in 1 week. Your facility wants to make the decision about which system to choose within 3 months. Your assignment is to evaluate the RFPs returned and to develop a plan to guide the team in the evaluation and selection of the final system.

Your plan should answer these questions:

1. What process(es) will be used to evaluate systems?

2. How will you evaluate the individual RFPs?

3. Who will be involved in the system selection process and what will be their roles?

4. Of all the evaluation methods used, which one do you believe should have the most impact on your decision? Why?

CASE 5-12

System Selection

Island Palms General Hospital has an existing admission discharge transfer (ADT)/master patient index (MPI) system that was implemented 20 years ago. It was developed in-house. By now, all of the original programmers have resigned or retired. It is cumbersome to manage and to update to meet the current needs of the hospital. Therefore, the decision has been made to purchase a new system.

An RFP was sent out to 2 vendors—System Patient Management, Inc., and System Patient Tracking, Inc. Key portions of the RFP have been summarized to allow for easy comparison. The responses to the functional requirements have also been provided for review.

Demonstrations were conducted at the hospital and both systems looked good. The MPI module is preferred on System Patient Management, and the ADT system is preferred on System Patient Tracking; however, both systems were received favorably. The committee went to see both systems in operation and liked them both. References were checked on both systems. The references for System Patient Tracking were glowing. All of them said that the system was good and the people were great to work with because they wanted their new company to succeed and to grow. The references on System Patient Management were excellent, too. The only negative about System Patient Management was that the company was too large and was sometimes slow to respond to what the company saw as minor problems.

The next release of System Patient Tracking is due out in 6 months and of System Patient Management is due out in 8 months. You expect to implement your system in 1 year. The Committee has used Tables 5-3, 5-4, and 5-5 to summarize and compare the information that was gathered, and is now ready to vote on which system to purchase. Based on the information below, which system would you select? Justify your response.

Table 5-3 *System Comparison*

System Comparison

Topic	System Patient Management, Inc.	System Patient Tracking, LLC
Cost of interface	$35,000	$27,000
Cost of software licensing	$147,000	$127,000
Cost of hardware	$245,000	$254,000
Implementation costs	$45,000	$47,000
Other costs	$80,000	$80,000
Annual maintenance	$56,000	$48,000
Number systems in use in hospitals	452	8
Length of time in business	25 years	3 years
Stability of company	Good	Good

Table 5-4 *Response from System Patient Management, Inc., RFP for ADT/MPI System*

Response from System Patient Management, Inc., RFP for ADT/MPI System

System Functions	Standard	Next Release	Not Available	Custom
Admit patient to ER	X			
Admit patient to inpatient status	X			
Admit patient to outpatient status	X			
Transfer patient from room to room	X			
Transfer patient from inpatient to outpatient	X			
Transfer patient from outpatient to inpatient	X			
Transfer patient from ER to inpatient status	X			
Discharge patient from ER	X			
Discharge patient from inpatient status	X			
Discharge patient from outpatient status	X			
Notify housekeeping when patient discharged		X		
Notify HIM when patient admitted		X		
Meets Uniform Hospital Discharge Data Set (UHDDS) requirements	X			
Meets HIPAA requirements		X		
Contains Joint Commission–required demographics	X			
Automated verification of insurance			X	
Graphical user interface (GUI) technology	X			
User friendly	X			
Delete patient from system	X			
Multiple levels of security	X			
Password protected	X			
Audit trail	X			
Biometric capable				X
Reads barcodes	X			
Edit demographics	X			

Table 5-4 *(Continued)*

Response from System Patient Management, Inc., RFP for ADT/MPI System

System Functions	Standard	Next Release	Not Available	Custom
Edit insurance	X			
Allows for 4 insurances		X		
Prints standards reports at specified periods	X			
Ad hoc reporting	X			
Admission list	X			
Discharge list	X			
Transfer list	X			
Looks for potential duplicate medical records		X		
Quality edits built into system	X			
Oracle database			X	
Runs on Windows NT	X			
Enterprise-wide ready		X		
Merge medical record numbers	X			
Allows for aliases	X			
Maintains old medical record numbers	X			
Maintains former names	X			
Allows at least 999 patient visits	X			
Data dictionary	X			
Three-character service field	X			
Allows housekeeping to notify admission that room is ready for patient	X			
Online no-bed list	X			
Sends out announcements to employees/staff	X			
Generates list of patients by physician	X			
Generates list of patients by unit	X			
Calculates census statistics	X			
Performs medical record number queries	X			
Performs patient name queries	X			

Table 5-5 *Response to System Patient Tracking, LLC, RFP for ADT/MPI*

Response to System Patient Tracking, LLC, RFP for ADT/MPI

Function	Standard	Next Release	Not Available	Custom
Admit patient to ER	X			
Admit patient to inpatient status	X			
Admit patient to outpatient status	X			
Transfer patient from room to room	X			
Transfer patient from inpatient to outpatient	X			
Transfer patient from outpatient to inpatient	X			
Transfer patient from ER to inpatient status	X			
Discharge patient from ER	X			
Discharge patient from inpatient status	X			

(Continued)

Table 5-5 *(Continued)*

Response to System Patient Tracking, LLC, RFP for ADT/MPI

Function	Standard	Next Release	Not Available	Custom
Discharge patient from outpatient status	X			
Notify housekeeping when patient discharged	X			
Notify HIM when patient admitted	X			
Meets UHDDS requirements	X			
Meets HIPAA requirements		X		
Contains Joint Commission–required demographics	X			
Automated verification of insurance				X
GUI technology	X			
User friendly	X			
Delete patient from system	X			
Multiple levels of security	X			
Password protected	X			
Audit trail	X			
Biometric capable		X		
Reads barcodes		X		
Edit demographics	X			
Edit insurance	X			
Allows for 4 insurances	X			
Prints standards reports at specified periods	X			
Ad hoc reporting	X			
Admission list	X			
Discharge list	X			
Transfer list	X			
Looks for potential duplicate medical records	X			
Quality edits built into system	X			
Oracle database	X			
Runs on Windows NT	X			
Enterprise-wide ready	X			
Merge medical record numbers	X			
Allows for aliases		X		
Maintains old medical record numbers		X		
Maintains former names	X			
Allows at least 999 patient visits	X			
Data dictionary	X			
Three-character service field	X			
Allows housekeeping to notify admission that room is ready for patient	X			
Online no-bed list	X			
Sends out announcements to employees/staff	X			
Generates list of patients by physician	X			
Generates list of patients by unit	X			
Calculates census statistics	X			
Performs medical record number queries	X			
Performs patient name queries	X			

CASE 5-13

System Testing Plan

You are in the process of implementing a new release of information (ROI)/accounting of disclosure system. You have an existing computerized release of information system, so the employees are comfortable with the technology—they just have to learn how to use the new one.

As part of the implementation plan for the new ROI/accounting of disclosure system, you will need to develop a testing plan that should include the following:

1. Testing that needs to be conducted prior to implementation.

2. A minimum of 6 scenarios that you would encounter when using the system during testing.

3. List of resources needed to complete the testing.

4. What to do when a problem is identified.

5. How you will know the system is ready for implementation.

6. Who should be included in the implementation of the testing plan.

CASE 5-14

Workflow Technology

You started as the new Director of HIM last week. Your department began using workflow technology 6 weeks ago with a relatively new EDMS, which was implemented a year ago. With the implementation of workflow, the department started coding and analyzing charts online. Other tasks involved in the workflow are:

- Notifying risk management of issues identified
- Communications with physicians
- Communications with business office
- Communications with supervisor
- Routing charts that meet criteria to performance improvement

One of the first things that you noticed when you started work was the stress level of the coders—they are panicking. You also found that the billing hold report is at $2.4 million, when the expected level is below $800,000. In a meeting with the coders, they all tell you that they hate using the new system. You also learn that much of their distress is a result of the fact that they were not involved in the selection or implementation of the new system. In addition, they had only a short training period, so they do not feel comfortable using the system.

1. How would you proceed to resolve the problems?

2. What will you do with future system selections to ensure that these same problems do not occur?

CASE 5-15

Developing a Workflow Plan

You just started as the new Director of HIM at a 200-bed hospital. This hospital is in the process of developing a new EDMS. One of the key benefits of this system is workflow technology. Charts will be routed to coding, analysis, documentation improvement, quality improvement, and risk management, as appropriate.

Make your recommendations for the system by answering the following questions:

1. Should we use push or pull workflow? Justify your decision.

2. What specific tasks would you recommend being included in the workflow?

3. What order of these tasks would you recommend? Justify your recommendation.

4. Draw a diagram showing the flow of the tasks, including both linear and nonlinear steps in the diagram.

5. What rules could you establish to route charts to each of the areas?

6. Why did you choose these rules?

7. As the HIM director, what reports would you want to receive on a regular basis?

CASE 5-16

Goals of the Electronic Health Record (EHR)

Your facility, Good Samaritan Hospital, is implementing a new EHR. You are excited about the positive impact that the EHR will have on your organization. During the planning stage, the hospital developed goals that it would like to accomplish with this implementation. Administration has said that these goals are firm expectations for the team and the system. The goals of the system are to:

- Reduce HIM staff
- Reduce time required to access health information
- Improve quality of care
- Decrease the number of duplicate and unnecessary tests
- Reduce the cost per case

1. Critique the goals provided.

2. How can the goals be improved?

3. Rewrite the goals based on your evaluation.

4. How can you monitor to determine if you met the goals?

CASE 5-17

Computerized Provider Order Entry Implementation

Your facility has made the decision to implement a new CPOE system. The Steering Committee has to decide which of the following implementation strategies to utilize:

a. Implement the CPOE on all units at the same time
b. Implement the CPOE unit by unit
c. Implement the medication orders unit by unit
d. Implement the medication orders on all units at the same time

1. Which of the implementation strategies would you choose?

2. Justify your decision.

CASE 5-18

Normalization of Data Fields

You have recently been hired at Black Hills Hospice to help with report generation. On your first day, you start investigating the databases that you will be working with. You see room for improvement in the first database that you look at—Human Resources. This database does not include payroll. Normalize the data fields to allow for more flexibility in reporting. Identify gaps in the human resources data collected and present the results of your investigation in a table with 1 column for the original data fields and 1 column for the normalized data fields. Include recommendations for additional fields to be collected. Data fields to consider are:

1. Full name
2. Address
3. City, state, zip
4. Phone
5. Social Security number
6. Race
7. Gender
8. Degree/major
9. Date of last evaluation
10. Department
11. Start date
12. Credentials

CASE 5-19

Human Resource Database

You are Director of the HIM Department of a home health organization. You constantly have to ask Human Resources for reports on your staff. Because of the frequency of these requests, you have asked for access to the Human Resources system. Unfortunately, their response is that the system will not allow you to access only your HIM staff, but would instead provide you access to all employees. Because administration will not allow you to have access to all Human Resources data, you have decided to create your own mini-database. This mini-database will help you in many ways. The following are examples of how you will use this database:

- Track salaries
- Track open positions
- Track when performance evaluations are due
- Track anniversary dates
- Track birthdates
- Identify employees on probation

Use Microsoft Access to create the database. Design a data entry screen that utilizes good screen design. Populate the database with 5 test employees and generate 2 reports: a list of all employees by anniversary date and a list of employees on probation.

CASE 5-20

Tumor Registry System Questionnaire

You have been asked to develop the questionnaire that will be used to collect functional requirements for the new tumor registry system at a cancer treatment facility. This questionnaire will be sent to the tumor registrars and the tumor registry supervisors and their customers, including the Cancer Committee, the Cancer Program director, oncologists, and the Vice President of Research. The questionnaire should use good design principles, be comprehensive, and should address accreditation, state cancer reporting, institutional needs, and user needs.

CASE 5-21

Bar Code Standards

You have been given the responsibility of developing the standards for using bar codes on medical record forms. Your facility plans to implement an EHR in 5 years and wants to take the intermediary step of purchasing an EDMS system. They want to implement the imaging system in about 2 years. They believe EDMS is an important step, since they want to stop microfilming and the images can be linked to the EHR. Because it will take a while to implement the EDMS system, your facility has time to revise all medical record forms to add bar codes so that when the system is implemented, the time required to scan and index the records will be minimal and the quality of the indexing will be high.

1. What bar code format do you recommend? Why?

2. What other forms design and bar code issues should you take into consideration?

CASE 5-22

Bar Code Policy

You have been given the responsibility of developing the standards for bar coding the forms that will be scanned into the new imaging system your facility is implementing in about a year. You have 6 months to have all of the forms redesigned to accommodate the bar code.

Research the use of bar codes and use the information that you find to develop your policy. The policy should be written in the policy and procedure format and should include specific guidelines that forms developers should follow.

CASE 5-23

Conversion of Admission Discharge Transfer (ADT) System

The service codes for your existing ADT System and the new system do not match. The old system uses a 2-digit numeric code to indicate service, while the new system will accept up to a 4-digit alphabetic code. The hospital has decided that it will use 2- to 4-digit codes depending on which format is more user recognizable. Review the codes utilized by both systems, as shown in Tables 5-6 and 5-7, and develop a map that will be used by the programmers to convert the data from the old system to the new system.

Table 5-6 *Codes in Old ADT System*

Codes in Old ADT System

Old System Code	Service Description
01	Medicine
02	Surgery
03	Obstetrics
04	Gynecology
05	Cardiology
06	Cardiovascular Surgery
07	Dermatology
08	Orthopedics
09	Endocrinology
10	Neonatology
11	Nephrology
12	Infectious Disease
13	Pulmonology
14	Gastroenterology
15	Otorhinolaryngology
16	Ophthalmology
17	Neurology
18	Neurosurgery
19	Trauma

Table 5-7   *Codes in New ADT System*

Codes in New ADT System	
New System Code	Service Description
	Allergy
	Burn
	Cardiology
	Cardiovascular Surgery
	Dermatology
	Endocrinology
	Otorhinolaryngology
	Gastroenterology
	Gynecology
	Infectious Disease
	Neonatal
	Nephrology
	Neurology
	Neurosurgery
	Obstetrics
	Orthopedics
	Pulmonology

CASE 5-24

Admission Report Design

Your facility is about to implement a new hospital information system. The reports have been distributed to the members of the team for design. You have been given the responsibility of designing the admission report, which will come from the Hospital Information System and be used by multiple departments in identifying the patients who have been admitted to the hospital as an inpatient each day. You do not like the current report, so you are essentially developing a new one. It should include the appropriate data elements, date, title of report, time ran, and other data as needed.

1. What recommendations do you have for this report regarding:

- Print orientation
- Timing of printing
- Content of report
- Ad hoc versus standard report
- Who receives report
- Other

2. Based on these recommendations, design the administrative report.

CASE 5-25

Choosing Software Packages

Technology Support is installing new computers throughout the HIM Department. The existing computers are slow and many freeze up several times a day. You receive an e-mail from the Supervisor of Technology Support relaying that Technology Support wants to install the same systems on all of the computers to make things easier. This is fine with you because that gives you flexibility in moving employees around the office, plus employees will only be able to access the data if they have the proper access controls. Technology Support is planning to load the following software packages on all of the computers:

- Chart locator system
- Hospital information system
- Financial information system
- Chart deficiency system
- Release of information system
- Encoder/grouper
- Electronic health record

You then read in the e-mail that Technology Support plans to install Microsoft Office only on the secretary's and the director's computers. You know that the facility has a site license for Microsoft Office, so expense is not the issue.

1. As director, how would you respond to the Technology Support supervisor's plan for Microsoft Office? Justify your stance by providing specific HIM tasks that require this software.

2. What other software/systems would you request?

CASE 5-26

General Office Software

The staff in the HIM Department uses general office software just like any other office. The general software used includes spreadsheet, calendar/e-mail, word processor, database, and presentation applications. The management team uses these products the most.

Identify 5 specific ways that each of these general office software products can be used by the HIM staff.

CASE 5-27

Selecting an Internet-Based Personal Health Record (PHR)

You are a patient advocate. A patient of your facility has come to you and asked for advice in selecting an Internet-based Personal Health Record (PHR). She saw a physician talking on the news during the aftermath of a recent devastating tornado about how hard it was to treat patients without basic health information. The patient has not been able to get this out of her mind. She wants to ensure that her patient information is available if she finds herself or her family members in a similar situation.

Go to http://www.myphr.com to review 3 of the Internet-based PHRs that are available on the market.

1. Create a table for use in comparing the various functions of the PHRs. For each PHR reviewed, determine if you would recommend the product to the patient. Justify your recommendations.

2. The patient asks which of the 3 you would choose for your own PHR. What would you tell her?

CASE 5-28

Data Warehouse Development

Your facility is developing a data warehouse. You have been asked to determine which of your current systems should be included. You have also been asked to write a justification for each system, stating why or why not you would want to include it. The administrator has indicated that she plans to use the data warehouse for business, research, and clinical data analysis. Examples of the usage of the system include identifying which physicians make/lose money for the facility, determining the most profitable services, and analyzing best practices in patient care. Based on how the system will be used, complete this information for the current systems using Table 5-8.

Table 5-8 *System Justification*

System Justification		
System	Included Yes/No	Justification for Decision
Patient satisfaction		
ADT		
Lab information system		
Radiology information system		
Picture Archiving and Communication Systems (PACS)		
Nursing information system		
Fetal monitoring		
Financial information system		
Human resources system		
Patient acuity system		
Chart deficiency system		
Quality indicator system		
Chart locator system		
Release of information system		

CASE 5-29

Data Tables

You have been given the responsibility of populating the deficiency and form types that will be used by your new chart deficiency system. The old system has such poor data quality that you are starting from scratch. In the current system, the deficiency type and form number have no logical meaning. For example, the form type of "X" means operative note and "P" is cancer staging form. You have been provided with the templates in Tables 5-9 and 5-10. Choose logical codes whenever possible.

Table 5-9 *Deficiency Type*

Deficiency Type	
Deficiency Code	Deficiency Description

Table 5-10 *Form Type*

Form Type	
Form Code	Form Description

CASE 5-30

Electronic Forms Management System

The facility where you work is completely paper except for laboratory, radiology, and dictated reports. The facility wants to implement an EHR in about 5 years. Time and money are preventing you from doing it sooner. In the meantime, you want to get a better handle on your forms management. Currently you are still creating your forms. You are having the forms printed off by your local printing company in large bulk and storing them in your materials management department. This is costly but effective. You tried just-in-time inventory, but this failed miserably because departments constantly failed to order supplies in advance. You are considering replacing the current method with an electronic forms management system. This system would allow you to design the forms and store the files on a centralized server. When a patient is admitted, a packet of admission forms would be printed based on the patient type. For example, physician order sheet, graphics, nursing notes, nursing assessments, and progress notes would be printed out for inpatient admissions. Individual forms could also be printed on demand. The patient name and other identifying information would print out on the form.

1. What are the pros of implementing a forms management system?

2. What are the pros of implementing a forms management system when you are planning to go to the EHR in 5 years?

3. What are the cons of implementing a forms management system at this stage?

4. Would you recommend doing this if you expect to implement an EHR in about 5 years? Justify your response.

CASE 5-31

Failure of an Electronic Health Record (EHR) System

Magnolia Hills Hospital implemented an EHR about 6 months ago. Your administrator decided to pull the plug on the project a week ago because of all the problems that you were experiencing. Physicians refused to use the system. They made the nurses print out everything so they could review the patients' medical records. The physicians would write orders on a piece of paper and ask the nurses to enter them into the order entry system. The few physicians who did try to use the system were still having problems. The system was down at least 2 hours a day, and many days for 4 to 5 hours. When the HIM Department printed out reports to satisfy release of information requests, what they received was more like screen prints than forms.

This system was the brainchild of Dr. Anderson. He is a retired transplant surgeon whose name is on the new transplant center building. He and a small group of his cronies were the ones who picked and controlled the implementation of the system. There was no input from anyone else other than the information technology (IT) staff. The screens are cluttered and difficult to use and do not have data quality built in. The system does not meet Condition of Participation, state licensing, and privacy requirements.

The HIM director, physicians, nurses, and other staff learned about the system 3 weeks before implementation. The HIM director was so angry at being left out of the loop that she took early retirement and left with only 2 days' notice. Physicians' training on the new system consisted of a demonstration of the system at the quarterly medical staff meeting. Nursing and other staff were given only 1 hour of training. Since the implementation of the system, there has been turnover in the hospital administrator position and a new HIM director has been hired.

1. What failures can you identify from the history of the EHR implementation?

2. What should the hospital have done to prepare the staff for the EHR implementation?

3. The hospital wants to salvage the system if possible. What should they do now to prepare to reimplement the system?

CASE 5-32

Preparation for an Electronic Health Record (EHR) System

An EHR is scheduled for implementation at Tres Rios Hospital in 3 years. The hospital is beginning to conduct the initial planning. They want to ensure that users are prepared for the changes that the EHR will bring to the facility. As you would expect, not all of the staff and medical staff are excited about the implementation of the EHR.

1. What change in management issues should be addressed?

2. What can you do to help prepare the medical staff and employees for the new system?

CASE 5-33

Employee System Access Termination Procedure

Edward, an HIM clerk, was terminated last week. The quality of his work was unacceptable and he was constantly late or absent. Three days after his termination, an audit trail review identified something strange. The information on 100 patients had been deleted from the MPI. It is rare to delete even 1 patient and the deletion of 100 patients was unheard of. Further investigation revealed that someone using Edward's user name and password had been the person to delete the data. After this incident is turned over to the appropriate authorities for investigation, you turn your attention to ensuring that this situation does not happen again.

Write a policy and procedure to discontinue access to the system when an employee is terminated or resigns. Use sound policy and procedure rules and format.

CASE 5-34

Intranet Functionality

Your hospital has been discussing the possibility of an intranet for the past year. The Chief Information Officer (CIO) has asked you to create a list of functions that could be included in the intranet. It is to be used as a tool to get the discussions started. The only guidance that he has given you is that the intranet should be useful to staff, management, and the medical staff.

1. Create a list of functions to be provided to the CIO.

2. Write a memo to the CIO describing your recommendations.

CASE 5-35

Evaluating Systems for Health Privacy Regulations Compliance

You are the privacy and security officer for your facility; your background is HIM and you are an RHIA with the Certified in Healthcare Privacy and Security (CHPS) credential. You are part of a team that is reviewing the RFPs received from various EHR vendors. Your emphasis in the review will be the privacy and security issues. You know that there are many privacy requirements, some of which are policy related; however, many impact the functionality of information systems. You are in the process of reviewing the RFPs that were returned to you by various EHR vendors. One of the RFPs states that they are HIPAA compliant, so you decide to compare their product to the HIPAA security regulations to determine if this is true.

1. What privacy functions should you look for in the EHR?

2. What security functions should you look for in the EHR?

3. Is the fact that the vendor claims to be HIPAA compliant adequate for the system you choose?

CASE 5-36

Website Resources

Your HIM director has asked you to identify 10 Internet sites that could be used by the HIM staff as resources in their job.

You are to provide the URL address, which staff would find the site useful and how the website can be used. Enter the information you have gathered into Table 5-11. One example is listed in the table to get you started.

Table 5-11 *Website Resources*

WEB RESOURCES

Name of Website	URL	Which Staff Would Find the Website Useful?	How the Website Can Be Useful to the HIM Staff
Joint Commission	http://www.jointcommission.org	All HIM Staff	This website provides educational materials on the accreditation standards, general information on the Joint Commission and the accreditation. There are also videos and resources for purchase.

CASE 5-37

Voice Recognition Editing

Baja Medical Clinic is a 20-physician multi-disciplinary practice. The clinic has decided to implement a voice recognition system. Approximately 275 patients are seen each day. A vendor has been selected and the system is scheduled to go live in 6 months. Currently the health record is completely paper-based. The decision has to be made as to whether front-end or back-end editing should be used. You have been given the responsibility of researching the pros and cons of each and making a recommendation.

1. What are the pros and cons of each?

2. Which do you recommend? Justify your recommendation.

CASE 5-38

Storage Requirements

The long-term care facility that you work at is implementing an EDMS. The decision has been made to scan the documents at discharge. You discharge an average of 25 patients a month. The average health record averages 750 pages at discharge. You have been given the responsibility of determining the scanner to be used, the number of scanners, the number of CDs needed for long-term storage each year, and the jukebox(s) needed for 1 year of storage. The CDs hold 500 MB each. Your choices are as follows:

Scanner options   Option 1: Scans 50 sheets per minute
                         Option 2: Scans 100 sheets per minute
                         Option 3: Scans 200 sheets per minute
Jukebox options   Option 1: Holds 50 CDs
                         Option 2: Holds 250 CDs
                         Option 3: Holds 500 CDs

1. Which scanner(s) do you recommend?

2. How many scanners would you purchase?

3. How many CDs will you need for the first year?

4. Which jukebox would you recommend?

5. How many jukeboxes will you need for the first 2 years?

CASE 5-39

Quality Control of Scanning

You are implementing a new EDMS in about a month. As excited as you are about the new system, you are still concerned about the quality of scanned images. You are familiar with other facilities that implemented an imaging system and had serious quality problems. One of the facilities even ended up having to shut down their EDMS due to the problems. You want there to be a firm policy and procedure from the beginning to minimize system clean-up later.

1. What issues would you address in the policy and procedure regarding the quality control process?

2. Is there anything else that you can do to help ensure quality in the scanning process?

CASE 5-40

Contingency Planning

You work in a facility that was affected by a recent flood. You were more fortunate than most because only your basement was flooded. The problem is that your data center was in the basement. The data on the computers has been completely lost because the computers were destroyed. Unfortunately, the back-up tapes were located in the room next to the data center and were also destroyed.

Fortunately, the HIM Department is on the second floor and the charts are intact. Although your lab, radiology, dictated reports, and nursing notes were electronic, the reports had been printed out and filed in the medical record. The HIM director has been trying for a year to get the Information System Department to develop a contingency plan because she wants to stop filing the reports that are stored electronically. The IS staff had not recognized the need for the contingency plan, but the flood was the catalyst that convinced them.

1. What recommendations do you have to ensure that your facility will not lose everything if another flood hits the area? Include both contingency and business continuity plans in your recommendations.

2. The failure to implement contingency and business continuity plans could result in what types of problems?

CASE 5-41

Business Continuity Planning

Unfortunately, your facility does not have an EHR yet. In the HIM Department, you have become dependent on computers to function. You still have paper records, but chart requests, disclosure management, transcription, dictation system, chart locator, MPI, and chart deficiencies are all computerized.

Write a policy that outlines how your department would operate if one or more of these systems went down for an extended period.

CASE 5-42

Audit Triggers

Since the HIPAA privacy rule was implemented, you have been drowning in your audit trail reviews. You have finally obtained permission from administration to develop and use triggers to help with the review. These triggers, although not eliminating review of the audit trail, can be used to identify potential problems much more quickly and easily than using a manual review. Now that you finally have approval, you have to develop the triggers to be used. Administration wants to review your proposed triggers before they are implemented.

Identify 10 triggers that you will present to administration for approval.

CASE 5-43

Password Management

Several managers have reported concerns about how passwords are used in your facility.

Problems reported include the following:

- Passwords are being written down and placed near the computers. (For example, passwords have been taped to the bottom of phones.)
- Passwords are sometimes called across the nursing unit.
- Users do not log out when leaving a computer. Then someone else sits down and uses the computer with the previous user's passwords still in place.

You suspect there are other problems with the protection of passwords but you cannot provide them at this time.

What password management rules can you put in place to eliminate these problems? Include any other password problems that you suspect but cannot prove.

CASE 5-44

Electronic Health Record (EHR) Security Plan

You are the Data Security officer for Brownsville Town Hospital. The hospital is preparing to implement an EHR. You have been asked to determine the security measures that your facility will take to maintain confidentiality and prevent loss of data.

Write a security proposal to be presented to the CIO. Areas to be covered include, but are not limited to:

- Physical security of hardware
- Data security
- Confidentiality
- Access
- Disaster recovery
- Back-ups
- Business continuity planning
- Penalties for violating policies
- Network security
- Integrity controls
- Other

This is not a paper—it is a proposal. Write a cover letter to the CIO to introduce the plan, and begin the proposal with an executive summary.

CASE 5-45

Electronic Health Record (EHR) Training Plan

The EHR is being implemented in 6 months. Attention has turned to the training plan. Develop a training plan that will ensure that everyone who needs to be trained will be trained in a timely manner. Currently there are 500 employees, 350 of which are clinical staff. Sixty physicians will need to be trained. You currently have access to 2 training classrooms and can get access to another room if needed. The vendor recommends 2 hours of training for nonclinical staff and 4 to 6 hours for clinical staff.

The plan should include:

- Content (What will the content of the training include?)
- Classes for employees (How will you break the students into different types of classes?)
- A schedule for training
- The skills that the trainers need
- Number of classes required
- Amount of time needed for course
- Number of trainers needed
- Format of class (online, lecture, etc.)
- Resources needed
- When you should start training to be ready for a December 1 implementation, assuming that today's date is July 10
- When the training should be completed

CASE 5-46

Strategic Planning

Bayside General Hospital is in a community that is changing. It had been an industrial city, but many of the industries have closed. The local college is growing and is now the number one employer. Other major businesses include healthcare and a local amusement park. The population is also changing. There is a great increase of young people because of the college and work available at the amusement park.

A new hospital is opening up in a year. It will be a high-tech facility. The only currently existing hospital competing against you has the trauma center for the area and is opening an OB service. There is no children's hospital in the area. Both existing hospitals treat some pediatric patients; however, seriously ill pediatric patients are sent to the closest children's hospital, which is located 2 hours away.

Bayside General Hospital has recently added physician offices, home health, and an occupational health center to their network. They have not networked and implemented existing systems to these organizations. Administration developed the following business objectives:

- Improve quality of care provided to patients
- Use hospital resources effectively and efficiently
- Increase market share of healthcare services provided within Bayside

Bayside General Hospital has the following information systems implemented:

- Lab information system was implemented 5 years ago
- Radiology information system was implemented last year
- Nursing information system was implemented 3 years ago
- Hospital information system was implemented 10 years ago
- Decision support system goes live in 6 months
- Financial information system was implemented 2 years ago
- Electronic health record

The hospital does not have the following systems:

- Knowledge-based system
- Order entry/results reporting
- Intensive care unit
- Data repository

Based on the information above:

1. How well are systems in place to meet the objectives?

2. Determine possible projects to ensure that the objectives are met.

3. How can you use technology to prepare for the changes in the community?

4. How will HIM be affected by your proposed projects?

CASE 5-47

Single Vendor or Best of Breed

You are HIM Director of a 500-bed facility. Two of your HIM systems are outdated, so you've decided to update. These systems are the encoder/grouper system and the tumor registry system. You have submitted a capital budget request and received approval to purchase the new systems that you need.

Before you can submit an RFP or even an request for information (RFI), you have a decision to make. You have to decide if you want to purchase systems from your existing vendor, or use the best of breed model. You are considering the pros and cons of each choice of vendors. You want to have the RFP submitted to the vendor(s) in 3 months and you cannot finish writing it until this decision is made.

1. Which would you choose: a single vendor or best of breed?

2. Why did you choose this model?

3. What are the downsides to the model that you selected?

4. What if you selected a single vendor that has most but not all of the products you need? Will you send the vendor an RFP?

CASE 5-48

Functional Requirements of a Transcription System

As the transcription supervisor, you have been given the responsibility of developing the functional requirements for a new transcription system that you hope to purchase and install in the next year. You have met with your staff and done some brainstorming to come up with a comprehensive list of functions that you need and whether or not each of the functions is mandatory, desirable, or a luxury. The functional requirements must be comprehensive and include data entry, interfaces, data fields, reporting, and other functionality.

Develop the list of functional requirements in the format of Table 5-12.

Table 5-12 *Functional Requirements of a Transcription System*

Function	Mandatory	Desirable	Luxury

CASE 5-49

Health Information Exchange

Your physicians have asked you to identify the health information exchange (HIE) in your area and to provide the following information about that HIE:

1. Name of HIE

2. HIE model used

3. City where the HIE is located

4. When the HIE was established

5. The advantages and disadvantages of participating in the HIE

6. How the HIE would impact their practice

CASE 5-50

Personal Health Record

You work for Healthcare Insurance. Your organization has decided to provide a PHR to the company's insured. Your database has claims data, some clinical data, and more. You want the system to go live in 1 year.

1. What issues do you have to address before the go-live date?

2. What data should you give patients access to?

CASE 5-51

Public Health

You work for the state department of health. You receive reports of notifiable diseases from healthcare providers around the state. This information is tracked so that you can watch for epidemics and other health hazards. You are purchasing a new population health system to be used for these purposes.

What functionality should you look for in the new system?

CASE 5-52

HL7 EHR System Functional Model

You are the CIO of a 300-physician practice. The board of directors has decided to purchase an electronic medical record (EMR). You have been asked what the role of the HL7 EHR System Functional Model should have on your decision.

1. Explain the direct care functions of the HL7 EHR System Functional Model.

2. Explain the supportive functions of the HL7 EHR System Functional Model.

3. Explain the information infrastructure of the HL7 EHR System Functional Model.

4. Do you recommend that the HL7 EHR System Functional Model should be the basis upon which you evaluate the EMRs?

CASE 5-53

Data Mining

The facility you work for has grown rapidly and has run out of space. Your administrator is considering constructing a new building. He is considering moving the emergency room to the new building. You have been asked to retrieve some information for him.

Go to the OASIS Web Query Tool, which can be found at http://oasis.state.ga.us/.

For the last 5 years, identify the number of ER visits in Georgia, in the North Central Health District, and in Bibb County (or another site specified by your instructor).

1. Trend these data in the appropriate data display.

2. What is the trend for the ER services in these 3 geographical areas?

3. When your administrator asks you for your recommendation on whether or not to continue investigating moving the ER into the new building, what will you say?

CASE 5-54

Database Queries

You are an RHIA who is working in the compliance department of a long-term care corporation. You have been asked to create a database to capture data on privacy training efforts. This database will be used to collect data from all of the corporate facilities.

Your instructions are as follows:

1. Identify the data elements required.

2. Build the data dictionary.

3. Design a data entry screen that builds data quality into the database.

4. Design reports.

5. Enter 5 training sessions in the database as examples so that you have data to present to the Chief Privacy Officer for approval.

CASE 5-55

Meaningful Use

You have been asked to consult for a physician who is applying for meaningful use. He works for a small practice with 3 other physicians. One of the other physicians is also applying for meaningful use. The physician plans to apply for Medicare rules. He does not understand the standards and has asked you to help.

1. Provide the physician with a list of stage 1 and stage 2 standards.

2. What would you tell the physician about meaningful use?

3. Is the physician eligible for the meaningful use incentive payments?

CASE 5-56

Clinical Vocabularies

You have been hearing the subject of clinical vocabularies discussed frequently at several meetings. Since the concept will impact the HIM department of your ambulatory surgical center, you recognize the need to research the subject more thoroughly to be able to articulate the needs not only of your department, but also of the facility in general.

1. What vocabularies do you have to choose from?

2. What are the functions of each of these vocabularies?

3. Is the vocabulary appropriate for your setting and purposes?

4. Based on your description, which vocabulary or vocabularies would you choose? Justify your decision.

Management and Health Information Services

Developing an Organizational Chart for Health Information Management (HIM)

Before you can begin recruiting personnel, you will need to develop an organizational chart for the Health Information Management (HIM) Department.

Use the list of employees and the classifications in the department provided in Table 6-1 to develop your organizational chart.

Table 6-1 *Department Employees by Classification*

Classification	Number of Employees
Director	1
Coding Supervisor	1
Release of Information (ROI) Coordinator (contracted employee through ROI services)	1
Transcription Supervisor	1
Transcriptionists	4
Coders	3
Chart Completion Supervisor	1
HIM File Clerks	2
Secretary	1

CASE 6-2

Writing a Policy and Procedure

Write a policy and procedure for customer service for use by the receptionists at the front desk. Include procedures for dealing with voicemail messages from overnight and telephone calls, and for handling walk-in customers. See Figure 6-1 for the formal format of the usual components found in a written policy and procedure. Include these elements in your final written policy and procedure. Remember, effective procedure writing requires great attention to detail.

You may use the format in Figure 6-1 for your policy and procedure.

PORT BISMARCK HOSPITAL

Department Policy:

Subject:

Title of Policy and Procedure:

Policy Number:

Approved by: _____

Effective Date: __/__/__ .   Approved Date: __/__/__ .   Revision Date: __/__/__ .

Policy:

Procedure:

Figure 6-1 *Policy and Procedure Form*

CASE 6-3

Work Measurement Study

Select a simple HIM-related task or task you perform at your current job to complete this exercise. You may need to get assistance in conducting the study to measure "how long" it takes to complete the task at least 6 different times.

1. Use Table 6-2 to record your work measurement study results. Then, use your data to calculate the average time to use in establishing a standard for a person performing the task. Remember to allow for external influences and fatigue when conducting the time study.

2. Design a productivity report on this task for a person to log and report weekly production to the supervisor.

Table 6-2   *Work Measurement Study Form*

WORK MEASUREMENT STUDY		
Task under Study: _____		
Times Task Was Studied		Amount Completed
Time 1	Start	
	Stop	
Time 2	Start	
	Stop	
Time 3	Start	
	Stop	
Time 4	Start	
	Stop	
Time 5	Start	
	Stop	
Time 6	Start	
	Stop	
Total Amount Completed		
Average Productivity		
Productivity Expected per 8-Hour Day		
Comments/Calculations		

CASE 6-4

Evaluating Employees' Skills

You are the assistant HIM director of a regional medical center. The HIM director has asked you to develop a general competency form that can be used when conducting HIM employees' performance appraisals. The competency form would be used to determine if the employees are meeting requirements necessary on an annual basis. The director explains that her goal is to maintain an Employee Competency and Staff Development Record that will provide evidence of the hours of continuing education and of staff training programs completed by employees. This form will be maintained throughout the year and reviewed with each employee at their annual evaluation period.

1. Which organizational agencies should be considered in determining what competency standards should be established?

2. Identify elements that should be met to remain competent.

CASE 6-5

Recruiting Resources

You have had trouble recruiting coders. You have advertised in the county *Herald Tribune* without success. The only applicants are people off the street without any coding background.

1. How should you proceed?

2. What are your options?

3. Who would you pick and why?

CASE 6-6

Recruitment Advertisement

You have been discussing the difficulty in recruiting coders with your director of Human Resources. She has agreed to place an advertisement in the local newspaper for you. After the ad is placed, you receive many job applicants for the coding position. In reviewing the advertisement, you find that the ad misrepresented the job and the salary.

What should you do?

Interviewing Job Applicants

A variety of scenarios have been provided for interview simulations in Interview Situation 1 through Interview Situation 6. Select one of the interview situations and present it with a classmate, adding either appropriate or inappropriate questions according to compliance with employment laws.

Allow the class to analyze and critique the interaction by identifying the compliance or noncompliance with employment laws. In turn, you will critique each role-play portrayed by your classmates and identify compliance or noncompliance with employment laws.

Interview Situation 1   Vacant Position—Coder

The applicant has 2 years of experience in an acute care facility as a Tumor Registrar. She is a registered health information technician (RHIT) and now wants to get into coding. You have been unable to find an experienced coder, even though your salary is competitive. This person has noted on her application that she was terminated from her last position.

Interview Situation 2   Vacant Position—Health Information Management Director

The applicant has 10 years' experience managing HIM Departments but has spent the past 4 years as a consultant. The HIM Department is responsible for the traditional HIM functions, including tumor registry and birth certificates. The department is preparing to implement an electronic health record (EHR) system and will be involved with implementation of a data warehouse.

Interview Situation 3   Vacant Position—Coder for Outpatient Records
(Emergency Room and Ambulatory Surgery)

The applicant has no work experience in an HIM Department and desires employment at this small acute care facility in her hometown. She is a recent graduate of a Health Information Technology (HIT) program and has registered to take her national RHIT exam this coming fall. Her application reflects previous employment as a bank teller for 2 years following high school graduation. The application lists her supervisor from the bank as a work reference. The only other references are 3 personal references.

Interview Situation 4   Vacant Position—Evening Chart Analyst

The applicant has never worked in a HIM Department. However, she has experience in 2 healthcare settings, most recently in a nursing home as the Medical Records Coordinator. She maintained records at the nursing home for 6 years prior to leaving approximately 1 year ago. Her job prior to the nursing home was in a doctor's office as an office receptionist.

Interview Situation 5   Vacant Position—Transcription Supervisor

The applicant has many years' experience in an HIM Department. Her latest position was as a transcriptionist at a large medical center in another state, which she held for the past 14 years. Prior to that, she worked as an assembler/analyst for 10 years at the same facility. Her application reflects that she graduated from high school in 1986 and that she obtained her Certified Medical Transcription (CMT) credentials in 1998.

Interview Situation 6   Vacant Position—File Clerk

The applicant has never worked in an HIM Department; however, she has worked in an insurance company for 6 months. She has held 5 jobs in the past 3 years. She performed filing in 2 of these positions. One position was working in a fast-food restaurant, another was at a day-care, and the fifth was in retail.

CASE 6-8

Job Applicant and the Americans with Disabilities Act (ADA)

An applicant has interviewed for the tumor registry position. He is in a wheelchair and has vision problems. He is an RHIT with tumor registry experience. You have several candidates with the same or fewer qualifications. No one has more qualifications than this applicant.

1. How should you proceed?

2. How would you determine who gets the position?

CASE 6-9

Developing a Training Plan

Most of your entry-level employees were hired with very little work experience. They are a good group in that they are hardworking and want to learn. Unfortunately, they do not have all the skills needed to perform their jobs. This has resulted in breaches of privacy, subpoenas not arriving in court on time, wrong charts being pulled, misfiles, and deficiencies assigned to the wrong physician. Their frustration level is high, which sometimes manifests in rudeness to the customers.

1. Develop a training plan for each of the following HIM functional areas:
   - Record analysis
   - Documentation improvement
   - Release of information
   - Reception and customer service
   - Maintaining the file area (either paper records or electronic management for information collection and retrieval)
   - Processing loose material (either filing in paper record or scanning information)
   - Coding

2. Include the specific topics to be covered, the amount of time that you plan to devote to training for each group, and how you will cover their responsibilities during the training.

3. How do you prioritize who gets trained first and what type of training is conducted first?

CASE 6-10

Department Coverage

You have problems with phone coverage when someone calls in sick or is on vacation. Administration and physicians have complained that there continue to be times when they have trouble reaching the department by telephone. The current policy is that whoever is available covers the phone.

1. What are your options?

2. What would you recommend and why?

CASE 6-11

Decision Making

The HIM Department is small and has very limited resources. Normally the director goes to the American Health Information Management Association (AHIMA) national meeting, but this year she will be unable to go because she will be on maternity leave. The director feels that the new employee, a registered health information administrator (RHIA) who will be covering while she is on maternity leave, should go. Another employee, who is also an RHIA and has been with the department longer, feels she should go.

How should the director choose which employee will go?

Progressive Disciplinary Approach

HIM managers may experience a variety of disciplinary situations.

How would you handle the following situations if you were an effective HIM manager who practices progressive discipline measures?

Disciplinary Situation 1

Jean is 30 minutes to 1 hour late 2 to 3 days a week. You have talked to her about it repeatedly and even given her a written warning. It is now 2 weeks since the written warning and there has not been an improvement.

   1. How would you discuss this situation with Jean?

   2. What would be your next step?

Disciplinary Situation 2

The quality of Carla's work has recently deteriorated. You have discussed this with her and have given her a verbal warning. There has not been any improvement.

   1. How would you discuss this situation with Carla?

   2. What would be your next step?

Disciplinary Situation 3

You have been at a meeting and return to the department. As you walk in, you hear the ROI coordinator, Susan, talking on the phone to a requester. Susan becomes very upset with the person on the phone and tells him off. This is the first time that Susan has done this that you are aware of.

  1. Discuss what happened with Susan. How would you handle the situation?

Disciplinary Situation 4

The HIM Department has a policy of no personal calls. You know that employees make short calls to let family know they are working late and the like. Pam has begun to spend a lot of time on the telephone discussing personal business. You know she is going through a divorce, but employees are starting to talk.

  1. How would you discuss the situation with Pam?

Disciplinary Situation 5

Cindy and Barbara work in the Analysis area. They got into an argument today that disrupted the workplace. They were both written up for this same behavior a month ago. You told them they would be suspended for 3 days if another incident happened.

  1. Discuss this situation with them. What would you bring out in your meeting with them?

Disciplinary Situation 6

Kim is a new employee who is having problems with her performance. She is still in her probationary status.

1. How would you discuss this situation with Kim?

Disciplinary Situation 7

Kelly is your coding supervisor. She was berating one of her subordinate coders. She called the employee stupid and said that she was going to make the coder's life miserable. Your transcription supervisor overheard the conversation and reported it to you.

1. How would you discuss the situation with Kelly?

CASE 6-13

Falsification of Information on Employment Application

Jeremy is the director of the HIM Department. Laura, a transcriptionist, has been a wonderful employee. Through the grapevine, Jeremy heard that Laura had put on her employment application that she had an associate's degree, but that she did not actually have one. He called the college and found that she was 2 classes short of her degree. This was grounds for dismissal.

1. What should Jeremy do?

2. How should he handle the meeting with Laura?

Time Management

You are the HIM Director for a small 140-bed county-owned hospital in a rural area. The department has become backlogged in ROI since your correspondence coordinator's resignation was received 2 weeks ago.

The correspondence coordinator resigned following an extended leave due to injuries received from a car accident that occurred 3 months prior. She was out of work for major surgery and rehabilitation, with the intent to return when she was able. She worked for you for 3 years and was rarely out of work until the accident. In the interim, you had employees cross-trained to help cover the ROI work.

You approached administration about hiring a temporary employee a month after your employee was out on leave, but administration did not give approval. When the employee turned in her resignation, you submitted a request to replace her position and administration has approved it. You are in the process of accepting applications and scheduling interviews.

The business office claims manager has been calling regarding "bills held" due to pending copies needed of medical records to support the claim. The business office manager called just this morning, concerned that an increase in accounts receivable (AR) is due to the backlog in ROI.

Two days ago, the hospital administrator requested that you submit a detailed report on the ROI status. It is due today. You are gathering the necessary data to compile the report for administration when your inpatient coder comes into your office and asks to meet with you. Your report is due in 2 hours and still needs a lot of work before it is complete.

1. Might an alternative means be available that you could consider (other than hiring a replacement full-time employee [FTE]) in providing ROI service? If so, what?

2. How should you respond to the business office manager?

3. What elements do you feel should be included in the report for administration?

4. How should you respond to the coder?

CASE 6-15

Interdepartmental Communications

Dr. Jenkins arrived in the operating room (OR) suite at 8:45 a.m. to perform surgery on an elective surgery case scheduled for 9:15 a.m. The OR supervisor requested to speak with the surgeon to explain that the case would have to be canceled because a history and physical (H&P) report had not been completed for the patient's record.

Dr. Jenkins became visibly upset and began making accusations, saying that he had dictated the H&P 3 days ago and that the HIM Department was at fault. The OR supervisor was already aware that her secretary had phoned Mr. Rheems, the HIM director, the day prior to inquire on the H&P report. The dictation system transcription report reflected that no dictation was available then. The OR supervisor informed Dr. Jenkins that as of yesterday afternoon there was no dictation found in the system, but that she would inquire again with the HIM Department.

The transcription supervisor searched the dictation system again immediately upon receiving the call and noted the H&P report had been dictated 45 minutes earlier, at 8:15 a.m., by Dr. Jenkins, and informed the HIM director that it would be typed as soon as possible and delivered to the OR.

The transcription supervisor informed Mr. Rheems that Dr. Jenkins had done this on 2 other occasions during the past few months. Mr. Rheems knows the dictation system has tracking and audit capability for reports that reflects the date, time, and author of dictation, as well as identifies the date, time, and transcriber of each dictation.

1. How should Mr. Rheems respond to the OR regarding Dr. Jenkins' H&P report?

2. Should this individual incident be taken to administrative staff?

3. If so, to whom?

4. Should this individual incident be taken to a medical staff committee?

5. If so, to which committee?

6. If not, what actions should Mr. Rheems take to prevent recurrence of such activity against the HIM Department in the future?

CASE 6-16

Merit Raise

You graduated from a Baccalaureate Health Information program 3 years ago. You obtained your RHIA credentials 6 months after graduation and have been coding at the county hospital since graduation. There are 4 inpatient coders, including you. The coding supervisor has a long tenure with the hospital and has acquired her certified coding specialist (CCS) credentials, but she does not have a college degree to accompany it. Your short-term career goal is to advance in salary and obtain a managerial position. You suspect, and have heard, that your coding supervisor is paid a salary much greater than yours.

How might you seek an increase in pay from your current employer that is a more comparable salary to the market scale for RHIA inpatient coders?

CASE 6-17

Incentive-Based Compensation Programs

There are several different payment scales for incentive-based transcription programs presented in Incentive-Based Compensations Programs 1 through 5. Review each program and complete the computation of incentive pay based upon the payment scale given for each program.

Incentive-Based Compensation Program 1

The incentive pay is $1.00 per dictated minute transcribed.

Calculate the incentive pay for each transcriptionist using Table 6-3.

Table 6-3 *Transcriptionist Incentive-Based Pay: Program 1*

Transcriptionist Incentive-Based Pay: Program 1				
Transcriptionist	Number of Hours Worked	Number of Minutes Transcribed	Minimum Required Biweekly Production	Amount of Incentive Pay
Jeana	80	1,145	1,200	
Meagan	80	1,200	1,200	
Sandra	80	1,264	1,200	
Julia	80	1,320	1,200	
Tenille	80	1,410	1,200	

Incentive-Based Compensation Program 2

The incentive pay is $0.15 per line transcribed, based upon 65 characters per line.

Calculate the incentive pay for each transcriptionist using Table 6-4.

Table 6-4 *Transcriptionist Incentive-Based Pay: Program 2*

Transcriptionist	Number of Hours Worked	Number of Lines Transcribed	Minimum Required Biweekly Production	Amount of Incentive Pay
Jeana	80	7,400	8,200	
Meagan	80	8,010	8,200	
Sandra	80	8,215	8,200	
Julia	80	8,575	8,200	
Tenille	80	8,885	8,200	

Incentive-Based Compensation Program 3

The incentive pay per dictated minute is $1.00. You are given the daily production in Table 6-5.

Calculate the weekly incentive pay for each transcriptionist using Table 6-6.

Table 6-5 *Weekly Transcription Totals for Incentive-Based Pay: Program 3*

Weekly Transcription Totals for Incentive-Based Pay: Program 3

Transcriptionist	Monday Minutes	Tuesday Minutes	Wednesday Minutes	Thursday Minutes	Friday Minutes	Total Minutes
Jeana	90	90	90	90	90	450
Meagan	90	90	89	95	122	486
Sandra	112	110	124	98	106	550
Julia	105	123	145	107	131	611
Tenille	157	132	137	123	116	665

Table 6-6 *Transcriptionist Incentive-Based Pay: Program 3*

Transcriptionist	Total Hours Worked	Total Completed Dictated Minutes	Minimum Required Minutes per Week	Total Amount of Incentive Pay
Jeana	40	450	600	
Meagan	40	486	600	
Sandra	40	550	600	
Julia	40	611	600	
Tenille	40	665	600	

Incentive-Based Compensation Program 4

The incentive pay per line, above required production, is $0.15. You are given the daily production in Table 6-7.

Calculate the weekly incentive pay for each transcriptionist using Table 6-8.

Analyze the production of each transcriber and determine if minimum lines of transcription are met for incentive pay.

Table 6-7 *Program 4 Weekly Transcription Totals*

Weekly Transcription Line Totals: Incentive-Based Compensation Program 4						
Transcriptionist	Monday	Tuesday	Wednesday	Thursday	Friday	Total
Jeana	1,070	1,250	1,135	1,030	1,290	5,775
Meagan	1,260	1,395	1,315	1,205	1,300	6,475
Sandra	1,325	1,415	1,300	1,205	1,395	6,640
Julia	1,140	1,255	1,230	1,335	1,230	6,190
Tenille	1,175	1,265	1,380	1,290	1,185	6,295

Table 6-8 *Transcriptionist Incentive-Based Pay: Program 4*

Transcriptionist Incentive-Based Pay: Program 4					
Transcriptionist	Total Hours Worked	Total Completed Dictated Minutes	Minimum Required Lines per Week	Incentive Pay above Base	Weekly Incentive Production Met? Y/N
Jeana	40	5,775	6,000		
Meagan	40	6,475	6,000		
Sandra	40	6,640	6,000		
Julia	40	6,190	6,000		
Tenille	40	6,295	6,000		

Incentive-Based Compensation Program 5

The daily incentive pay per line is $0.13 from 800 to 1,099 lines; $0.15 for 1,100 to 1,399 lines; and $0.20 for 1,400 and more. Use the information in Table 6-9 to calculate the daily incentive pay for each transcriptionist. Enter the daily incentive pay for each transcriptionist in Table 6-10.

Table 6-9 *Program 5 Daily Transcription Totals*

Daily Lines of Transcription: Incentive-Based Compensation Program 5					
Transcriptionist	Monday	Tuesday	Wednesday	Thursday	Friday
Jeana	990	990	990	990	990
Meagan	990	990	989	995	1,122
Sandra	1,112	1,110	1,124	998	1,106
Julia	1,105	1,123	1,145	1,107	1,131
Tenille	1,157	1,132	1,137	1,123	1,116

Table 6-10 *Program 5 Daily Incentive Pay*

Daily Incentive Pay Earned: Program 5					
Transcriptionist	Monday	Tuesday	Wednesday	Thursday	Friday
Jeana					
Meagan					
Sandra					
Julia					
Tenille					

CASE 6-18

Payroll Budget Decisions

The HIM directors in the following situations have been approached by administration with personnel budget concerns and given constraints to apply. Review the 4 budgeting issues presented and make calculations as appropriate.

Budget Decision 1

The HIM director, Linda, has been given $15,000.00 for the overtime needed to catch up on the loose filing.

If the average salary of the HIM clerical staff is $15.75, how many hours of overtime can be worked?

Budget Decision 2

The HIM director, Carlotta, has been given $23,500.00 to hire temporary employees.

If the temporary agency is charging $28.00 per hour, how many hours of temporary help will be available to Carlotta's department?

Budget Decision 3

The HIM director, Jose, has been given instructions that he cannot go over $8,100.00 in salary (overtime) for the week of June 2-8.

Based on the information provided in Table 6-11, how close is he to using the allotted overtime budget for loose filing?

Table 6-11 *Salary Expense Calculation*

Salary Expense for June 2–8			
Employee	Number of Hours Worked	Salary/Hour	Total Earnings
Michaela	40	$15.35	
Glenn	40	$18.46	
Jerome	22	$17.78	
Natasha	32	$16.88	
Sarah	40	$19.66	

Budget Decision 4

As the HIM imaging coordinator, you are in charge of reporting your staff payroll. Overtime is based on 80 hours per 2 weeks. The weekly hours for the past 2 weeks are shown in Table 6-12 and Table 6-13.

1. Your HIM director has asked you if you have had any overtime for this payroll.

2. If so, who worked overtime and how many overtime hours did they work?

Table 6-12 *Hours for Week 1*

Hours Worked per Employee in Week 1						
Employee	Monday	Tuesday	Wednesday	Thursday	Friday	Total
Michaela	8.0	7.5	8.5	6.25	8.0	
Glenn	8.0	8.5	9.0	10.5	8.0	
Jerome	8.0	7.5	3.0	10.0	8.0	
Natasha	9.0	8.0	9.0	8.0	7.5	
Sarah	8.0	9.0	8.0	8.0	7.5	

Table 6-13 *Hours for Week 2*

Hours Worked per Employee in Week 2						
Employee	Monday	Tuesday	Wednesday	Thursday	Friday	Total
Michaela	8.0	8.0	8.0	8.0	7.75	
Glenn	10.5	8.0	8.0	8.0	8.25	
Jerome	9.0	8.0	8.0	8.0	8.5	
Natasha	8.0	8.0	8.0	8.0	9.0	
Sarah	7.75	8.0	8.0	8.0	7.75	

CASE 6-19

Budgeting for Reducing Payroll

Two of the facilities in the healthcare corporation you work for are going through a transitional period. As the divisional HIM director, you have been given the assignment to help with corporate finances by reducing payroll in the HIM Department in each of these facilities.

Follow the instructions and complete the calculations so that you can report the results for each of the HIM Departments undergoing reductions.

Facility 1

You have been given the difficult assignment of reducing your payroll by 4% per week.

1. If the payroll is $15,348.45 for the week, how much will have to be eliminated?

2. What will be the new weekly payroll?

Facility 2

All of the departments have been given instructions to reduce payroll costs.

The HIM Department has been instructed to reduce payroll by 6% per week.

1. If your payroll is $20,149.99 for the week, how much will have to be eliminated?

2. How much should the new reduced payroll be?

CASE 6-20

Calculating Salary Increases

The 5 HIM Departments that you manage have just completed the annual evaluations for your staff. Now you need to calculate the increase in payroll for each one.

Facility 1

The hospital has just announced a 3.5% raise across the board. What would be the new salaries after the 3.5% increase? Use the information in Table 6-14 to calculate the new salaries (round to the nearest cent).

Table 6-14 *Facility 1 Salary Increase Calculation Form*

Salary Increase Calculation Form: Facility 1 HI Tech Department			
Employee	Current Salary	Amount of Raise	New Salary
Michaela	$15.35		
Glenn	$23.46		
Jerome	$16.78		
Natasha	$18.88		
Sarah	$26.66		

Facility 2

The hospital has just announced a 5% raise across the board. Use the information in Table 6-15 to calculate the new salaries (round to the nearest cent).

Table 6-15 *Facility 2 Salary Increase Calculation Form*

Employee	Current Salary	Amount of Raise	New Salary
Nicole	$38.54		
Brad	$25.53		
Jared	$15.22		
Sophie	$21.22		
Elizabeth	$21.66		

Facility 3

The hospital has just announced raises. The amount of the raise is based on the employee's performance evaluation. Based on the employee information in Table 6-16, calculate the new hourly salary for each employee (round to the nearest cent) and enter the information in Table 6-17.

Table 6-16 *Facility 3 Evaluation Score and Amount of Raise*

Evaluation Score and Corresponding Amount of Raise	
Evaluation Score	Amount of Raise
5	5.0%
4	4.0%
3	2.5%
2	1.0%
1	0.0%

Table 6-17 *Facility 3 Calculation Form for Increase in Salary*

Calculations for Increase in Hourly Salary: Facility 3				
Employee	Current Hourly Salary	Evaluation Score	Amount of Raise	New Hourly Salary
Toni	$38.23	5		
LaSha	$32.54	3		
Lori	$15.75	2		
Gloria	$16.22	5		
Thaddeus	$25.85	3		
Gregg	$30.22	4		

Facility 4

The hospital has just announced raises. The amount of the raise is based on the employee's performance evaluation. The evaluation score and corresponding raise amount is shown in Table 6-18. Using the information in Table 6-18, calculate the new hourly salary for each employee and enter the information in Table 6-19.

Table 6-18 *Facility 4 Evaluation Score and Corresponding Amount of Raise*

Evaluation Score and Corresponding Amount of Raise	
Evaluation Score	Amount of Raise
5	6.0%
4	5.0%
3	3.0%
2	1.0%
1	0.0%

Table 6-19 *Facility 4 Calculation Form for Salary Increase*

Calculation Form for Salary Increase				
Employee	Current Hourly Salary	Evaluation Score	Amount of Raise	New Hourly Salary
Jennifer	$35.55	5		
Grant	$29.65	2		
Flora	$16.61	2		
Louise	$18.55	5		
Laura	$17.69	5		
Mark	$21.93	4		
Abigail	$24.22	3		

Facility 5

The hospital has just announced raises. The amount of the raise is based on the employee's performance evaluation as shown in Table 6-20.

Table 6-20 *Facility 5 Evaluation Score and Corresponding Amount of Raise*

Evaluation Score and Corresponding Amount of Raise	
Evaluation Score	Amount of Raise
5	5.0%
4	4.0%
3	2.5%
2	1.0%
1	0.0%

Based on the employee information in Table 6-21, calculate the new annual salary for each employee and the total salary budget (round to the nearest cent).

Table 6-21 *Facility 5 Calculation Form for Salary Increase*

Calculation Form for Salary Increase: Facility 5				
Employee	Current Annual Salary	Evaluation Score	Amount of Increase	New Annual Salary
Toni	$79,248.77	5		
LaSha	$45,599.47	3		
Lori	$31,657.44	2		
Gloria	$31,555.95	5		
Thaddeus	$45,578.33	4		
Gregg	$44,558.04	3		
Total Salary Budget				

The salary budget is based on the fiscal year (FY), which begins June 1. Salary increases will not take effect until October 1. Based on the employee information that you have calculated in Table 6-21, determine your payroll budget for the rest of the calendar year (beginning in June and ending in December). Then enter the information by month in Table 6-22.

Table 6-22 *Payroll Budget for Year Beginning June 1*

Name	Jun	Jul	Aug	Sep	Oct	Nov	Dec	Total
Toni								
LaSha								
Lori								
Gloria								
Thaddeus								
Gregg								
Totals								

CASE 6-21

Planning for Paper-Based Record Retention

You have been given the task of planning for paper-based record retention needs for each of the departments given below. Calculate the information needed to generate your report to administration.

Department 1

Use the information in Table 6-23 to calculate the average chart thickness (round to 1 decimal place).

Table 6-23   *Samples Taken to Determine Average Size of Chart Thickness Department 1*

Sample Inch Measurements to Determine the Average Chart Thickness					
0.2	4.0	0.5	3.5	0.5	0.25
0.5	0.4	0.25	2.75	0.5	0.75
0.75	0.75	0.75	4.0	0.5	0.75
1.25	1.25	1.25	1.5	1.75	1.0
3.25	1.5	1.75	3.75	0.25	0.75

Department 2

Calculate the linear filing inches required for 175,000 charts with an average size of 0.5 inch each.

Department 3

Calculate the linear filing inches required for 576,000 charts with an average size of 0.75 inch each.

Department 4

Calculate the linear filing inches required for 326,000 charts with an average size of 0.2 inch each.

Department 5

Calculate the linear filing inches required for 175,000 charts with an average size of chart 0.5 inch and a 25% allowance for future growth.

Department 6

Calculate the linear filing inches required for 576,000 charts with an average size of 0.75 inch and a 20% allowance for future growth.

Department 7

Calculate the linear filing inches required for 326,000 charts with an average size of 0.2 inch each and include a 35% allowance for future growth.

Department 8

Use the information in Table 6-24 to calculate the average chart thickness. Then calculate the linear filing inches required for 217,000 charts, including a 25% allowance for growth.

Table 6-24 *Samples Taken to Determine Average Size of Chart Thickness Department 8*

Sample Measurements (in Inches) to Determine the Average Chart Thickness

0.75	3.0	0.75	2.25	4.0	1.5
0.25	0.5	0.25	2.50	4.0	1.75
0.10	1.75	0.75	3.0	4.0	0.75

Department 9

Use the information in Table 6-25 to calculate the average chart thickness (round to 2 decimal places). Then calculate the linear filing inches required for 452,000 charts, including a 25% allowance for growth.

Table 6-25 *Samples Taken to Determine Average Size of Chart Thickness Department 9*

Sample Measurements (in Inches) to Determine the Average Chart Thickness

1.0	2.25	0.25	1.75	3.75	2.50
3.0	2.5	0.75	2.75	2.25	0.50

Department 10

Macon General Hospital has 248,000 medical records with an average size of 0.75 inch per chart.

How many shelving units are required if the shelves are 36 inches wide and there are 7 shelves in each unit?

Department 11

Atlanta General Hospital has 758,200 medical records with an average size of 1.0 inch per chart.

How many shelving units are required if the shelves are 36 inches wide and there are 6 shelves in each unit?

Department 12

Perry Medical Center has 150,000 medical records with an average size of 0.5 inch.

How many shelving units are required if the shelves are 33 inches wide, there are 8 shelves in each unit, and a growth rate of 25% is desired?

Department 13

Birmingham Pediatrics currently has 467,000 linear filing inches. The current shelves are nearing capacity. They want to increase filing capacity by 40%. They want to continue utilizing shelving units that are 33 inches wide and 7 shelves tall.

How many new shelving units will be required?

Planning for Electronic Record Retention

You have been given the task of planning for electronic record retention needs for each of the departments given in the following sections. Perform the calculations necessary to report to administration.

Department 1

You must decide how many CDs you will need to store the scanned images of the existing medical records. Each CD stores 12,000 images. It is estimated that there are 750,852,214 images to store on the CDs.

How many CDs would you need?

Department 2

You must decide how many CDs you will need to store the scanned images of the existing medical records. Each CD stores 12,000 images. It is estimated that there are 1,538,535,515 images to store on the CDs.

How many CDs would you need?

Department 3

The 12-inch platters that have been selected for the new imaging system will each store 1,400,000 images via computer output laser disk (COLD). It was calculated that over the next 5 years there would be 129,956,493,345 images via COLD.

How many of these platters should be purchased for the department?

Department 4

The platters that have been selected for the new imaging system will store 14 gigabytes. There are 2,000,000 images and a scanned image averages 199 KB.

How many platters will be needed?

CASE 6-23

Calculating Department Operations Budget

As HIM Divisional Manager over 4 facilities, you are responsible for submitting the operations budgets for the HIM Departments. Use the information that is provided for each of the HIM Departments to calculate the budgets for reporting to administration.

Facility 1 Operations Budget

You have been asked to calculate the operations budget for the HIM Department for the new FY. The hospital has announced that there will be a 2% increase in the operations budget across the board. Based on the current line items and FY budget shown in Table 6-26, calculate the new budget.

Table 6-26 *Line Items—Facility 1 Operations Budget*

Line Items for Operations Budget		
Line Item	Current Budget	New Budget
Supplies	$7,500.00	
Maintenance	$2,000.00	
Equipment	$12,000.00	
Software Licensing	$1,000.00	
Copy Machines	$5,000.00	
Folders	$15,000.00	

Facility 2 Operations Budget

You have been asked to calculate the operations budget for the HIM Department for the new FY. The hospital has announced that there will be a 2% increase in the operations budget across the board. In addition, there will be a 5% increase in the maintenance costs and your software. Based on the current FY budget shown in Table 6-27, calculate the new budget.

Table 6-27 *Line Items—Facility 2 Operations Budget*

Line Items for Operations Budget		
Line Item	Current Budget	New Budget
Supplies	$5,500.00	
Maintenance	$2,000.00	
Equipment	$15,000.00	
Software Licensing	$1,500.00	
Copy Machines	$3,000.00	
Folders	$8,000.00	

Facility 3 Operations Budget

You have been asked to calculate the operations budget for the HIM Department for the new FY. The hospital has announced that there will be a 6% decrease in the operation budget across the board. Based on the current FY budget shown in Table 6-28, calculate the new budget.

Table 6-28 *Line Items—Facility 3 Operations Budget*

Line Items for Operations Budget		
Line Item	Current Budget	New Budget
Supplies	$6,000.00	
Maintenance	$3,000.00	
Equipment	$20,000.00	
Software Licensing	$1,500.00	
Copy Machine	$2,500.00	
Folders	$5,500.00	

Facility 4 Operations Budget

You have been asked to calculate the operations budget for the HIM Department for the new FY. The hospital has announced that there will be a 5% decrease in the operation budget across the board. The budget must be cut even though maintenance and software licensing is being increased by 2%. Based on the current FY budget shown in Table 6-29, calculate the new budget.

Table 6-29 *Line Items—Facility 4 Operations Budget*

Line Items for Operations Budget		
Line Item	Current Budget	New Budget
Supplies	$4,500.00	
Maintenance	$3,000.00	
Equipment	$4,500.00	
Software Licensing	$750.00	
Copy Machine	$800.00	

CASE 6-24

Net Present Value (NPV) Method of Evaluating a Capital Expense

You are requesting approval of a capital expenditure for a new dictation system. The cost of the system is $65,000.00. You expect that the system will save the HIM Department $20,000.00 per year by eliminating the cost of outside contract transcription. You anticipate that the system life will be 5 years. Your facility uses straight line depreciation for the life of any capital expenditure. Assume that management requires the use of a net present value (NPV) of capital at 10%. Use the NPV shown in Table 6-30.

1. Calculate the net cash flow.

2. Would the dictation system meet the criteria to have a 10% return and exceed the initial capital outlay?

Table 6-30 *Net Present Value at 10.0%*

Net Present Value at 10%			
Years	Net Cash Flow	Factor for NPV at 10.0%	Present Value of Cash Flow
1		$0.909091	
2		$0.826446	
3		$0.751315	
4		$0.683013	
5		$0.620921	

CASE 6-25

Accounting Rate of Return Method of Evaluating a Capital Expense

You want to get approval for a capital expense to bring the copy service back in house. You estimate that it will bring in a net cash flow of $40,000.00 over the next 5 years. An initial outlay of $24,000.00 cash will be needed for 2 networked, dedicated computers and a new copy machine to support the ROI staff you already have.

1. Use straight-line deprecation in calculating the average net income and enter the information in Table 6-31. The accounting rate of return needs to be at least 10% for the project to be accepted.

2. Will the accounting rate of return for the capital expense be acceptable?

Table 6-31 *Accounting Rate of Return*

Accounting Rate of Return		
Net cash flow per year	Cash flow/number of years	40,000/5 = 8,000
Depreciation	Cost/number of years	
Average net income	Net cash flow per year less depreciation	
Investment	Cost of project	
Accounting rate of return for project	Average net income/investment	

CASE 6-26

Payback Method of Evaluating a Capital Expense

You want to get approval for a capital expense to bring the copy service back in house. An investment of $24,000.00 for a dedicated computer and a new copy machine will support the ROI staff you already have. You estimate that it will bring in a cash income of $40,000.00 over the next 5 years. Your facility uses straight-line depreciation to calculate the average net income.

1. Use Table 6-32 to figure the rate of return on the NPV and Table 6-33 to determine the number of years it will take for the payback.

2. Then, use the formula in Figure 6-2 to calculate the payback period.

3. How many years will it take to pay back the investment?

Table 6-32 *Net Present Value at 10.0%*

Net Present Value at 10.0%			
Years	Net Cash Flow	Factor for NPV at 10.0%	Present Value of Cash Flow
1	$2,000	$0.909091	
2	$5,000	$0.826446	
3	$9,000	$0.751315	
4	$11,000	$0.683013	
5	$13,000	$0.620921	

Table 6-33 *Payback Method of Evaluating the Capital Expense for the In-House Copy Service*

Payback Method of Evaluating the Capital Expense for the In-House Copy Service			
Year	Average Net Income	Initial Investment	Remaining
0		$24,000	
1			
2			
3			
4			
5			
6			
Total			

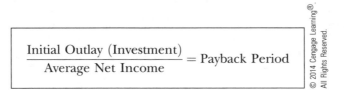

$$\frac{\text{Initial Outlay (Investment)}}{\text{Average Net Income}} = \text{Payback Period}$$

Figure 6-2 *Formula for the Payback Method*

CASE 6-27

Developing the HIM Operations Budget

Develop the HIM Department operations budget on a spreadsheet for the next FY. Allocate the funding throughout the FY on a monthly basis. The FY at General Hospital begins July 1.

First, create a spreadsheet folder with the Salaries and Wages information, and then create a spreadsheet folder with the Operating Expenses.

Personnel Salaries and Wages

Calculate amounts for

1. Salaries with fringe benefits

2. Allowed overtime

Second, calculate total personnel budget.

Use the information in Table 6-34 to calculate the payroll costs for the new FY. New salaries include:

1. A new approved Analyst/Coder/Abstractor position that will go into effect at the beginning of the new FY with a salary of $48,500.00.
2. Fringe benefits of 30% of monthly salaries.
3. A merit raise of 5% that will go into effect in December.
4. Overtime limits not to exceed $4,000.00 for the year.

Table 6-34 *Personnel Salary Information*

Personnel Salary Information			
Classification	Number of Employees	Current Salaries	Salaries for New FY
Director	1	$79,450.00	
Assistant Director	1	$67,478.00	
Coding Supervisor	1	$55,971.00	
Receptionist/Clerk	1	$31,502.00	
Transcription Supervisor	1	$56,800.00	
Transcriptionists	4	$46,000.00	
Coders	3	$47,500.00	
Chart Completion Supervisor	1	$50,000.00	
HIM Technicians	2	$44,052.00	
*Analyst/Coder/Abstractor	1	New position	
SALARIES & FRINGE BENEFITS			
BUDGETED OVERTIME			
SUBTOTAL PERSONNEL			

*Denotes new approved position

Operating Expenses

Operations expenses are shown in Table 6-35 and should be allocated throughout the FY.

What would be the operations budget for the new FY, including line items given?

Table 6-35 *Operations Expenses for New FY*

Operations Expenses for New FY	
Expense	Budget
Telephone	$1,000.00
Supplies	$10,500.00
Folders	$10,000.00
Equipment	$25,000.00
Copy Machine	$8,000.00
Education	$2,500.00
TOTAL	

CASE 6-28

Developing the HIM Department Budget

Develop a budget for the HIM Department for the next FY at Sea Crest Healthcare Center. The FY begins July 1. Utilize spreadsheet software to develop the budget parts and then develop the department budget for the next FY.

There are 3 parts to the budget:

- Personnel (see Table 6-36)
- Operational (see Table 6-37)
- Capital Equipment (see Table 6-38, Figure 6-3, and Figure 6-4)

1. Calculate the budget for each month and a total for the year. Line items to be included are identified in each of the 3 parts of the budget. Any limitations/instructions from administration are also provided.

2. Use the Capital Expenditure Approval Form (Figure 6-4) in completing and submitting a capital expenditure request for a new dictation system.

Personnel Budget

The FY personnel budget is indicated in Table 6-36. Remember that the salary raises will not go into effect until October of the FY.

Instructions: Calculate fringe benefits as 25% of monthly salary. A 5% raise will go into effect in October.
Limitations: Overtime cannot exceed $4,000.00 for the year. No new employees.

Use a spreadsheet to calculate and reflect the monthly personnel budget.

Table 6-36 *Information for Salary Budget*

Personnel Budget		
Position	Current Salary	20XX-20XX Salary
Director	$82,000.00	
Assistant Director	$74,000.00	
Receptionist/Clerk	$31,000.00	
Analyst/Coder/Abstractor	$46,000.00	
Analyst/Coder/Abstractor	$48,500.00	
Assembly Clerk	$30,000.00	
Transcriptionist	$45,000.00	
Transcriptionist	$47,000.00	
Part-time File Clerk	$16,500.00	
Line Items Total Salaries		
Total Salaries and Fringe Benefits		
Overtime		

Operational Budget

Table 6-37 *Operational Budget*

Operational Budget Fiscal Year 20XX-20XX	
Operation	Budgeted
Telephone	$2,000.00
Supplies	$1,050.00
Folders	$10,000.00
Equipment	$22,000.00
Copy Machine	$5,000.00
Education	$ 5,000.00
TOTAL	

Capital Equipment Budget

Instructions: Complete the HIM Department's Capital Equipment Budget for the FY.

Note: The only major equipment request is to replace your current dictation system.

Administration has distributed budget requests to each department at General Hospital with a memo indicating a due date of 1 month.

Instructions state that the capital budget is "zero-based," requiring justification of any proposed capital expenditures. You have listed some justifications for a new digital dictation system for the upcoming year in Figure 6-3. You need to complete the Capital Expenditure Approval Form shown in Figure 6-4 and return it to administration with your budget.

As the HIM director, you know that after administration's review of submitted department budgets, only those foreseen as most important will be approved and funded. **For this exercise, include the dictation system in your capital budget as if it had been approved.**

Table 6-38   *Capital Equipment Information*

Capital Equipment	
Item: New Dictation System	
Cost for System	$65,000.00
Annual Income Produced	$20,000.00
Depreciation over 5 Years	

Justification for New Transcription System

- The current dictation system is 15 years old. It requires service a couple of times per month. The downtime of the system averages fifty minutes each time the serviceman comes out to service it.
- The medical staff has complained of not being able to access the system due to getting busy signals.
- Dr. Delinco complains that his Operative Reports are taking 1 to 1½ weeks to be typed.
- Dr. Smith has complained that the current system doesn't allow him to call in and listen to his dictations as an alternative when the report is not available on the patient chart.
- Prioritizing reports among the transcriptionists is not as automated as newer systems allow, therefore consuming transcribers' time and impacting production.

Figure 6-3 *Justification for New Transcription System*

Capital Expenditure Approval Form	
Description: <u>Digital Dictation System</u>	
Budget Year: <u>20XX</u>	Budget Cost: <u>$65,000.00</u>

Type of Expenditure: <u>Capital</u>	Replacement: <u>Y</u>	New: <u>N</u>

Briefly define function of capital expenditure:

Perfecto Digital Dictation System has state of art capabilities with a 15-year full warranty. The system is capable of 42 simultaneous dictators to call in, while 16 transcribers can access system for output. Access can be made from direct-wired dictation units, phone call-in, or cellular call-in with security of proper access codes. There is functionality to call in and listen by authorized users with secure access passwords (numbers). User-friendly edit functions are available to authorized users for backup, stop, record-over, add-in, and save functionalities. The system has monotype audio technology for clear recording of dictator. In addition, the new system has excellent functionality for queuing STAT and workflow of medical dictations for transcriptionist. This will equate to better prioritization and turnaround of medical dictations.

Briefly describe why item is needed (students may choose to add variation to justification):

The current dictation system is 15 years old and requires service a several of times per month causing the system to incur an average of fifty minutes of downtime. The system is not capable of having simultaneous dictators. The medical staff has complained of not being able to access the system due to getting busy signals. The system does not have a method of effectively prioritizing STAT and workflow of dictations for transcriptionists. Dr. Delinco complains that his operative reports are taking 1 to 1½ weeks to be typed. The system does not have the technology that will enable physicians to call in and listen to dictations. Dr. Smith has complained that the current system does not allow him to call in and listen to his dictations as an alternative to when the report is not available on the patient chart. Prioritizing reports among the transcriptionists is not as automated as newer systems allow, therefore consuming transcribers' time and impacting production.

Figure 6-4 *Capital Expense Approval Form*

Financial Analysis	Annual
A) Gross Revenue	$_____
B) Less Depreciation	(_____)
C) Gross Profit	_____
D) Asset Cost	$_____
E) Return on Asset	_____%
F) Payback- years	_____

Requested by:_____ (Department Manager)

Approved by:

_____ (Operations Manager)   Date_____

_____ (Finance Manager)   Date_____

_____ (Administrator)   Date_____

Figure 6-4 *Capital Expense Approval Form (continued)*

CASE 6-29

Filing System Conversions

As an HIM assistant director, you have been asked by administration to help with the filing system conversions at 2 of the outpatient service facilities of your healthcare system. They have asked you to help them in calculating the number of employees needed to complete their projects.

Project 1

Orthopedics of Central Omaha is converting the filing system from alphabetic to terminal digit. The front office staff consists of 8 FTEs. The practice manager has given instructions that the work can begin on Friday afternoon as soon as the last patient leaves, which is typically 5:00 p.m. The project must be completed by 8:00 a.m. Monday morning.

The HIM coordinator has been collecting information for you to use in the planning process. There are 8,950 medical records. It takes 2 minutes per chart to convert from alphabetic to terminal digit.

1. Determine the number of hours that you expect the project to take.

2. Can everything be done by working the day shift, or will you need an evening and/or night shift to get the job completed on time?

3. How many people will be needed to complete the project in the time frame given?

Project 2

Eastern Omaha Neurology Center is converting its filing system from alphabetic to terminal digit. There are 15 office staff members. The practice manager has given instructions that the work can begin on Friday afternoon as soon as the last patient leaves, which is typically 2:00 p.m. The project must be completed by 8:00 p.m. Sunday night.

The HIM coordinator has been collecting information for you to use in the planning process. There are 54,760 medical records. It will take 3.5 minutes per chart to convert from alphabetic to terminal digit filing.

1. How many hours do you expect the project to take?

2. How long will a shift be?

3. How many people will be needed to complete the project in the time frame given?

4. Can everything be done by working the day shift, or will you need an evening and/or night shift to get the job completed on time?

Project and Operations Management

CASE 7-1

Organizational Chart

The current organizational chart for the Health Information Management (HIM) Department is shown in Figure 7-1.

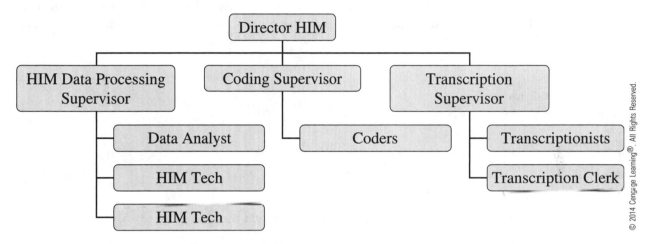

Figure 7-1   *HIM Department Organizational Chart*

The hospital has just undergone a massive restructuring in which the HIM Department has added 3 new functions: quality improvement, birth certificates, and research/institutional reporting. With these functions, the positions being moved to the HIM Department include Quality Improvement Coordinator, Physician Advisor, Quality Improvement Clerk, Research Coordinator, Report Writer, and Birth Certificate Coordinator. You have also received approval to hire 2 Assistant Directors. You plan to have 2 Supervisors moving with the new staff to the HIM Department.

Update the organizational chart to indicate the changes.

CASE 7-2

Job Description Analysis

You are the coding supervisor at a hospital that just increased its number of beds from 75 beds to 150 beds. The facility offers inpatient services, outpatient surgery, ancillary services, and emergency room services. As the volume increases with the increased bed capacity, you will have to increase the number of coders who are in your department. Currently there is only 1 coding job classification—HIM Coder. This position is responsible for coding all services. You are evaluating this practice to determine if you want to continue with the single job classification.

1. What would you recommend?

2. If you recommend more than 1 job classification, what would they be?

3. How would you divide the workload?

CASE 7-3

Productivity Study

Your inpatient coders are always behind. The supervisor has asked for more staff and the HIM director agrees with the request. When the director submitted her request to administration, the vice president asked her to conduct a productivity study of the local hospitals. She called 4 hospitals, and her findings are shown in Table 7-1. The director knows that if she shows this data to the vice president, not only will she not get the positions she requested, but she will also be asked to increase her productivity. She can see that she needs to do some more research. You know that the coders at your facility code the charts and also abstract quality indicators. Your research shows that at the other hospitals, the quality indicators are abstracted by staff in the Quality Management Department.

Table 7-1 *Productivity Study of Local Hospitals*

	Our hospital	Hospital A	Hospital B	Hospital C	Hospital D
Inpatient charts per day	15	20	22	23	21

1. Do you need any additional information?

2. If so, where would you go to get the information?

3. What arguments can you use to support your request for the additional staff?

CASE 7-4

Performance and Quality Improvement in a Coding Department

Molly, the coding supervisor of Homer General Hospital, has a problem. Her Discharged Not Final Billed (DNFB) report is staying significantly over the limit that administration desires. She is also behind in some of the compliance monitoring that needs to be completed. Molly has been given the mandate to determine what needs to be done to bring the DNFB down and still maintain quality, as well as to keep current in the compliance monitoring. She pulls together the information shown in Table 7-2. Analyze this situation from every angle, including but not limited to quality, legal, and management, and answer the following questions:

1. What additional information should Molly gather?

2. What are Molly's options?

3. How can you ensure quality of coding while at the same time emphasizing volume?

4. What solution would you recommend to Molly's problems?

Table 7-2 *Analysis for Discharged Not Final Billed (DNFB)*

Number of current employees	Coding Supervisor	1
	Coders (all types of charts)	3
Number of vacant positions	Coders	1
Volume (average per day)	Inpatient	70
	Outpatient	177
	Emergency Room	122
	Outpatient Surgery	90
Productivity Standards (per 8-hour day)	Inpatient	25–28
	Outpatient	170–185
	Emergency Room	120–125
	Outpatient Surgery	85–100
Time currently spent on compliance issues	Hours per week	10
Time that Molly feels should be dedicated to compliance to do it right	Hours per week	32
Current DNFB	$1.2 million	
Desired DNFB level	$600,000	
Aging	Current charts (3-day bill hold)	35%
	4–10 days old	20%
	11–21 days old	15%
	22–30 days old	15%
	More than 30 days old	15%

Performance Improvement for a File Area

You are the new archives (file area) supervisor. The previous supervisor was terminated for incompetence, and the position remained vacant for 6 months before you were hired. There are major problems with the quality of the work provided by your staff, resulting in a lot of time spent searching for misfiled charts. Many of the misfiled charts are not just transposed numbers or 1 to 2 charts off, but are grossly misfiled. The loose material on the chart has been found filed in the wrong order and, in addition, frequently in the wrong chart.

The customers have several complaints:

- They are not getting the charts as requested.
- The records that they do receive are in shambles.
- Sometimes the charts are never provided.
- Sometimes they get the wrong patient record.
- At times, the requested visit is not in the volume that they received.

Your staffing is currently structured as follows:

- Six full-time employees (FTEs) on the day staff. The day staff retrieves charts for the ER, finishes up anything not completed by the night shift, and files loose material.
- Two FTE evening staff. The evening shift files back all of the charts returned throughout the day and pulls for the ER.
- Two FTE night staff. The night shift pulls for the clinic, for scheduled admissions, for the ER, and for administrative purposes.

The daily work assignment can be described as follows:

- Staff members grab the first stack(s) of charts that they get to, sort them into terminal digit order, and then file them.
- Staff members grab the first stack(s) of loose material that they get to, sort the sheets into terminal digit order, and then file them.
- There is no control over the number of charts picked up by the employee or the area in which the charts are filed.

The first thing that you evaluated is the work volume, and you found that the number of staff is appropriate. You also looked at the overall flow of the process and found that to be appropriate as well. However, as an experienced supervisor, you realize that there is no accountability for quality in this method of work distribution. By the end of the first week, you need to give a proposal to the HIM director regarding your plan to solve the quality problems in the department.

1. What changes would you recommend?

2. How would you implement your plan, if it is approved by the director?

Instituting Productivity and Quality Standards for Imaging or Scanning Records

You are the new imaging supervisor. The previous supervisor recently retired after 35 years of service to the hospital. The facility has had the imaging system only for the past 6 months.

The scanners are responsible for prepping the medical record as well as the actual scanning. They do not index, nor do they conduct quality checks. If the quality control clerks find more than 1–2 pages in a chart that need to be rescanned, the chart is returned to the scanners for rework.

The first thing that you noticed is the significant backlog of charts to be scanned. You learn that the previous supervisor did not want to create productivity standards until the system had been used for at least a year. The scanners do not even turn in a report of their work each day. It is going to take some time to develop the appropriate productivity standards. In the meantime, you plan to have the scanners report their productivity each day.

1. Use form design principles to develop the productivity report required.

2. What would you recommend to get the scanners caught up in their work?

3. How will you establish productivity standards?

CASE 7-7

Evaluation of Transcription Department

Because you have been having difficulty recruiting transcriptionists, you are considering outsourcing the transcription services. You have the responsibility of making the decision.

Based on the information that has been collected, you have to decide which option is more cost-effective. Table 7-3 shows the current in-house transcription services with the transcriptionist positions and salaries. The following list includes additional information regarding in-house transcription:

- Expenses caused by overhead are $4,500.00 per year
- 500 square feet of space have been allocated
- Number of lines transcribed a month: 225,000
- Benefits are 24% of salaries
- If you retain transcription in-house:
  - You will have to increase salaries by 20% to be competitive. (This figure is based on salary surveys of local hospitals and major transcription services.)
  - You will need an additional 50 square feet to accommodate 2 more transcriptionists.

Table 7-3 *In-House Transcription Positions and Salaries*

Transcriptionist Positions and Salaries	
Position	Current Hourly Salary
Transcriptionist 1	$21.76
Transcriptionist 2	$18.23
Transcriptionist 3	$19.47
Transcriptionist 4	$18.72
Transcriptionist 5	$19.06
Transcriptionist 6	$17.76
Transcriptionist 7	$18.84
Transcriptionist 8	$17.37
Transcriptionist 9	$19.27
Transcriptionist 10	$19.84
Transcriptionist 11	Vacant position
Transcriptionist 12	Vacant position
Supervisor	$29.02
Transcription Clerk	$15.75

An RFP was utilized to gather information on several transcription companies. You have decided which company you will go with if the decision is made to outsource.

Key information regarding outsourcing transcription and your projected volume is shown in Figure 7-2.

Information Needed for Outsourcing Transcription

- A transcription coordinator will be needed to handle problems, monitor quality, and be the contact for the transcription company.
- The annual range for the transcription coordinator is $40,000–$55,000.
- The current Transcription Supervisor would probably be placed in the transcription coordinator role.
- A 12% increase in the work load over the next year is expected.
- Fifty square feet of space will be needed to support the transcription functions (not including the servers in the computer room).

Figure 7-2 *Outsourcing Transcription*

1. Which method would you recommend from a strictly financial aspect?

2. What other issues should be reviewed before making this decision?

3. What additional information do you need to make a decision?

Performance and Quality Evaluation and Improvement of the Health Information Management (HIM) Department

You have just been hired as the HIM quality coordinator. This is a new position in the HIM Department. Your job tasks read as follows:

- Develop and implement the HIM Department Quality Plan.
- Develop data collection, data analysis, and data presentation tools for use in the quality plan.
- Report findings to the HIM director and medical staff director and administration, as well as medical staff committees, as appropriate.
- Other duties are as assigned.

The facility is a 338-bed hospital with active ER and outpatient services. There are 45 employees in the HIM Department. About 75% of the medical record is electronic. Those documents are not printed out. The remaining 25% of the record is paper and is scanned into the system by the HIM Department. These documents are scheduled for destruction 60 days from scanning.

The former director of HIM was successful in working with administration to get the Electronic Health Record (EHR) and imaging in place and to get approval to destroy the paper records. However, she failed at managing the day-to-day operations of the department. Now the department has quality issues in the HIM functions. The former director also did a great job preparing the medical staff for the EHR, and the transition went smoothly; however, many physicians and other users are frustrated by the quality issues. Administration is also becoming concerned with the high billing hold report. The director's position was vacant for 5 months before the new director started work. She has only been here a month.

Today is your first day. The HIM director has her instructions from administration and the medical staff. She has passed these instructions on to you. Your instructions boil down to two words—FIX IT. While the director will be actively involved in this clean-up, she cannot do it by herself with the other demands on her time. This is why she requested your position. It is almost unheard of for a new position to be approved in the middle of the fiscal year. Adding the extra position shows how serious administration is about getting the problems solved. The problems are as follows:

- Scanning:
  - There is a 2-month backlog in scanning the paper records.
  - The quality of the scanning has problems.
    1. Sometimes pages are fed 2 at a time, and the backs of pages are not always scanned.
    2. This requires 100% audit, which is 3 months behind.
    3. The staff members conducting the quality audits do not catch all of the errors.

- Billing:
  - The billing hold report is over $2,000,000.00.
  - Administration wants the billing hold report held at $500,000.00.

- Coding:
  - Coding is 2 weeks behind.
  - There are 3 vacancies in the coding area.
  - One of your coders is a new graduate of the local HIT program and is slower than the experienced coders.
  - The last coding audit conducted by corporate showed an 80% coding accuracy report.

- Release of Information:
  - The release of information area is 2 days behind.
  - The release of information area has received repeated complaints that the wrong information is being sent. The errors include:
    1. Not everything requested was released.
    2. Wrong admissions are being released.
    3. Information on wrong patients is being released.
    4. Wrong documents are being released.

- Transcription:
  - An outsourcing company is used since the hospital had trouble recruiting and retaining qualified transcriptionists.
  - Although the transcription is current, the quality of the work is inconsistent. Most of the reports are perfect, but a significant number of reports are totally inaccurate due to:
    1. Multiple typographical errors
    2. Abbreviations that are not spelled out
    3. Poor grammar
    4. Wrong medications with names similar to the right medications

Your assignment for this project is to develop a plan to solve the problems identified above and to prevent them and other problems from occurring in the future. Your plan should include at least the following:

- Who should be involved
- What reporting mechanism you should have
- Who you should report to
- What accuracy rates you expect
- What you will do to solve problems (training, outsourcing, new policies, etc.)
- What will be monitored
- Frequency of monitoring
- Frequency of reporting
- What investigations you will perform
- How you will build quality into your process
- How you will prioritize problems to be addressed
- Forms
- Graphs

Be creative, but use sound HIM principles as the foundation for your project. If you make assumptions, identify the assumptions in your narrative. Please take into consideration all aspects of the issues involved in this situation, including but not limited to legal, data quality, compliance, and quality improvement.

CASE 7-9

Creating a Workflow Diagram for Discharge Processing

You have been asked to draw a workflow diagram to illustrate the discharge processing workflow in your HIM Department. Show key steps in the process, not every step.

The process is:

- The charts are picked up at midnight on the day of discharge.
- The charts are brought to the HIM Department via a buggy.
- The charts are checked off the discharge list.
- The charts are sorted based on the primary terminal digits into the following stacks: 00-24, 25-49, 50-74, and 75-99.
- The charts are placed on the appropriate assembly clerk's desk.
- Each chart is assembled into proper chart order.
- The person assembling the chart writes his or her initials on the facesheet.
- The chart is placed on the analyst's desk.
- The analyst reviews the medical record for deficiencies.
- Colored tags are placed on the page where signatures are required.
- The deficiencies are entered in the chart deficiency system.
- The deficiency sheet is placed on the chart.
- The person analyzing the chart writes his or her initials on the facesheet.
- The charts are placed on the shelf in coding (terminal digit filing) by discharge date.
- Each chart is pulled from the shelf for coding.
- Each chart is reviewed.
- Codes are assigned.
- Discharge disposition abstracted, service, and attending physician are confirmed.
- Code summary is printed out.
- Information is filed in chart folder.
- If complete, chart is sent to permanent files.
- If incomplete, chart is sent to incomplete chart room.
- Chart is filed in terminal digit order on wall.
- Incomplete charts are pulled for physician.
- Deficiency sheet and system are updated.
- If complete, chart is sent to permanent files.
- If incomplete, chart is returned to incomplete files.
- Process is repeated until chart is complete.
- Chart is filed.

CASE 7-10

Improving Workflow Process for Performance Improvement for Discharge Processing

The current workflow process has worked well for the past 10 years. The new CFO wants the DNFB to drop from $2.4 million to $750,000.00. Coding is the only thing preventing the bill from being dropped within 3 days. In addition, there are complaints from some of the new physicians on staff that they have to wait too long to get charts to dictate. They want to be able to dictate the discharge summary within 48 hours after patient discharge. To satisfy the CFO and the physicians, you will need to make changes. You need to speed up the process to get the codes entered into the system faster, as well as to get charts to the incomplete chart room quickly. To accomplish this, you need to reengineer the current workflow. The current process is:

- The charts are picked up from the unit at midnight of the day of discharge.
- The charts are checked off the discharge list.
- The charts are placed on the "wall" to await loose material that is needed for analysis, coding, and quality indicator monitoring.
- Loose material is filed in the charts for 3 days.
- On the fourth day, each chart is coded.
- On the fifth day, each chart is assembled.
- On the sixth day, each chart is analyzed.
- On the seventh day, the quality indicator abstracting is conducted and the charts are sent to the incomplete chart room or the permanent file.

1. What changes can you recommend to accomplish your goals?

2. What impact (positive and negative) do you expect?

3. What could you do to diminish the impact of the negative outcomes?

CASE 7-11

Physical Layout Design for the Health Information Management (HIM) Department

Design the physical layout for the HIM Department for a 250-bed acute care hospital. When designing the department, consider the equipment needs, the workflow, and the tasks involved. The department has implemented an imaging system for scanning records upon discharge; however, it still retains 2 years of old records on the completed shelf. Records older than 2 years are stored on microfilm for access. The department houses 2 main areas: the Physician's Incomplete/Research Room and the HIM Room. The Physician's Room serves as an area for digital completion of patient records and dictating by telephone, as well as access to the Internet for purposes of research into knowledge-based healthcare information. The specifications for both areas of the HIM Department are shown in Figure 7-3.

Data for HIM Department Layout Design

I. HIM Department

Size: 65 feet by 45 feet

Staff: 1 Director

1 Imaging Coordinator

1 Receptionist/Secretary

2 Analysts

2 Coders/Abstractors

1 ROI Coordinator

1 Assembly Clerk

2 Transcriptionists

4 File Clerks

II. Physician's Incomplete/Research Room

Size 10 feet by 20 feet

III. Guidelines

Equipment needed for each HIM employee includes, but not limited to the following:

1. Desk with overhead file shelf

2. Chair

3. Computer

4. Telephone

IV. Equipment needed elsewhere in department includes, but not limited to the following:

- Open file shelving units (stationary or mobile units)
- 1 Imaging System
- 1 Microfilm/Reader Printer
- 1 Copy Machine
- 2 Chairs for visitors near correspondence desk
- 1 Network printer in transcription
- 2 Network printers in main area
- 1 Printer for director
- 1 Printer for secretary
- 4 Computer workstations for Physician's Incomplete Room/Research Room

---

V. Other Pertinent Information

- Labeling: Identify each piece of equipment (legend or text labeling).
- Title of Project: The floor plan should include facility and department name.
- Offices: Include Private Office Areas for Director and Transcriptionist.
- Scale: 1/4 inch per 1 foot
- Complete Shelf: Design area for 30 open shelf filing units. Units are 36 inches wide, 8 shelves high and 12 inches deep.
- Aisle space: 36 inches

Figure 7-3 *Data for HIM Department Layout Design*

CASE 7-12

Revision of the Information Management Plan

As the HIM director, you have been assigned the responsibility of revising the outdated information management plan. Although the Joint Commission conducts unannounced surveys, you know that you can expect a visit in about a year. The information management plan has to be revised and in place before the surveyors arrive. You only have 6 months in which to have the new plan developed, approved, and implemented. Obviously you cannot do this alone. You do not know how Physical Therapy (PT) and other departments use information. After reflection, you decide to make each department head responsible for developing the portion of the information management plan applicable to them. You will write the overall information management portion of the plan as well as the HIM Department's portion. You decide to have a training session for all of the department heads who will be involved. There are 30 people to be trained on what needs to be included, the time table, and the format.

1. Develop a project plan for the revision of the information management plan.

    - What steps need to be done?
    - Who is responsible for each?
    - How long will you allocate to each step?

2. Develop a Program Evaluation Review Technique (PERT) chart of the project.

CASE 7-13

Defining a Project

One of your employees is confused about what is a project and what is a new process/procedure. She has given you a list of changes going on at your facility and asked you to help her understand. Review the situations described in Table 7-4. Indicate whether each situation meets the definition of a project or not. Explain to her why it is or is not a project.

Table 7-4 *Which Scenarios Are Projects*

Scenario	Project	
	Yes	No
1. The assistant director is ordering the annual supply of medical record folders. He is taking bids from vendors to get the best price.		
2. You are developing a new Performance Improvement (PI) program. Data will be abstracted into an information system with reports being generated monthly.		
3. You are converting your filing system from alphabetic to terminal digit.		
4. You are installing new cubicles in the HIM Department.		
5. The state is updating its electronic birth certification software. It will be rolling out to all of the hospitals over the next 6 months.		
6. The Information Management plan is being revised. The HIM special projects coordinator has been given sole responsibility of the revision.		
7. You are developing new productivity standards for your HIM functions.		
8. Your Joint Commission survey is scheduled sometime around the end of the year. You have a lot of work to ensure that everything is in place.		
9. The annual coding update has been sent to you for installation.		
10. The monthly employee newsletter is being written for release next week.		

CASE 7-14

Job Description for Project Manager

It is time to review all of the job descriptions in the organization to determine if they are still valid. The next one in your stack to review is for Project Manager.

What problems do you see with the Project Manager Job Description in Figure 7-4?

Taos General Hospital

Job Description

Department:	HIM
Title:	Project Manager
Classification:	Level 36
Education:	Master's Degree preferred, BS, HE required.
	RHIA certification required
Experience:	1 year of management experience.
Skills:	Leadership and computer skills.
Job Responsibilities:	
	Manage assigned projects efficiently and effectively.
	Develop project plans.
	Manage large budgets.
	Supervise large numbers of people on project team.
	Ensure the quality of the projects assigned.
Revised: 4/5/XX	

Figure 7-4 *Project Manager Job Description*

Forming Committees

You are the chairperson of a large Information Systems (IS) committee in charge of implementing a new EHR. The committee is so large that you are not getting anything done. For example, you met for 4 hours yesterday and only got through 3 of the 15 items on the agenda because everyone wants to have his or her say on each issue. The committee makeup is as follows:

- Project leader
- HIM Director
- Vice President, Finance
- Vice President, Clinical Services
- Chief Information Officer
- Director, Lab
- Director, Radiology
- 4 computer programmers
- Vice President, Nursing
- 2 vendor representatives
- Director, Cardiopulmonary Services
- Director, Materials Management
- Director, Research
- 3 systems analysts
- 2 database administrators
- Director, Training

The decision has been made to create subcommittees. The subcommittees will be:

- Training
- Data Management (data quality, data collection, and data retrieval)
- Development (programming, customization)
- Conversion
- Interfaces

All representatives should be on at least 1 subcommittee.

1. Who would you place on each subcommittee?

2. Why did you choose them?

3. What charge would you give to each subcommittee?

CASE 7-16

Committee to Perform System Benefits Analysis

As the HIM director of a large medical center, you employ 88 FTEs in your department. Your hospital still maintains a paper medical record, although it has several systems throughout the hospital that could directly feed into an EHR. You are certain that the efficiency of your department and the hospital can be achieved with the implementation of an EHR. The efficiencies that can be achieved in the HIM Department alone are abundant if the EHR can interface directly to the dictation and transcription system, coding, release of information, and chart completion systems.

You chair the intradepartmental Clinical Information System Committee for the hospital, which is represented by every clinical department, as well as by administration and Information Services staff. In developing the criteria for sending a Request for Proposal (RFP) out to various vendors, it is important to identify benefits and efficiencies the hospital expects to achieve from an EHR. The task assigned was to have the committee identify benefits to be achieved to help in justifying the EHR for the hospital.

1. What benefits can be achieved with the implementation of an EHR for the HIM Department?

2. Which benefits might impact the delivery of patient care?

CASE 7-17

Project Management and Program Evaluation Review Technique (PERT) Chart

You have been given the responsibility of conducting a purge of your files. You have just developed a first draft of the PERT chart for the project.

Review the PERT chart shown in Figure 7-5.

1. What is the critical path?

2. What problems can you identify?

3. How can you improve on this plan?

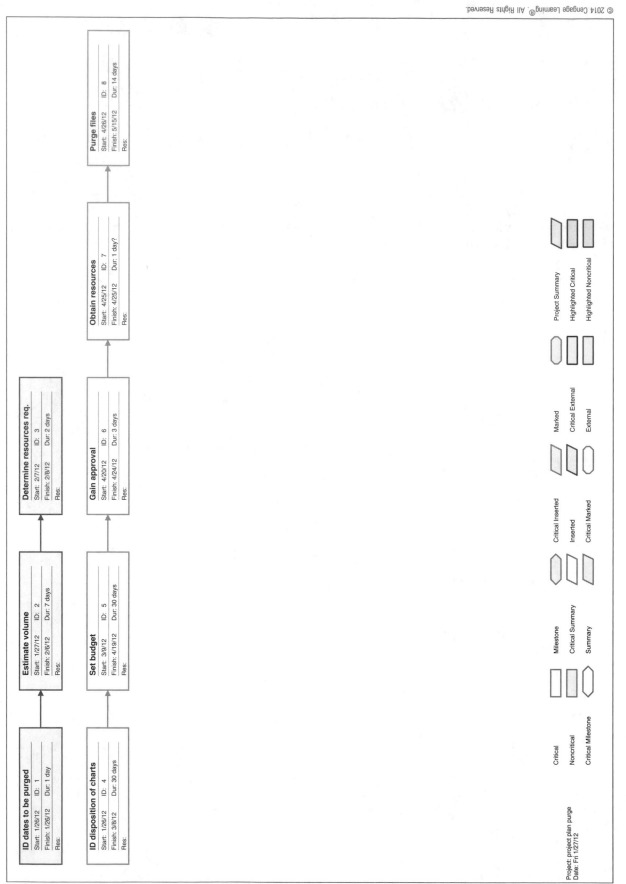

Figure 7-5 *PERT Chart for File Purge*

CASE 7-18

Project Management and Analysis of a Gantt Chart

Review the Gantt chart in Figure 7-6 and identify any problems with the project plan.

How can the Gantt chart be improved?

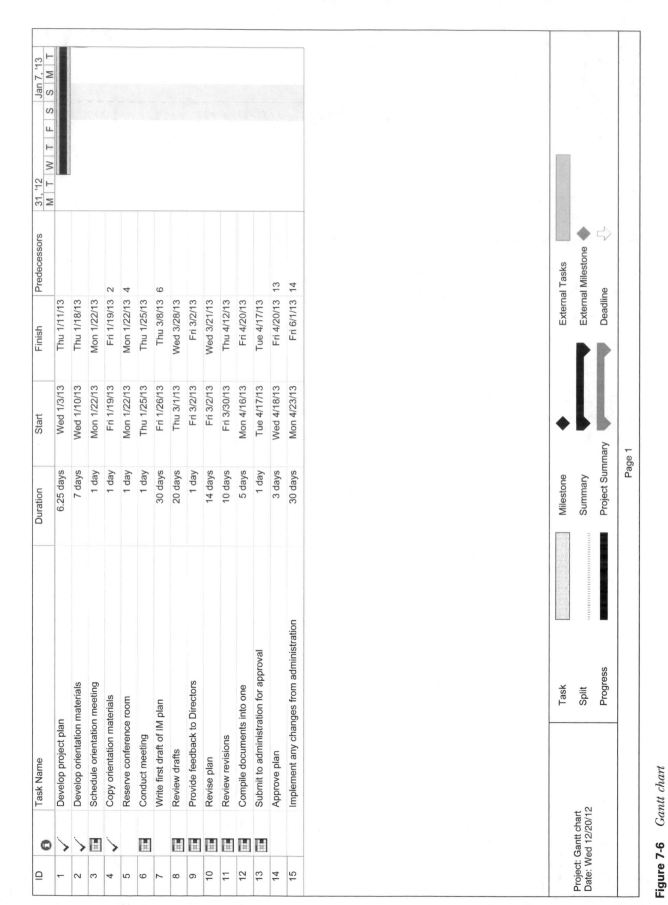

ID	●	Task Name	Duration	Start	Finish	Predecessors
1		Develop project plan	6.25 days	Wed 1/3/13	Thu 1/11/13	
2		Develop orientation materials	7 days	Wed 1/10/13	Thu 1/18/13	
3		Schedule orientation meeting	1 day	Mon 1/22/13	Mon 1/22/13	
4		Copy orientation materials	1 day	Fri 1/19/13	Fri 1/19/13	2
5		Reserve conference room	1 day	Mon 1/22/13	Mon 1/22/13	4
6		Conduct meeting	1 day	Thu 1/25/13	Thu 1/25/13	
7		Write first draft of IM plan	30 days	Fri 1/26/13	Thu 3/8/13	6
8		Review drafts	20 days	Thu 3/1/13	Wed 3/28/13	
9		Provide feedback to Directors	1 day	Fri 3/2/13	Fri 3/2/13	
10		Revise plan	14 days	Fri 3/2/13	Wed 3/21/13	
11		Review revisions	10 days	Fri 3/30/13	Thu 4/12/13	
12		Compile documents into one	5 days	Mon 4/16/13	Fri 4/20/13	
13		Submit to administration for approval	1 day	Tue 4/17/13	Tue 4/17/13	
14		Approve plan	3 days	Wed 4/18/13	Fri 4/20/13	13
15		Implement any changes from administration	30 days	Mon 4/23/13	Fri 6/1/13	14

Project: Gantt chart	Task		Milestone		External Tasks
Date: Wed 12/20/12	Split		Summary		External Milestone
	Progress		Project Summary		Deadline

Page 1

Figure 7-6 *Gantt chart*

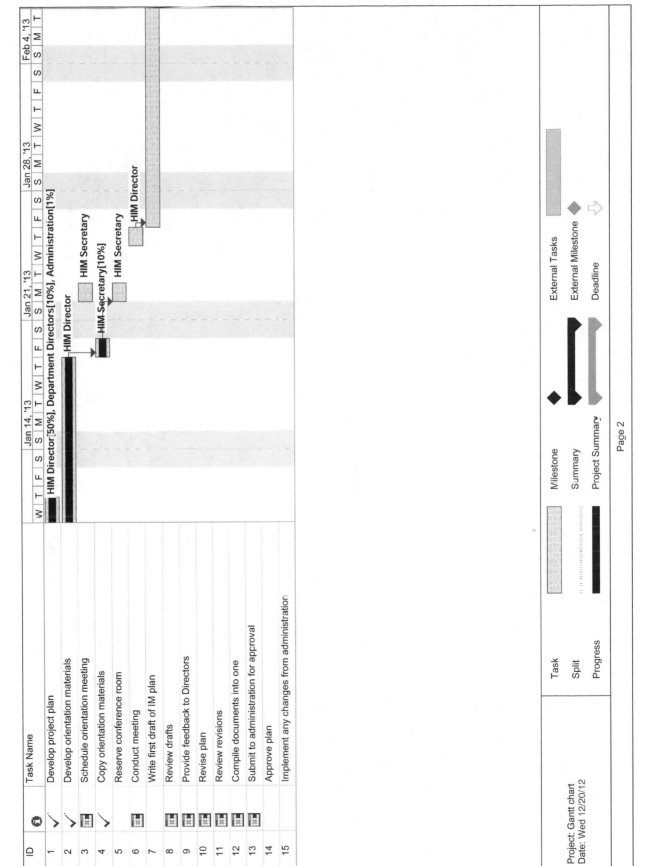

Figure 7-6 *Gantt chart (continued)*

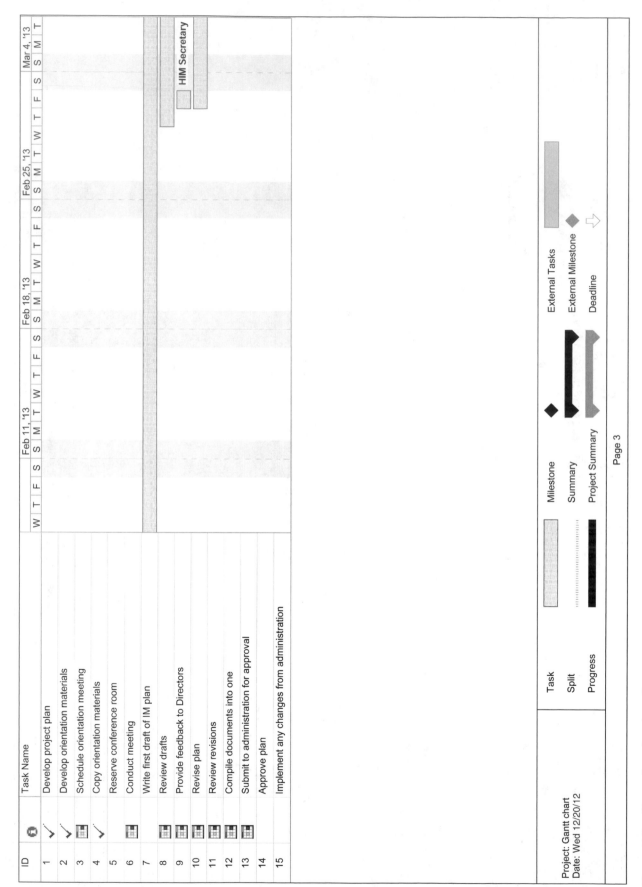

Figure 7-6   *Gantt chart (continued)*

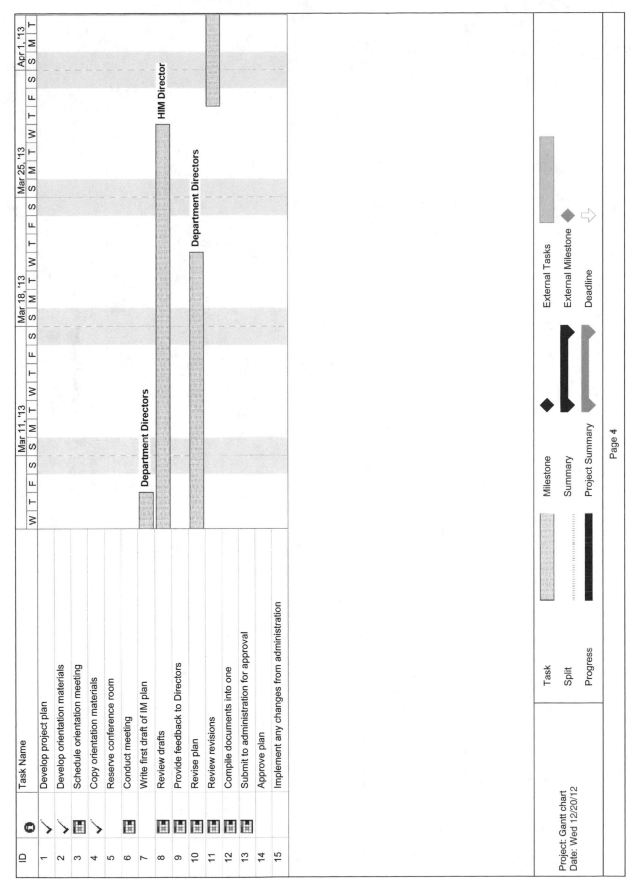

Figure 7-6 *Gantt chart (continued)*

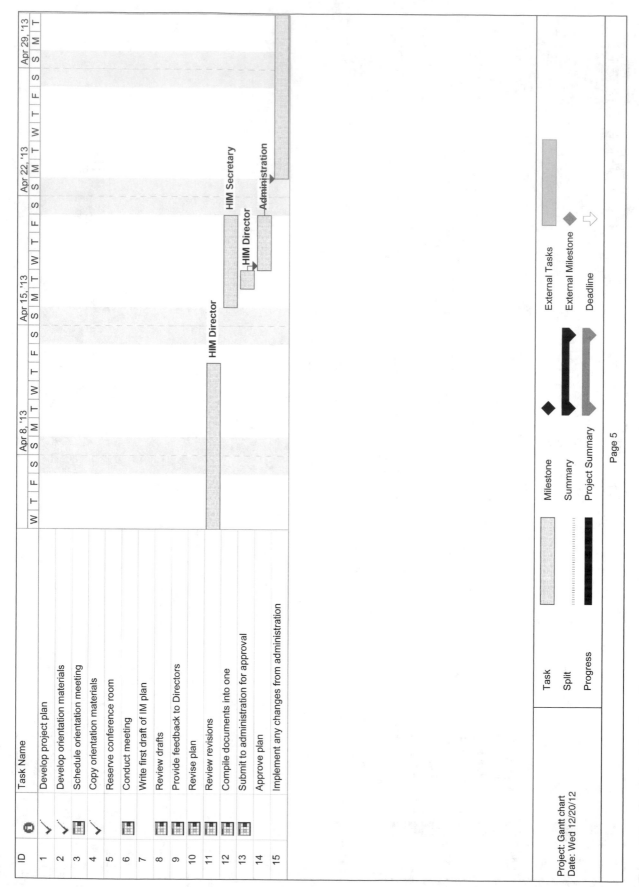

Figure 7-6 *Gantt chart (continued)*

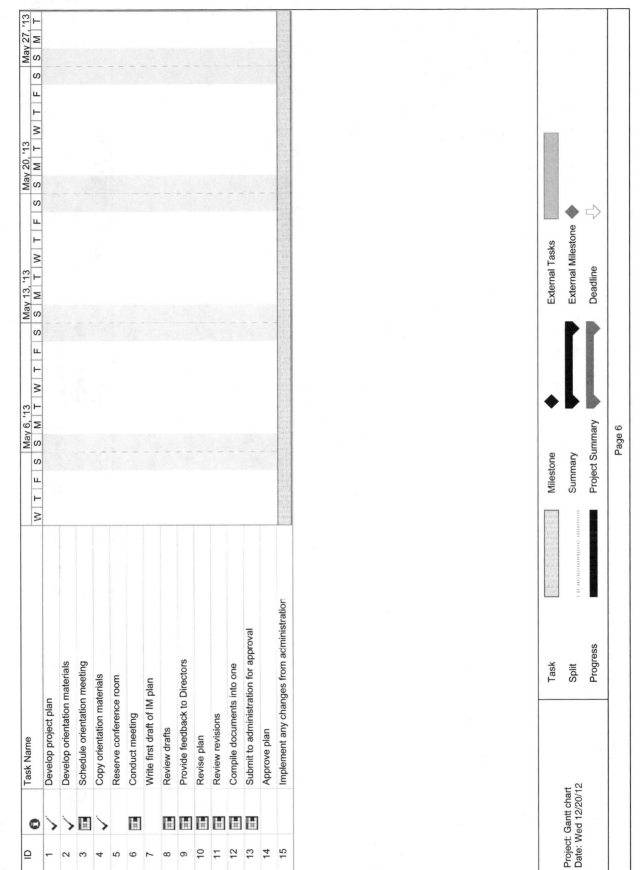

ID		Task Name
1		Develop project plan
2		Develop orientation materials
3		Schedule orientation meeting
4		Copy orientation materials
5		Reserve conference room
6		Conduct meeting
7		Write first draft of IM plan
8		Review drafts
9		Provide feedback to Directors
10		Revise plan
11		Review revisions
12		Compile documents into one
13		Submit to administration for approval
14		Approve plan
15		Implement any changes from administration

Project: Gantt chart
Date: Wed 12/20/12

Task Split Progress Milestone Summary Project Summary External Tasks External Milestone Deadline

Figure 7-6 *Gantt chart (continued)*

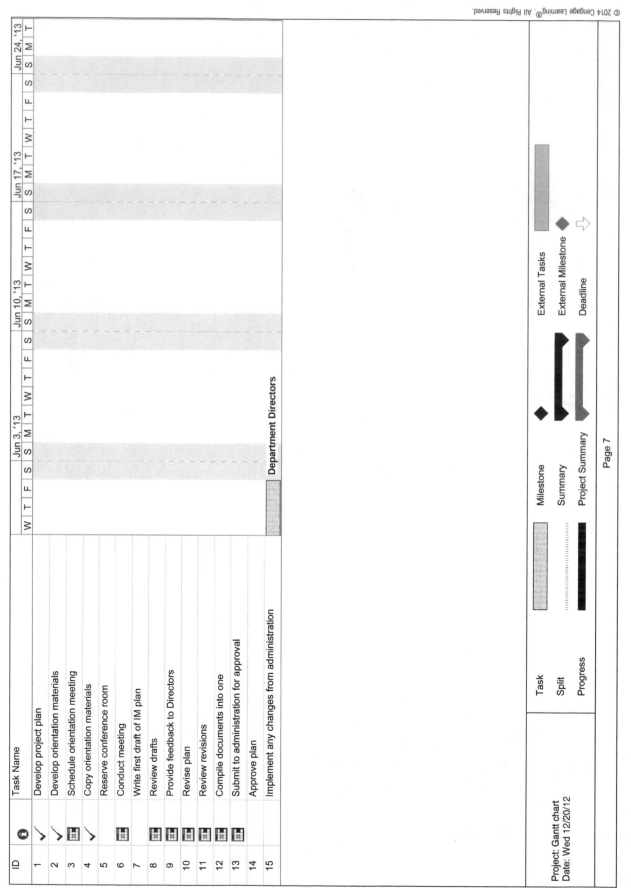

Figure 7-6 *Gantt chart (continued)*

CASE 7-19

Creating a Gantt Chart

You are in charge of the implementation of the new Admit Discharge Transfer (ADT)/Master Patient Index (MPI) installation. Your go-live date is December 1. Today's date is March 3. The contract has been agreed to but not officially signed. Assume that the contract will be signed within the week. You have been asked to create a first draft of a Gantt chart for the implementation process.

Use Microsoft Project to develop a Gantt chart that will include, at a minimum:

- A list of tasks that must be completed
- The date each task must be started
- The date to be completed, with estimated number of days to completion
- Who will be responsible for each task (can include more than just the employees listed below)
- Enter any predecessors (what has to be done before the step can be done; for example, you cannot start implementing the computer system until a contract is signed and hardware has been installed)

In order to develop the Gantt chart, you have been asked to work with a committee consisting of the following:

- HIM Director
- Admissions
- Business Office Director
- Project Manager
- Network Administrator
- Chief Information Officer
- Vendor Representative
- Programmer

CASE 7-20

Evaluation of Project Management Budget Variance

Your hospital has a major problem with duplicate medical record numbers. You are implementing a new EHR and need to get this problem solved before implementation. You decide to hire a consultant to act as the project manager and to use temporary staff to do the actual work. The use of temporary staff is at the suggestion of the consultant. You have to train the registration staff on ways to avoid creating duplicate medical record numbers. Some of the temporary staff members have to be trained to pull and file charts. Other temporary staff members are trained to review the charts and determine if there is a duplicate and combine the physical chart where appropriate. A temporary Registered Health Information Administrator (RHIA) is responsible for conducting data quality checks. You have a significant amount of temporary staff turnover, resulting in constant training and fluctuation of productivity on a daily basis. This results in the RHIA having to do a 100% audit for the entire project, instead of just at the beginning as planned. You really have had to speed up the process over the last 2 months to complete the project on time. The project is completed 2 days ahead of time; the quality of the work is great. Now you need to review the final budget for the MPI clean-up.

1. Based on the project description and the budget shown in Table 7-5, what problems do you see?

2. From a project management standpoint, what could have been done to make this project work better?

3. To what do you contribute the budget variance?

4. Does the budget reflect the description of the project?

5. If you had to do this project again, what would you do differently?

Table 7-5 *Master Patient Index (MPI) Clean-Up Budget*

	MPI Clean-Up Budget						
	Actual Monthly Expenses						
Line Item	April	May	June	July	Budgeted	Actual	Variance $
Temp Staff	12,345.44	13,764.45	21,546.63	24,454.44	60,000.00	72,110.96	(12,110.96)
Equipment	602.67	0	0	0	1,000.00	602.67	397.33
Project Manager	5,000.00	5,000.00	5,000.00	5,000.00	20,000.00	20,000.0	0
Training	2,000.00	1,200.00	300.00	300.00	8,000.00	3,800.00	4,200.00
Total	19,948.11	19,964.45	26,846.63	29,754.44	89,000.00	96,513.63	(7,513.63)

CASE 7-21

Developing a Filing System and Evaluating Equipment Needs

South Utah Community Hospital is a new hospital that is opening on January 2. The facility will have an active clinic and Emergency Room in addition to inpatient services. Unfortunately, it will not have an EHR when it opens because of budget constraints. You have been hired as the HIM director. You are developing a filing system and determining the number of shelves and related items that you will need. The hospital has asked you to keep hard copy records for 4 years.

To simplify the project, the number of discharges includes inpatient, outpatient, and ER.

- Expected number of discharges, year 1:   25,000
- Expected number of discharges, year 2:   28,000
- Expected number of discharges, year 3:   32,000
- Expected number of discharges, year 4:   40,000
- Average expected size of chart   3/4 inch

1. Determine the following:
   - Amount of filing space required
   - Type of shelving desired
   - Number of shelves per unit
   - Number of shelving units required
   - Number of guides required
   - Type of filing system to be used (centralized, decentralized, terminal digit, alphabetic, etc.)
   - Method used to get information from HIM Department to the requestor
   - Type of equipment needed to file and retrieve records
   - Method of chart location system
   - If outguides will be used
   - Security measures to be taken
   - Design of medical record folder

2. Justify your decisions. Include the advantages and disadvantages of the system that you select, where appropriate.

3. Identify how you will work around the disadvantages of the system, where appropriate.

Project Planning for Conversion from Alphabetic to Terminal Digit Filing

You work in a physician office as the office manager. Several new physicians have been added to the practice over the past year. There are approximately 32,000 records. Based on time and motion studies, one employee can convert 50 records from alphabetical to terminal digit filing in an hour. The alphabetic filing system is no longer working for your office. Your job is to plan the conversion from alphabetic to terminal digit filing.

Create a plan for this conversion that includes the following:

- Number of staff
- Space
- Supplies required
- Staff training required
- Time schedule
- The process that will be followed

CASE 7-23

Planning the Health Information Management (HIM) Department for a New Facility

You have been hired by West Texas Hospital as their HIM department director. West Texas Hospital is a new 200-bed hospital that will open on January 1. The hospital has several parts of the record that will be maintained in an electronic format; however, for the first 2 years, the majority of the health data will be paper based. The HIM Department will contain the following functions: assembly, analysis, coding, tumor registry, filing charts, chart completion, filing loose material, transcription, and birth certificates.

Use data in Table 7-6 to determine number of employees needed, their job titles, and their job descriptions.

Table 7-6 *Data for Health Information Management (HIM) Functions*

Description	Expected Amount for 2013
Discharges	25,000
Admissions	24,750
Outpatient admissions	57,000
ER	36,000
Number of pages per discharge	125
Number of pages per ER visit	10
Number of pages per outpatient visit	7
Number of different patients	62,000
Number of births	700
Number of new cancer cases	145
Amount of loose reports	250,000
Expected records to file/pull	300,000
Number of requests for information expected	3,000
Transcription lines expected	7,000,000
Time assemble charts—inpatient per chart	10 minutes
Time assemble charts—outpatient per chart	2 minutes
Time assemble charts—ER per chart	2 minutes
Time analysis—inpatient per chart	15 minutes
Time analysis—outpatient per chart	2 minutes
Time analysis—ER per chart	2 minutes
Transcription lines per hour per transcriptionist	300
Time—release of information	20 minutes
Time—tumor registry abstract records	1 hour
Loose material per day	800 reports per day
Time—birth certificates	45 minutes
Time—pull/file chart	2 minutes

CASE 7-24

Planning Release of Information (ROI) Department Functions for a New Facility

You have been hired as the director of HIM for a new 100-bed hospital that opens 6 months from now. As part of the planning for the HIM Department, you are responsible for designing the ROI functions from the ground up. Write a detailed proposal to the hospital administrator outlining what functions must be performed, why they must be included, and what needs to be done to prepare for the implementation of the ROI desk.

Expectations are that you will average 5 requests per day for medical information during the first 6 months, and after that you expect 15 requests per day.

Tasks should include, but not be limited to the following:

- Policy and procedure
- Equipment required
- Training
- Form design
- Information systems
- Management systems

You are not expected to conduct the development, just the planning. Be specific in developing your plan. For example, list all of the policies and procedures that must be written and forms that must be designed. You do not actually have to write policies and procedures, design the forms, and so on.